"It's hard to believe that all the key ingredients ⸱ into one book, but that's what Steve Spinelli, Sue Birley and Bob Rosenberg have done with *Franchising: Pathway to Wealth Creation*. From the idea stage to the sophisticated world of IPOs, it's all carefully laid out in fine detail. This is an essential collection of valuable information that is long overdue."

—Don DeBolt, President, International Franchise Association

"A lot of books talk about getting rich. This book takes an analytical approach to wealth creation. It uses analysis and quantification in articulating how value is created by the franchisor and the franchisee. There's no buying a job here. Spinelli, Birley and Rosenberg take you through the process of examination, execution and delivery that is sophisticated and, based on my experience, right on target."

—Harry D. Loyle, President and CEO, MotoPhoto®

"By using actual examples from well-known companies, this book is certain to become one that everyone involved in franchising, or contemplating it, will want to own. A fascinating and extremely useful mix of theory and reality, this book tells it the way it is, for franchisors, franchisees and entrepreneurs."

—Steve Siegel, COO and CFO, KaBloom Ltd. and Immediate Past Chair of the International Franchise Association

"*Franchising* nails it like nothing we've seen before. Spinelli, Birley and Rosenberg not only perform a fascinating dissection of the nature of franchising, but they bring color to an underlying story of successful small business growth in America. *Franchising* should be in the hands of all of us in the business, as well as those considering the plunge!"

—Clifford Hudson, Chairman and CEO, Sonic, America's Drive-In

Franchising:

Pathway to Wealth Creation

FT Prentice Hall
FINANCIAL TIMES

In an increasingly competitive world, it is quality
of thinking that gives an edge—an idea that opens new
doors, a technique that solves a problem, or an insight
that simply helps make sense of it all.

We work with leading authors in the various arenas
of business and finance to bring cutting-edge thinking
and best learning practice to a global market.

It is our goal to create world-class print publications
and electronic products that give readers
knowledge and understanding which can then be
applied, whether studying or at work.

To find out more about our business
products, you can visit us at www.ft-ph.com

Pearson
Education

Franchising:
Pathway to Wealth Creation

Stephen Spinelli, Jr.
Robert M. Rosenberg
Sue Birley

An Imprint of Pearson Education
London ▪ New York ▪ San Francisco ▪ Toronto ▪ Sydney
Tokyo ▪ Singapore ▪ Hong Kong ▪ Cape Town ▪ Madrid
Paris ▪ Milan ▪ Munich ▪ Amsterdam

Library of Congress Cataloging-in-Publication available

Editorial/production supervision: *Kathleen M. Caren*
Cover design: *Nina Scuderi*
Interior composition: *Sean Donahue*
Cover design director: *Jerry Votta*
Manufacturing manager: *Alexis R. Heydt-Long*
Marketing manager: *Laura Bulcher*
Executive editor: *James Boyd*

© 2004 Prentice Hall PTR
Pearson Education Inc.
Upper Saddle River, NJ 07458

Prentice Hall books are widely used by corporations and government agencies for training, marketing, and resale.

The publisher offers discounts on this book when ordered in bulk quantities.
For more information, contact Corporate Sales Department, Phone: 800-382-3419;
Fax: 201-236-7141; E-mail: corpsales@prenhall.com
Or write: Prentice Hall PTR, Corp. Sales Dept., One Lake Street, Upper Saddle River, NJ 07458.

Printed in the United States of America
10   9   8   7   6   5

ISBN 0-13-009717-9

Pearson Education LTD.
Pearson Education Australia PTY, Limited
Pearson Education Singapore, Pte. Ltd.
Pearson Education North Asia Ltd.
Pearson Education Canada, Ltd.
Pearson Educación de Mexico, S.A. de C.V.
Pearson Education—Japan
Pearson Education Malaysia, Pte. Ltd.

FINANCIAL TIMES PRENTICE HALL BOOKS

For more information, please go to www.ft-ph.com

Executive Skills

Cyndi Maxey and Jill Bremer
It's Your Move: Dealing Yourself the Best Cards in Life and Work

Finance

Aswath Damodaran
The Dark Side of Valuation: Valuing Old Tech, New Tech, and New Economy Companies

Kenneth R. Ferris and Barbara S. Pécherot Petitt
Valuation: Avoiding the Winner's Curse

International Business

Peter Marber
Money Changes Everything: How Global Prosperity Is Reshaping Our Needs, Values, and Lifestyles

Fernando Robles, Françoise Simon, and Jerry Haar
Winning Strategies for the New Latin Markets

Investments

Zvi Bodie and Michael J. Clowes
Worry-Free Investing: A Safe Approach to Achieving Your Lifetime Goals

Harry Domash
Fire Your Stock Analyst! Analyzing Stocks on Your Own

David Gladstone and Laura Gladstone
Venture Capital Investing: The Complete Handbook for Investing in New Businesses, New and Revised Edition

D. Quinn Mills
Buy, Lie, and Sell High: How Investors Lost Out on Enron and the Internet Bubble

D. Quinn Mills
Wheel, Deal, and Steal: Deceptive Accounting, Deceitful CEOs, and Ineffective Reforms

John Nofsinger and Kenneth Kim
Infectious Greed: Restoring Confidence in America's Companies

John R. Nofsinger
Investment Blunders (of the Rich and Famous)…And What You Can Learn from Them

John R. Nofsinger
Investment Madness: How Psychology Affects Your Investing…And What to Do About It

H. David Sherman, S. David Young, and Harris Collingwood
Profits You Can Trust: Spotting & Surviving Accounting Landmines

Leadership

Jim Despain and Jane Bodman Converse
  And Dignity for All: Unlocking Greatness through Values-Based Leadership

Marshall Goldsmith, Vijay Govindarajan, Beverly Kaye, and Albert A. Vicere
  The Many Facets of Leadership

Marshall Goldsmith, Cathy Greenberg, Alastair Robertson, and Maya Hu-Chan
  Global Leadership: The Next Generation

Management

Rob Austin and Lee Devin
  Artful Making: What Managers Need to Know About How Artists Work

J. Stewart Black and Hal B. Gregersen
  Leading Strategic Change: Breaking Through the Brain Barrier

William C. Byham, Audrey B. Smith, and Matthew J. Paese
  Grow Your Own Leaders: How to Identify, Develop, and Retain Leadership Talent

David M. Carter and Darren Rovell
  On the Ball: What You Can Learn About Business from Sports Leaders

Subir Chowdhury
  Organization 21C: Someday All Organizations Will Lead this Way

Ross Dawson
  Living Networks: Leading Your Company, Customers, and Partners in the Hyper-connected Economy

Charles J. Fombrun and Cees B.M. Van Riel
  Fame and Fortune: How Successful Companies Build Winning Reputations

Amir Hartman
  Ruthless Execution: What Business Leaders Do When Their Companies Hit the Wall

Harvey A. Hornstein
  The Haves and the Have Nots: The Abuse of Power and Privilege in the Workplace... and How to Control It

Kevin Kennedy and Mary Moore
  Going the Distance: Why Some Companies Dominate and Others Fail

Robin Miller
  The Online Rules of Successful Companies: The Fool-Proof Guide to Building Profits

Fergus O'Connell
  The Competitive Advantage of Common Sense: Using the Power You Already Have

W. Alan Randolph and Barry Z. Posner
  Checkered Flag Projects: 10 Rules for Creating and Managing Projects that Win, Second Edition

Stephen P. Robbins
  Decide & Conquer: Make Winning Decisions to Take Control of Your Life

Stephen P. Robbins
  The Truth About Managing People...And Nothing but the Truth

This book is dedicated to the thousands of franchisees who have worked to make their franchise systems successful, with special recognition to the many friends and colleagues at Jiffy Lube and Dunkin' Donuts.

Contents

Introduction

This book provides an in-depth and comprehensive look at franchising. The authors' combined 75 years of franchise practice and 55 years in academia forged an authors' alliance that resulted in *Franchising: Pathway to Wealth Creation*. We argue that franchising embodies entrepreneurial zeal, a scalable business model, a complex and dynamic strategic alliance between franchisor and franchisees, and great wealth creating potential. Franchising also uniquely fulfills a wide spectrum of entrepreneurial appetites. If you wish to grow your idea into an international behemoth, franchising may serve as a vehicle. However, if your dream is to operate a single outlet in your hometown, franchising may also be right for you.

The word "franchise" is one of the most misunderstood and abused words used in the conduct of commerce. It is used to describe the value of an individual or a brand, or to describe a relationship. Seldom, if ever, is it used to expound on the potential to build a robust professional and economic life. Some of the confusion rests on the fact that franchising always involves at least two entities, the franchisor and the franchisee. The popular press tends to focus on the tension and litigation in franchising. Many business schools tend to ignore it. Most people are confused as to the difference between the two. But franchising has been an important part of new venture growth and expansion for almost half a century. Have no doubt, we believe there is vast wealth creating potential in franchising.

But even for those who agree with us, there is a tendency to focus attention of the franchisor and ignore the entrepreneurial aspirations of the franchisee.

The three of us are often asked the question: Is franchising entrepreneurship? Certainly, most people would agree that Ray Kroc, founder of the giant restaurant chain MacDonald's, or Anita Roddick, The Body Shop founder, were entrepreneurs. But their companies are the franchisors, the owner of the trademark and business model. What about the franchisees, those individuals who buy a franchise, implement the concept on a local basis, and serve customers? Are they entrepreneurs?

The answer to the question is based on more than linguistics. The central issue regards the ability of the franchise to create wealth. Clearly, there are no guarantees of wealth when a new venture is founded. Return *and* risk are the balancing force controlling the entrepreneurial process and therefore the potential of failure looms in any business start-up, balanced by the prospect of wealth. However, if the buyer of a franchise is simply purchasing employment, then a franchise is no more than an alternative to an employment agency. Most people invest a substantial portion of their personal assets to buy a franchise. It would be irrational to do so just for a job.

We wrote this book to answer a number of key questions about franchising. Yes, franchisor and franchisee are entrepreneurs. If they are to be successful entrepreneurs, they must understand the skills and motivations of each other and work together. And the best franchises are driven to create wealth for both of the strategic partners. This book contends that focusing your intellectual lens on only one partner is analogous to covering one of your eyes while playing a sport. You lose depth perception and peripheral vision. You may still win the game but you unnecessarily stack the odds against yourself. The principal objective of this book is to turn those odds in your favor. We want you to consider franchising as a viable option for the creation of wealth. Our involvement with the establishment of franchise systems, the proliferation of new franchises, and profitability as franchisees spurs our efforts. Recently, we have seen an increasing number of multiple outlet franchisees. Some franchisees achieve both growth and diversification by operating multiple franchise concepts. There seems no end to the possibility for those who are dedicated to understanding the complexity and potential of franchising.

The authors of this book come from vastly different backgrounds but remarkably similar experiences with franchising. Each has been involved in the launch, growth, and financing of franchise companies. We have also been deeply committed to higher education. Teaching, researching, and writing about phenomenon in entrepreneurship and especially franchising at the graduate level has inspired our belief that would be entrepreneurs are ready for a rigorous discussion of franchising.

We hope you will find *Franchising: Pathway to Wealth Creation* a useful tool, a dynamic guide, and a challenging read. But mostly we hope you focus your passion on a franchising opportunity that fulfills your entrepreneurial dreams and results in wealth creation for you and your stakeholders.

Stephen Spinelli, Robert Rosenberg and Sue Birley
July, 2003

Acknowledgements

We started Jiffy Lube in 1978…a few college football players led by their coach (and experienced entrepreneur) Jim Hindman. We were young and inexperienced, but a hard working and dedicated group (special nod to John Saasser, Rich Heritage, Pete Clark, Craig Bourgeois, and Ann Santonastassi). Because we believed we had to grow fast, we turned to franchising and made a list of the best franchise companies in the world. We called the CEOs and asked for a meeting. One person, Bob Rosenberg, said, "Sure, come up to the Dunkin' Donuts headquarters and I'll meet with you for as long as you want." Writing this book with Bob is a privilege. He is the most sophisticated franchise executive entrepreneur and executive in the world. He is also a gentleman and friend.

After selling Jiffy Lube, I decided to pursue a doctorate. Following the advice of my MBA entrepreneurship professor, Bill Bygrave, I sought out interviews with the best entrepreneurship professors in the world. Studying for a PhD with Sue was an overwhelming privilege. A world-class mind combined with sophisticated research capability with textured experience defines Sue Birley.

Babson College is a unique and wonderful college defined by a population of students, faculty and administration that is focused, caring and supportive. My research assistant, Jeff Palter, embodies those attributes and adds writing skills that challenged every word in this book, adding great value. The franchise classes at Babson struggled with us to critique *Franchising*, especially the Spring 2003 group. Thank you.

I would be remiss not to comment on the team from Prentice Hall-Financial Times. Led by Jim Boyd, Executive Editor, and Kathleen Caren, I can say they are genuine professionals and partners.

1 Franchising as Entrepreneurship

Lincoln Speers spent 20 years building a successful career as an investment banker. He was living in New York, thriving professionally on Wall Street and making a lot of money. "So I quit and bought a Krispy Kreme franchise."

Derek Skeletsky had a newly minted MBA and a pocketful of job offers from big companies. He went right from graduation to Snip-Its, a three-store children's hair-care company. His role is to grow Snip-Its as a franchisor. "I believe in the product, and I think franchising is a way to make it big, very big."

The motivations of these two entrepreneurs are strikingly similar and consistent with key themes in this book. Both are interested in pursuing a life as an entrepreneur with its inherent freedom and creativity. They understand there are risks in starting a business. At the same time, they want to go beyond a basic lifestyle business to seek wealth. Their vision is of a professional life that offers the opportunity to engage ideas, employees, partners, and customers in a personal and direct manner. The best way to control your destiny is to confront it with action. They don't want to be just part of an opportunity—they want to seize it.

Two people at very different stages in their lives came to the same conclusion. They see franchising as a pathway to entrepreneurship and wealth. One is now a successful franchisee with 12 restaurants in Reno, Nevada. The other is in the midst of launching the franchise with visions of a national rollout. Both of them believe that franchising can help them achieve their goals. This book provides insights into franchising from a holistic perspective that allows you to see how the franchisee and the franchisor thrive together and to decide which aspect of the franchise partnership is best for you.

Franchising

Why is franchising such a powerful economic engine? Because it is a sophisticated, entrepreneurial alliance through which thousands of individuals create vast wealth. This is a book about entrepreneurship. More specifically, it is about franchising as a pathway to entrepreneurship and the creation of wealth. The franchise entrepreneurial spirit in the United States has never been more alive than today. Forty-five hundred franchise businesses with 600,000 outlets crowd the marketplace, accounting for a third of all retail sales nationwide. The International Franchise Association expects that franchise businesses will continue to thrive and prosper for the foreseeable future, growing to account for at least 40 percent of U.S. retail sales in the next decade.

What is franchising? Franchising happens when someone develops a business model and sells the rights to operate it to another entrepreneur, a franchisee. The company selling the rights is the franchisor. The franchisee usually gets the rights to the business model for a specific time period and in a specific geographic area. Franchising is sometimes referred to as *business format franchising* or *product franchising*. McDonald's is the classic business format franchise, and an auto dealership is the classic product franchise. In a business format franchise the way the product is delivered is as important to the brand as the actual product—for example, golden arches and red-roofed building for McDonald's. In a product franchise, the actual product—not the way that it is delivered—is the focus. An Audi can be sold from a standalone, single-brand store or from a multi-branded dealership. While business format franchises tend to form a more rigid relationship, obligating the franchisee, the distinction between business format and product franchises is becoming more and more blurred. If you understand the business format franchise, you'll have little difficulty with the product franchise relationship. The lessons of this book can easily be applied to both business format franchises and product franchises. The key feature of the franchise system is that the ownership of the brand and the modus operandi for the delivery of the product are retained by the franchisor, and execution is a franchisee responsibility. A wide range of services and products are delivered through a franchise: Some include oil lubrication, gas stations, automotive service, tax advice and preparation, landscaping, cleaning services, as well as the commonly recognized restaurant and fast-food industry. Normally, delivery is through a franchise outlet, or store, although there are several franchises that operate essentially without stores or with reduced real estate constraints. For example, Service Master and Snap-On Tools franchisees operate from a central office that provides support for back office needs and vehicles to deliver products.

What you gain in a franchise entrepreneurial alliance is a method for exploiting a business opportunity in a competitive manner. One of the biggest benefits to you is a dramatic compression of the long apprenticeship often necessary for entrepreneurial success. The would-be franchisor recognizes an opportunity and designs a service delivery system to exploit that opportunity in a unique way. The franchisor bears the burden of assessing the market, creating the product or service, establishing the brand, building the business plan, and measuring the competition. The franchisee can get down to the process of cultivating customers and an awareness that incremental changes may be necessary to assure the franchise's ongoing competitive advantage.

The trademark or brand of the franchise is what creates the bond between you and your franchise partner, the brand owner. You share a mission to maintain and build the brand, which already signals a price–value relationship in the minds of your customers. The franchisor brings the brand; you bring the entrepreneurial instincts to manage the day-to-day selling. It takes both of you to achieve market acceptance of the brand.

What It Means to Be Entrepreneurial

Entrepreneurship, according to Howard Stevenson of the Harvard Business School, is "exploiting an opportunity regardless of the resources currently available." Stevenson goes on to say, "The key to this perspective is the focus on opportunity" (not on resources).

What does it mean to focus on opportunity instead of on resources? Think about baking a pie. If we focus on resources, we first line up the required ingredients. The next step is to combine the ingredients in just the right amounts. But if we are looking at this as an opportunity, first we consider whether the pie is even what people want to eat. If the answer is yes, then we find out what kind of pie people want and figure out how to deliver a better, faster, cheaper one. Business development is not a zero-sum game. Where some see competition, or winners and losers, entrepreneurs see wealth creation for a larger set of stakeholders and ultimately for society.

By focusing on opportunity, the entrepreneur seeks to fill a need that has been previously ignored or underserved. The wealth he or she creates in the process elevates the lifestyles of a segment of the population, specifically the *stakeholders,* or people with vested interests in the success of the "pie"—that is, customers, suppliers, marketers, and retailers. Entrepreneurs focus on delivering value to the marketplace by seeking, analyzing, and shaping an opportunity, and only then concentrating on attracting resources. The opportunity is the primary concern, the resources secondary.

So, if you discover an opportunity, and you can create wealth, you've won the game, right? Clearly not. Discovering an opportunity is not the end of the process. We believe that "Entrepreneurship is a way of thinking and acting that is opportunity obsessed, holistic in approach, and leadership balanced—for the purpose of wealth creation."[1] Let's look more closely at this idea of entrepreneurship.

How do we define *wealth*? Although profit and capital gain are easily measured benchmarks, they are certainly not the only measures of wealth. The stakeholders in the opportunity—the founders, customers, employees, shareholders, and suppliers—must see intrinsic value in the exploitation of the opportunity for individual gain. Ultimately, the stakeholders must define wealth. "Opportunity obsession" brings a dynamic element to the focus on opportunity—we are never finished shaping the deal. The explicit link between "thought and action" suggests a rigorous planning process as opposed to gun-slinging, seat-of-the-pants business behavior. "Holistic" remind us that the business environment both within and outside the franchise firm is constantly changing, and we must always be taking its shifting patterns into account. Finally, "leadership" is the important human element underscoring that entrepreneurial activity is typically focused by the vision of a single person or a committed team.

Franchising is, at its core, an entrepreneurial alliance between two organizations, the franchisor and the franchisee. There is no franchise per se until at least one company store exists, the opportunity has been tested, and franchisees sought. Once the concept has been proven, the franchisor and the franchisee enter into an agreement based on their belief that there are advantages in the alliance. An advantage is when you can outperform the competition. Franchising clarifies which partner can best perform a certain job that is relevant to the end product or service. The key motivation behind franchising is that each partner seeks to create wealth for himself or herself by exploiting the opportunity together.

Franchising: Small and Big Business

One of the strengths of franchising is that it provides a wide breadth of options for individuals to find an opportunity to meet their financial goals and business visions, however conservative or grandiose. Franchising allows entrepreneurs to build wealth to varying degrees according to the scale of the business enterprise. For those whose life goal is to own a pizza restaurant and earn a comfortable income, the opportunity is there. They become small business owners. But franchising may afford the opportunity to build 300 pizza restaurants using a business model that allows a sharing of both risks and rewards with other "owners" in a system.

It's important, of course, to do your homework before choosing a franchise arrangement that suits your needs. If, for example, the company sells franchises only in small markets and keeps big markets for company stores, this may not send the best signals to the prospective franchisees. Or, if the company limits the growth potential of franchisees by tightly controlling the number of units, or if it expands with numerous franchisees in a high-potential market, mixed messages may also be perceived by prospective franchisees. You have to understand how big your appetite is and whether a franchise of interest will allow you to stay small or become big. The prospective franchise has to allow you the chance to be rewarded as desired without exceeding your tolerance for risk.

There are companies designed to encourage successful franchisees with the opportunity to buy more stores in a particular market or region. Franchisees who achieve prosperity with a single unit are rewarded with additional stores. The entrepreneurial process is encouraged, and greater wealth can be created. Please note that some franchisors push franchisees to grow beyond their capabilities. Boston Markets (formerly Boston Chicken) pushed franchisees to grow more quickly than the market (or maybe the franchisees' ability to operate) could sustain. The company ultimately went bankrupt and was bought by the McDonald's Corporation.

Although it is possible to enter into franchising with a small-business perspective, franchising is, at its core, a large-scale entrepreneurial growth strategy for the franchisor. That might mean a series of different relationships with franchisees based on the franchisees' appetite and capabilities. A franchisee might want to operate only one store because it fulfills his or her entrepreneurial ambitions. Another franchisee might want 10, 20, or 100 stores. The franchisor must understand that its total system growth and success is dependent on a combination of single and multiunit franchisees. The fundamental point is that both parties must be aware of each other's expectations for success and wealth creation.

Remember, the focus of our definition of entrepreneurship is opportunity. The franchisor's development of a business model that is offered as a franchise is a thoughtful approach to opportunity recognition followed by execution and shaping of the opportunity. Therefore, opportunity, thought, and action are key elements of a franchise company. Because each partner expects to create wealth from the relationship, the entrepreneurial definition is sealed.

Modeling Entrepreneurship[2]

Let's assume for a moment that you've selected a franchise opportunity and completed your investigation of its potential. How will you integrate your entrepreneurial goals with the mechanics of running a franchise? In a nutshell, you will recognize and shape the opportunity to identify both the resources required and the appropriate team. This opportunity is the cornerstone of the entrepreneurial process. Let's talk briefly about how to recognize an opportunity.

The Opportunity: The Core of Entrepreneurship

Bill Gates once said, "Vision is the easy part." But when you think you have the vision, the good idea, your very next question must be, Is it an opportunity? You must understand what separates an opportunity from an interesting idea. Think in terms of three subsets of opportunity recognition: market demand, market size and structure, and margin analysis. Let's examine each concept in turn and make the links to franchising.

When anyone approaches us with a concept that may be a franchise business, we ask a lot of questions about market demand—about who will buy the product. Assessment of an opportunity requires an articulate understanding of market demand. We want to know everything possible about these potential customers, beginning with who they are and why they will buy from us. A prospective franchisee should ask probing questions of the franchisor (and their franchisees) about their customer and how deeply the franchise systems understand the nature of the customer. Here are five important questions you should ask about your potential customers. The order of the franchise opportunity analysis is to first determine the viability of the opportunity, then to develop a mechanism (which we call the service delivery system, or SDS) to extract the demand in your local market.

Five Key Market Demand Questions

- **Who is the customer?** Describe the customer most likely to express a demand for your product or service. This analysis process consists primarily of collecting data about the customer's geographic, demographics, and psychographics, which we cover in the following sections.

- **Is the customer reachable?** The saying "Build a better mouse trap and the world will beat a path to your door" is misleading in an entrepreneurial context because even the best opportunity will be limited by the entrepreneur's ability to reach the customer. Customers will not beat a path—instead, you must build a roadway to them! You must plan a method of distribution to determine whether the customer is indeed reachable. Channel development (the process of building the roadway to the customer) is both acutely important and a particularly strong aspect of successful franchising when properly executed. Without a strong channel to reach more customers, there can be no growth. In later chapters we discuss this in detail.

- **Is the price–value relationship attractive to the customer?** The more quickly customers receive value from a product or service, the greater the likelihood of increased market demand. Therefore, the longer it takes for customers to identify the relationship between price and value, the greater is the risk to both the franchisee and franchisor. Some people may argue that immediate customer satisfaction (and therefore reduced risk of price–value imbalance) is one reason franchises tend to be retail focused.

- **Can the business achieve a 20 percent market share?** The proof of sustainable market demand is significant market share. Businesses that last become markets leaders, and history has defined leadership as being in the range of 20 percent market share. Market leadership is not necessarily a requirement for a successful venture, as the large number of businesses that are successful "intelligent followers" can attest. Just look at Meineke Muffler and Wendy's Old Fashioned Hamburgers, and the ability of an intelligent follower to achieve success in its own right is evident. However, leaders have market power that affects funding, pricing, and marketing issues that tend to positively affect return on investment.

- **Can the business grow at an aggressive annual rate?** The pace of growth over time determines the firm's projected life cycle and helps establish the richness of the opportunity. The consumer and capital markets dictate what rate of growth is considered aggressive. During the Internet boom, for example, annual growth rates were expected to exceed 100 percent. While rapid growth is a hallmark of high-potential ventures, a historical perspective indicates that something closer to 20 percent annual growth is more the norm. You must calculate how long it will take to clearly identify your customer and develop a plan to reach that customer.

Targeting the customer who has an expressed demand for your offer is the fulcrum of action in entrepreneurship and franchising. Let's look at some of the ways in which you will profile your prospective customers.

Geographic Profiles

The scope of a business concept is local, regional, national, or international. A sample national market is the United States, which is typically divided into nine regions: Pacific, Mountain, West North Central, West South Central, East North Central, East South Central, South Atlantic, Middle Atlantic, and New England. Regions are divided by population density and described as urban, suburban, or rural. Population densities in these subdivisions range from under 5,000 to 4,000,000 or more. Franchises define a market by the number of people necessary to support a single unit of operation or store.

Geography may in fact prove to be an advantage to franchisees, not a limitation, as some believe. Many regional franchisees limited by geography are free to develop other noncompetitive offerings in their local areas. In fact, many of the most successful emerging food service concepts, such as Krispy Kreme, Panera Bread, and Baja Fresh, will sell only to successful regional franchisees of other concepts who have demonstrated their knowledge of the area and ability to successfully run their operations.

Demographic Profiles

A demographic profile is a compilation of personal characteristics that enables the company to define the "average" customer. Most franchisors perform market research as a central function, developing customer profiles and disseminating the information to their franchisees. That research may include current user and non-user profiles. Typically, a demographic analysis includes age, gender, income, home and work addresses (driving or walking distance from the store), marital status, family status (number and ages of children), occupation, race and ethnicity, religion, and nationality. We put demographics into context by looking at data specific to the business concept we are considering, such as mean number of registered automobiles for a Midas Muffler franchise territory or percentage of disposable income spent on clothes for a Gap franchise.

Link your analysis of the data to your vision of the concept. For example, if you launched an earring company 10 years ago, you might have defined the target market as women ages 18 to 40 and the size of the market as the number of women in this age group in the United States. But what does that vision look like today, in the larger market that now exists? The target market for earrings could now be defined as women and men ages 12 to 32, who purchase an average of three earrings per individual, not two. Clearly, identifying your target market requires that you combine demographic data with a unique vision of the future for the venture.

Defining the target customer is essential because it dictates so many diverse functions of the business (see TIP 1–1). Most importantly, it measures the first level of demand, the customer with the greatest need. Once you've defined this primary target audience, you can also find your secondary targets: other customers who might want your product or service. The degree of market penetration in the secondary target is usually less than that of the primary target, because a secondary market is by definition a customer with a lower likelihood of using your service. You can make revenue projections from your definition of target audiences and the degree of market penetration you expect based on historical information.

Although measuring market demand is not an exact science, a franchisor continually collects data about its customers through point-of-sale data from franchisees and more typical market research tools, such as surveys, focus groups, and test marketing. Even after buying your franchise, you will continue to compare local market demographics with national profiles to help you decide the number of local outlets that can be developed. TIP 1–1 illustrates the principle of target markets and the significance of anticipating or modifying a concept to fit changing market needs.

Psychographic Profiles

Psychographic profiles segment potential customers based on social class, lifestyle, and personality traits. Information of this nature is defined both broadly, through industry research such as that of a trade group, and narrowly, as defined by individual companies through their own market research. This research is almost always conducted by a franchisor on an ongoing basis as the system grows. Following is an example of the more broadly defined pyschographic information. Franchise systems construct profiles of their customers to better understand their needs and to focus growth in areas with the highest density of targeted customers.

TIP 1–1 Theory into Practice: Radio Shack's Moving
Target Market

Target markets are dynamic, often changing organically in size and shape. Back in the 1970s and 1980s, for example, Radio Shack grew by addressing the needs of technophiles—young men with penchants for short-wave radios, stereo systems, walkie-talkies, and the like. The national retail chain supplied this audience with the latest gadgets and did very well.

Then, starting in the early 1990s, technology became more sophisticated. Personal electronic equipment began to include cell phones, handheld computers, and electronic organizers. The market for these products was expanding from a smaller group of technophiles to a larger group of middle-aged males who loved gadgets and who had more disposable income. Yet Radio Shack remained Radio Shack. Its audience dwindled while the personal electronics market boomed.

Radio Shack wisely refocused its business to target this new demographic. Its advertising addressed the needs of the 44-year-old upper middle-class male instead of the 29-year-old technophile. That 29-year-old who used to shop at Radio Shack was now 44! He was not going to build or repair a radio, but he would buy a cell phone. Radio Shack made dramatic changes in its marketing and inventory. As a result, it has also made dramatic improvements in its profitability and continues today as a major retailer for mobile phone product and service providers.

Social classes in America are generally divided into seven categories:

1. Upper uppers (1 percent)
2. Lower uppers (2 percent)
3. Upper middles (12 percent)
4. Middle class (32 percent)
5. Working class (38 percent)
6. Upper lowers (9 percent)
7. Lower lowers (7 percent)

Lifestyle addresses such issues as health consciousness, fashion orientation, and being a car enthusiast. Personality variables such as self-confident, conservative, and independent are used to further segment markets.

Behavioral Profiles

Behavioral variables segment potential customers according to their knowledge, attitudes, and use of products. A detailed understanding of the target market and why certain consumers will buy your product or service gives you great knowledge of the competitive landscape. Why will consumers spend their money with you instead of with someone else? Behavioral variables can come to bear in instances such as designing advertisements. In designing an ad for your highline automobile franchise, you may determine that the most important behavioral characteristics of the majority of your customers are concern about the car's pricing and concern about its appearance. Therefore, you would design your ad to be free of clutter, focusing on an image of the car and on an aggressive price. Once a customer has walked into your dealership to start a transaction, the individual salesperson can tailor the presentation to the specific needs and wants of the customer.

Opportunity Recognition: Market Structure and Competition

Now that you have an idea who your target customers are, ask who currently serves them. Identifying your competitors and their relative strengths helps you define the overall market structure. The market structure that usually provides the most fertile ground for the entrepreneur is fragmented or emerging. A fragmented market provides the opportunity to consolidate the market around a brand—that is, to provide the consumer with a product or service defined by a positive price–value relationship embodied in a trademark or brand. Jiffy Lube provides an example of this. Before the quick-lube industry was born, preventive maintenance for an automobile was ill-defined by providers and not well understood by consumers. The company's goal is to redefine preventive car maintenance as a "Jiffy Lube."

The other attractive market structure for an entrepreneur is one that is emerging. The aging population has created an emerging market in health care, for instance. Although some companies have been more successful than others, this emerging market has attracted a number of franchised medical clinics, vitamin retailers, assisted-living centers, and other health-care product and service companies, all seeking to ride a national or international tide of growing demand.

Opportunity Recognition: Market Size

Once you understand who the target customer is, you must calculate how many there are and then determine more specifically the size of any given local market. In other words, is the juice worth the squeezing? Do you believe enough customers will buy your product or service to make the potential for wealth creation reasonable? Understanding market size helps you to understand the scope of the opportunity—is it local, statewide, national, international, or global? When looking at market size in the United States, keep in mind that there are 300 standard metropolitan statistical areas (SMSAs), which is the U.S. government's title for a metropolitan area. International means having a presence in a country other than the home market. Global means having a marketing perspective that includes many national markets in a rational development and management plan. Market demand is time-dependent. Consumer trends imply changes over time, and therefore your measurement of market size must look into the future.

Jiffy Lube determined market size by the following calculation: When the company was started, there were approximately 120 million cars and light trucks in the United States. The average car owner required preventive maintenance service 2.8 times per year. Therefore, market size was defined as 336 million services per year.

Interestingly, in the midst of Jiffy Lube's analysis of market size, the founders saw a dramatic change occurring in market conditions that they believed would lead to changes in market structure. The existing supply of general "bay" maintenance was shrinking with the proliferation of self-serve gas stations. The opportunity existed to reintroduce bay maintenance with a more specialized service. This combination spawned the creation of a new industry (the quick-lube industry) and a corresponding new revenue growth curve in automotive services. In this example we see how markets move in certain directions. The size of a market is almost always changing (whether getting bigger or smaller). The fact that markets are always changing introduces time as an important qualifier of market size.

Too early in the life cycle, and there is not enough demand to sustain the firm. Too late, and brand position can be lost to a competitor. "Vision" in entrepreneurship is very much about where markets are *going*. Franchising is a mechanism that can allow for more efficient flexibility when market conditions dictate a contraction or rapid expansion. It also can more quickly contribute to the fulfillment of latent demand and therefore increase in market size. Because of the changes recognized by the Jiffy Lube founders, the 2.8 average oil changes per year soon grew to 3.2. The contraction of service bays because of the switch to self-serve gas stations combined with the increased convenience to customers because of Jiffy Lube's unique building and system allowed customers to get their oil changed more frequently.

The probability of success increases dramatically when your business is launched at the most appropriate point in the product life cycle. Consider the five stages of the business cycle: research and development, launch, growth, maturity, and decline. The most fertile entrepreneurial territory is clearly located within the growth stage. The growth stage is where you can see the power of franchising to reduce risk. Prospective franchisees should pay attention to what stage of growth the franchise system is in when making a decision to buy. The earlier the industry stage, the greater the risk—and likely the greater the potential return. When existing market demand is compared to market size, we have a fairly clear picture of the potential opportunity. TIP 1–2 takes a look at this calculation using the example of Jiffy Lube International, Inc.

Opportunity Recognition: Margin Analysis

Margin analysis is the final differentiator between an opportunity and an interesting idea. As part of your opportunity-assessment process, you must demonstrate that you can provide a product or service that is faster, better, or cheaper than what currently exists. If you provide better products or services, will the market pay for that offering, and will you gain a viable and sustainable profit margin?

Gross margin is the basic ratio you examine in the opportunity-assessment process. Net profit, cash flow, and consideration of the time necessary to break even are also vitally important. Common indicators of a competitive advantage are being the low-cost provider of a good or service and having a lower capital requirement than the competition. Many franchisors use a 20 percent return on investment (ROI) as their benchmark for successful store-level economics. However, everything starts with cash flow for the franchisee. The amount of positive cash generated beyond the breakeven point is the ultimate measure of a good opportunity. We discuss the financial ramifications and implications of a franchise's service delivery system in Chapter 8 when we compare two franchises: Bagelz and Panera Bread.

Resource Marshaling: The Establishment of the Service Delivery System (SDS)

When it comes to resources, the mantra of the successful entrepreneur is to "minimize and control rather than maximize and own." Remember, the objective is to create wealth through the exploitation of a defined opportunity. Your goal is not to own resources but rather to use resources to exploit the opportunity. Minimizing the required resources is often a competitive requirement for the startup venture. The well-assessed and well-shaped opportunity is your guide for marshaling the right resources. You must ask yourself, What are the minimum resources I need to exploit the opportunity?

The creative marshaling of resources can be the most challenging part of the entrepreneurial process. Sometimes you can gain flexibility by turning traditionally fixed costs into variable costs. Part-time help, commissioned sales, and facility rent determined as a percentage of sales are examples of making expenses fit better with the revenue they generate. Another mechanism is to outsource or lease underutilized assets. Before buying the Panera Bread franchise rights for

TIP 1–2 Theory into Practice: How Jiffy Lube Exploited
a Fragmented Market

Where there is no market leader, there is often an opportunity. Jiffy Lube was a classic "consolidation play." Before the company started, there was no dominant brand in the automotive oil-change market. It would have been difficult to name the key providers of preventive maintenance service. Car and tire dealers, gas stations, garages, and do-it-yourselfers split the market into small segments.

Men dominated automotive care decisions. The do-it-yourselfer was the most strident competitor for the startup. But by the time men were 29 years old, they tended to seek alternatives to doing it themselves. The initial target market was a 29- to 54-year-old male car owner.

Beyond this, the founders of Jiffy Lube identified a gap in the delivery of oil changes. First, what an oil change included varied significantly, from a simple oil change to changing the oil and oil filter. And what about fluids, such as transmission and brake fluid? Pricing varied from $9.95 to about $45. Second, delivery time was erratic at best and often extended through most of a workday. The assessment of the opportunity dictated a comprehensive preventive maintenance service, delivered in a defined period of time at a package price.

It is said that the well-defined opportunity can be described in a "30-second elevator pitch." The Jiffy Lube opportunity was as follows:

- Check fluid levels for the transmission, differential, brakes, battery, and power steering, and fill as needed.
- Fill the windshield washer fluid, vacuum the interior, wash the windows, and inflate the tires.
- Deliver all this within 10 minutes, at one fixed price, with no appointment, in a bi-level drive-through facility.

Although the scope of the market seemed significant, it told only half the story, the franchisor's half. The franchisee is the local implementer of the concept. Understanding the finest textures of the target market demand becomes essential at the point of execution for the franchisee.

At the time Jiffy Lube was launched, the per-unit breakeven was about 30 cars per day. Breaking even quickly was essential to the survival of the individual franchise. Many stores doubled or even tripled breakeven within the first year of their unit's operation. For those franchisees, the Jiffy Lube concept was quickly proven, and significant wealth was created. Other franchises never achieved breakeven and ultimately failed.

New Hampshire, franchisee Mitch Roberts and his partner assessed the cost of land and new building construction. He judged it might exceed $600,000 per outlet. If they had gone to a bank and obtained a mortgage, they would have had to put down between $120,000 and $240,000. Applying the mindset of minimize and control, they went to a landowner and said, "Would you build us this building and lease it to us?" The real estate costs were thereby reduced to $50,000 per year with no cash up front.

Another way to get into the minimize and control mentality is to "think cash last." When you have defined the appropriate resources for your opportunity, ask, How do I gain access to these resources without writing a check? We suggest that you begin by leasing the building and the equipment. Set up payment terms so that vendors can be paid with customers' cash if at all possible. Only when there simply is no other way, obtain cash from an investor to buy what you need.

You'll draw your roadmap for marshaling resources when you establish the service delivery system (SDS). The franchisor develops a method for delivering the product or service that fills customer demand. In its most basic form, the SDS is the way in which resources are arrayed so that demand can be extracted from the marketplace. This SDS has to be well defined, documented, and tested by the company. It allows a company to conduct a comprehensive analysis of the way it delivers its product or service to customers. The end result of the organization, execution, and transfer of the SDS is the firm's competitive advantage.

The Entrepreneurial Team

High-potential ventures are best brought to fruition by management teams, not individuals. Choosing the team is the most important part of the entrepreneurial process. Be sure you understand what constitutes "relevant experience" in a potential team member. Perfect relevance is a track record of having launched a new venture in the same industry with great success for all the stakeholders. But experience can still be relevant and significant if the team member has startup experience, has had bottom-line responsibilities in the past, and has managed people and hard assets. At Togo's Eateries[3] the founders required a team with knowledge of real estate, construction, specialty foods, franchising, and marketing. Other franchisors are concerned not to have franchisees with industry experience because they will need retraining to shed their "bad habits." However, experience in local markets and marketing may be critical. Franchisees have to look at the age and experience of the franchise system and the sophistication of training programs.

After considering the relevant general business and specific industry experience of the team members, consider characteristics that we call the "vital organs" of entrepreneurs: opportunity obsession, flexibility, and leadership. One of the potentially dramatic advantages of the franchise entrepreneurial alliance is that the definition of the team can and should be very broad. When the franchisee organizations and the franchisor organization are viewed as a team, then both can leverage the special skills and competitive advantages of each.

- One particularly pertinent question to ask yourself is, Do I view the world in terms of opportunity or in terms of resources? The "manager" tends to focus on the marshaling and allocation of resources. The entrepreneur's perspective is opportunity-obsessed.

- Can you deal with ambiguity? The nature of entrepreneurship is that the venture is always changing. If change is a reality, you must be able to embrace ambiguity and uncertainty, and find the opportunities they create.

- Do you have stellar leadership skills? Someone has to get out in front, steer the ship, and declare, "This is where we are going!"

Entrepreneurial teams must have business experience relevant to the venture as well as the entrepreneurial characteristics described here. When these attributes come together, there is a team locus of control. There cannot be any "it's not my fault" mentality—there must be mutual passion and shared responsibility. In an entrepreneurial alliance, such as franchising, it is important that the team is defined at the intersection of the two organizations. The delineation of tasks defined by the opportunity can and should be filled by leadership from each of the strategic partners. If the two teams are not able to work together, the alliance is likely to be ineffective. The two integrated teams should be able to take advantage of each other's competitive strengths and powerfully exploit the opportunity. Remember our comment early in the chapter about franchising providing a dramatic compression of the entrepreneurial apprenticeship. The great franchises transfer the knowledge and experience of the system to their new franchisees.

Conclusion

We have defined entrepreneurship, explained its specific components, and put the components into a process that is easily understood and easily applicable to various business ideas. Clearly, opportunity recognition and shaping is at the heart of the process—and there is a vast difference between a great idea and a viable opportunity. Eighty-five percent of all successful entrepreneurs spend at least three to five years in their industry learning the language and niches before setting out in that industry to start a business.[4] This is an incredibly powerful principle that is especially compelling in the franchise relationship. If the franchisor can transfer its experience and bundle it with the entrepreneurial talents of franchisees, then the opportunity is leveraged and scaled.

As discussed, the three most important elements of this opportunity recognition process are market demand, market structure and size, and margin analysis. Without substantially understanding these elements as they pertain to your opportunity, determining whether it is a viable one or just a pipe dream would be a wild guess at best. But once these elements are identified, studied, and analyzed, you can proceed to the second major component of the entrepreneurial process: resource marshaling. Remember the mantra of the entrepreneur, especially during startup phase: Minimize and control rather than maximize and own. Even with superior opportunity recognition and sophisticated resource marshaling, people with relevant experience drive the entire entrepreneurial process. Central to the issue of people is the consideration of the characteristics or vital organs of the entrepreneurial team. Are they opportunity-obsessed and able to deal with ambiguity, and do they have clear leadership skills? These are important questions with consequential answers. Ultimately, leadership in the entrepreneurial environment is the process of constantly evaluating and shaping the opportunity—and subsequently balancing the human, financial, and physical resource requirements that are needed for the venture to begin, launch, grow, and succeed.

Next, we move from the more general discussion of entrepreneurship and franchising to the specific examination of how the concept innovator (franchisor) and the concept implementor (franchisee) join together for the purpose of creating wealth. In Chapter 2 we introduce the franchise relationship model (FRM), the framework for creating and analyzing the franchise organization.

Endnotes

1. Jeffrey A. Timmons and Stephen Spinelli, *New Venture Creation for the 21st Century,* 6th ed., McGraw Hill, 2003.

2. Special thanks to Professor Jeffrey A. Timmons. For an in-depth discussion of modeling the entrepreneurial process, see *New Venture Creation for the 21st Century.*

3. Togo's Eateries is a specialty sandwich franchise that began on the west coast and has grown across the United States.

4. Timmons and Spinelli, *New Venture Creation for the 21st Century.*

2 The Franchise Relationship Model

In 1986 Pizza Hut was struggling with upstart competitor Domino's. Franchisor management was convinced that the competitor's pizza delivery was a real threat and that Pizza Hut needed to respond with its own delivery offering. But the franchisor had over a thousand franchises with territory rights that were highly successful sit-down restaurants. "Why fix what isn't broken?" was a common franchisee refrain. The delivery system added costs to the franchise operation with uncertain revenue. It also affected the way franchisees operated the sit-down business. Tension grew as the franchisor began to experiment with the Pizza Hut business model with centralized phone ordering and special procedures for home delivery orders. Pizza Hut teetered on the brink of massive litigation.

Eventually, the franchisor negotiated with franchisees and the firm embraced delivery. But why did the friction between the franchisees and franchisor rise to this level in what now seems an obvious need to respond to the competition? The complexity of the franchisor–franchisee relationship suggests that if you don't pay attention to key aspects of this partnership, the system will fray.

We make these details understandable through the franchise relationship model (FRM). The FRM takes the entrepreneurial framework established in Chapter 1 and incorporates specific processes that are unique to franchising. The FRM gives you a blueprint for developing and analyzing all aspects of the franchise format, from the physical building to the monitoring and control aspects. It asks the questions that become pertinent when designing the most ideal service delivery system (SDS) for any given franchise. It anticipates practical break-downs in the franchise relationship and suggests avenues for appropriate modifications for both the franchisor and franchisees.

Franchising is a powerful tool because it has the potential to create wealth for a large number of entrepreneurs. The FRM illustrates both how a potential franchisor can most efficiently construct a franchising company and how a prospective franchisee can determine which system to join. Among other things, the FRM also helps to distinguish between those tasks best executed under a corporate umbrella and those best done by the individual franchisee. The problems at Pizza Hut, for instance, began when corporate management started tinkering with the business format that franchisees were comfortable with. The changes disrupted the security of their revenue, and franchisees naturally became concerned about their financial futures. Confusion equals conflict in franchising. That confusion doesn't pertain only to the financial results. It can manifest in role responsibilities too. When the franchisor experimented with taking orders centrally and eliminating onsite phone orders, the franchisees became confused about who was responsible for delivery tasks.

Figure 2–1 is our first look at the FRM. This model depicts a series of franchise principles, each of which interacts with the others to form a powerful, interlocking business concept that solidifies itself as the links are implemented more efficiently. The process starts in the center with the customer and moves to the SDS. Any changes in your target customer, customer needs, or the SDS have consequences that affect the franchise alliance. The value of the FRM is that it enables you to identify the nature of these consequences. Once the causes are identified, the franchise can be improved by realigning transaction responsibility and reassessing the financial well-being and reliance on each partner. The dynamics of answering these questions, however, can often cause conflict in the relationship, because changes to the relationship have to be agreed upon between you and the franchisor.

The FRM suggests a series of questions. Both potential franchisors and franchisees can use it as a roadmap to success by asking the questions that we pose throughout the chapter. The answers offer a perspective that can help determine the entrepreneur's success. We cannot stress enough how important it is to understand the goals and objectives of both players in the franchise company for a healthy franchise relationship to develop. We consider each part of the FRM, the model as a whole, and how the parts interact. To best illustrate the parts of the FRM, we evaluate them in the following sections from the perspective of a prospective franchisor because the franchisor must deal with these issues first when developing the franchise. The discussion is also beneficial to prospective franchisees, as it illustrates how a franchise and the resulting FRM are developed, thus enabling franchisees to evaluate different franchise systems.

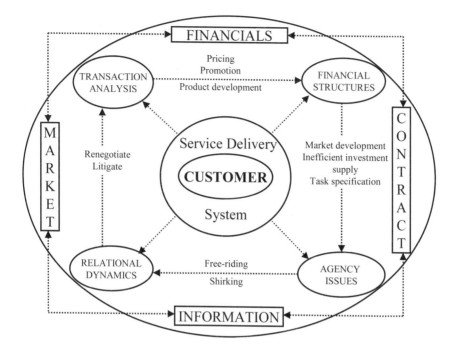

FIGURE 2–1 The franchise relationship model.

The Customer: How Does Opportunity Recognition Work in Franchising?

Time and again, hopeful entrepreneurs announce, "I have a great idea for a franchise." Unfortunately, there is no such thing as a great idea for a franchise. As discussed in Chapter 1, an idea is simply that: just an idea. Determining whether there is a great *opportunity* inherent in the idea is the crux of the entrepreneurial decision. Assessment of a concept starts with defining the opportunity and is validated in one or more outlets. The franchise relationship model provides a roadmap to apply the franchise context to the opportunity and to reassess the concept in the real-world marketplace to see whether it actually generates a profit. The customer is at the center of the FRM. The job of the franchisor is to develop a business format that will meet the needs of the customer in a way that makes money for both the franchisor and the franchisee. The SDS surrounds the customer in an attempt to meet the demands of the customer.

Franchisees and franchisors should assess and reassess often. The problems at Pizza Hut started when Domino's exposed pizza delivery as a customer need that Pizza Hut wasn't meeting. The Domino's 30-minute guarantee (later changed, but by then the brand had been established) changed the rules about how people could eat pizza in the USA. Clearly, a segment of the population wanted a pizza delivery option.

Once you know there is a market for your product, your next step in evaluating a potential opportunity is to estimate the size of the market. Your calculation can follow this formula:

Target Customer × Estimated Revenue per Transaction × Transactions per Year by Each Target Customer = Annual Revenue

Every business uses this type of formula to determine its revenue basis and to continually work toward honing in on average price. Forecasting specific amounts is difficult, however. For example, at Kinder Care, a franchised daycare center, the average revenue per transaction equals the base cost of care per day plus any extra service that can be sold. The next step in calculating the annual revenue is to take the number of days per year that the target customer is in the company's care and multiply this by the average price per day. The result equals the total expected yearly revenue.

Projecting revenue is a process of calculating the size of the customer base and the result of selling products and services to each member. The customer base is projected as a percentage of the primary target audience. Then, we must ask specifically. How many service/products can we sell? How many add-on sales will occur, and how many times per year will sales be made? These are the questions and layers of intricacy that that add texture and management direction to revenue projections.

With this projected annual revenue amount in mind, you can forecast the costs and expenses of the proposed franchise by developing the appropriate SDS. The FRM leads us to the next step.

Establishing the Service Delivery System (SDS): How Does the FRM Provide a Framework for Marshaling Resources?

Why is the SDS, which is also called the business format, often a proprietary design? Because it is not only the fundamental means by which customers' needs will be served, but it is also the way in which the service delivery resources are arrayed to create competitive advantage in the marketplace. Highly successful and visible examples of business format innovations are the drive-through windows in fast-food restaurants and bi-level facilities in quick-oil-change facilities. Every franchise has a well-defined SDS, however overt or transparent it may seem to an outside observer.

Don't underestimate the value of carefully planning the SDS. The expression "The devil is in the details" never takes on greater meaning than during the design of the franchise delivery mechanism. This was very clear from experiences that Jiffy Lube encountered while expanding the franchise. One particular component of the expansion plans paints a vivid picture of the intricacy of SDS development and reveals what a great benefit this design was to the founders over time. Steve Spinelli recalls the following:

> When we decided to open a new Jiffy Lube location, we had specific criteria for location that simply had to be adhered to: high volume of car traffic, on which side of the street the building was located (outbound or inbound), high-profile retail area, and the far corner of any given street or block, among others. Once these aspects were addressed, then came the building specifications. As overanalyzed as it may seem, through some trial and error, we were able to determine the optimal location of the Jiffy Lube structure on any given property. Once that was determined, we dealt with the structural specifications for the exact angle of the building, including the width, depth, and angle of the entrance and the degree bend of the driveway—all to allow for the optimal number of cars to "stack" in line, waiting for the car in front to complete the service. On several occasions we were confounded by locations that fit all of the above criteria but were still not performing as expected. Upon closer inspection it became apparent that the bend in the driveway was too sharp. This prevented customers from driving their cars completely onto the lot and into the queue; subsequently, this gave the impression to oncoming traffic that the lot was full—when in fact it was not. We quickly understood the devilish nature of the details and had to adjust several driveways to accommodate an increased number of cars.

It is this level of refinement and detail orientation, if not obsession, that you must adopt while looking at your planned and actual delivery system. Unless you examine it under a high-powered microscope, you might miss essential components. Steve continues:

> Another part of the "complete" Jiffy Lube SDS was the design of the inside of the Jiffy Lube maintenance bay. Considering the limitations inherent in the use of hydraulic lifts, we were confronted with the dilemma of how we could offer thirty minutes of labor in only ten minutes. To deliver this ten-minute service, we knew that we had to have three technicians work on a car at once without the use of a lift. This quandary led us to develop an SDS in which the cars would drive through the bay and stop above an opening in the floor. This allowed one technician to service the car from below, another to service the car underneath the hood, and a third to service the car's interior. We knew that without developing such a "disruptive"[1] system, we would not have been able to succeed as we did. The typical delivery system in automotive service standardized the physical setting (bays with lifts) combined with mechanics that were certified in many areas of automotive repair. We used a specialized facility with highly focused (versus broadly qualified) lube technicians. Our method "disrupted" the conventional thinking about automotive maintenance delivery.[2] The soundness of our decision to use the drive-through, bi-level system was confirmed when we saw

our competitors—gas stations and car dealers—insist that they could offer a "quick lube" in thirty minutes using hydraulic lifts and traditional bays. It quickly became apparent that they simply could not compete for the very reasons that Jiffy Lube became a success. It became clear to us that it was the sum of the intricately designed parts that created the value of the SDS. Moreover, it was clear to us from our competitors' failure to compete that if one of the parts were removed from the SDS, the result was not simply a slightly diminished return, but rather a complete lack of return.

Such is the level of detail needed for an SDS to deliver both value to the customer and cost efficiencies to the concept operator. Every franchise company bets the future of the company on having a better understanding of how to meet consumer needs through its business format. Eastman Kodak and the founder of Mail Boxes Etc. teamed to develop the Image Arts Etc. franchise. They believed that by combining technology and retail service, they were putting the company "on the cutting edge of the digital imaging revolution and [becoming] the first company to offer wide format printing and digital photography to the public in retail shopping center locations."[3]

TIP 2–1 provides a classic example of an SDS that creates value.

It is important to note the interrelationship between the SDS and the customer. Since the customer is at the center of the FRM, addressing customers' needs should be at the center of the SDS. This is particularly evident in the preceding Wendy's example, where Dave Thomas saw customer needs that were not being met by the market and developed an SDS accordingly. The more natural, seamless, or transparent the delivery of the product is to the customer, the more confident you can be that you have achieved the ideal business format.

Transaction Analysis: In the Franchise Relationship, How Are Responsibilities of the Franchisor and Franchisee Allocated?

So far, we have discussed market demand without reference to the individual responsibilities of the franchisor and franchisee. We call the assignment of these responsibilities *transaction analysis*. There can be no viable franchise until you have a financially sound business model for the single outlet. Franchising creates sound, single-store operations and economics in a unique way. The tasks and responsibilities necessary to deliver the product to the customer are clearly documented in the contract and allocated between the franchisee and franchisor based upon their respective capabilities and efficiencies. The sum of the transactions constitutes the brand equity shared by the parties to the license agreement. Those issues that stand outside the realm of foreseeable and definitive actions but that will play an ongoing role in the operation of the franchise will be documented

TIP 2–1 Theory into Practice: How Wendy's Used Its SDS to Enter a Saturated Market

In 1972 Dave Thomas entered what many experts called an already crowded hamburger fast-food market. His concept was to offer a "Cadillac hamburger" that was hot, fresh, and delivered more quickly than the competitions'. To execute Thomas's mission, Wendy's introduced the first drive-through in a national fast-food chain. Because Wendy's menu offered double and triple patties in addition to the traditional single-patty hamburger, its kitchens were designed to mass-produce hamburgers and deliver them to the front counter or drive-through window with minimal effort. To ensure a just-in-time hamburger, each Wendy's restaurant included a large front window that enabled grill cooks (who were placed in clear view of customers, not in a back-room kitchen) to observe the flow of customers onto the premises.

Notwithstanding the huge market share owned by McDonald's and Burger King, Wendy's was able to successfully enter the fray because of the manner in which it arranged its resources to create a competitive advantage. Dave Thomas, after spending years in the fast-food business, believed that the major players had lost sight of the benefits consumers most desired: fast, hot, custom-made hamburgers. Wendy's designed its system with these key benefits as its guideposts. In Wendy's the sum of the intricacies—the drive-through window increasing speed, the position of the cooks and kitchen allowing hamburgers to be cooked just in time, and the double and triple patties creating a custom feel for the consumer—has allowed the chain to compete and prosper in the fast-food hamburger market.

and continually updated in an extracontractual *franchise operations manual*. This manual gives both parties the opportunity to update rules, regulations, and procedures that will come to bear over time.

Thus, in setting up the franchise, you must ask, What are all the individual transactions necessary to deliver the prescribed SDS? These tasks must then be allocated between the franchisor and franchisee on the basis of whether the task is best executed at a national (franchisor) level or at a local (franchisee) level. As a general guide, the franchisor tasks are those that carry economies of scale. This usually implies a size or bulk requirement in the task, such as management training or bulk purchase of equipment. Franchisee responsibilities are based on the task being executed on site in the local market, such as local sourcing of raw materials and hiring employees. Critical to local entrepreneurial intensity is customer contact and local market knowledge. Some tasks are shared. For example, the franchisor has a national role in marketing, and the franchisee is responsible for local interpretation and execution of advertising and promotion.

Once you allocate the tasks associated with the SDS, the franchisee can continue to assess costs and revenues through the use of pro forma[4] financial statements that incorporate the information already gleaned by determining the market demand. Table 2–1 lists sample transactions that would be part of the development of a fast-food restaurant such as Wendy's.

TABLE 2–1 Sample Transaction List

Franchisor: Centralized economies of scale	Franchisee: Local entrepreneurial intensity
1. Establish site acquisition criteria.	1. Locate site that fits criteria.
2. Design building blueprint specifications.	2. Initiate local contractor bidding.
3. National contracts for inventory and equipment specification and purchasing.	3. Onsite installation of equipment and inventory management.
4. Centralized training of franchisee management.	4. Onsite training of franchise employees.
5. Detail marketing plan template for radio, print media, and television promotions.	5. Placement of promotions in local media.

As we see in Figure 2–1, the link between the transaction analysis and financial structure is very direct. Each transaction incurs a cost or requires investment. The costs and investment are put in place to make sales. The sales are *revenue* on the income statement. The costs are *expenses* incurred to generate the revenue. Investment in property plant and equipment to set up your SDS are the assets on the balance sheet. Dave Thomas had to buy land large enough to handle the traffic associated with a drive-through and then install windows and equipment to make it work properly. Therefore, the transaction analysis defines the financial status of both the franchisor and franchisee.

Financial Structure: What Is the Financial Model of the Franchise Concept?

By understanding the illustrated core of the FRM, the customer, and the SDS, we have gained an understanding of the whole financial structure of the concept. Let's step back for a moment to gain some perspective. The customer definition provides the basic understanding of revenue. Marshaling the resources to establish the SDS allows you to understand the costs involved in meeting market demand; the SDS defines the costs of acquiring the revenue. The known revenue and known costs bring you directly to a clear understanding of your project's net revenue.

Once you've established them, you can use the costs related to the acquisition of resources, such as a stove or ice cream machine, to develop a balance sheet. Again, you have a unit of analysis issue. This analysis is initially done at the operating unit level. By the same token, you can use the costs of the resources necessary to extract demand to develop an income statement. When the hamburger or ice cream is actually delivered, you also have a price paid for the product as well as costs associated with food and labor—this provides the information for the income statement. Pro forma financial statements allow you to better understand the viability of the franchise system's business model prior to launch.

Although you construct the financial statements from the results of the individual transactions, understanding the impact of the fully integrated system is equally important. As evidenced by Wendy's success, the whole concept is typically greater than the sum of the individual component parts (the drive-through, the visible kitchen, the double patties.) The successful combination of these parts is paramount to establishing the competitive advantages of a franchise's business format—the key ingredient that will lead to the franchise's competitiveness in the market. You go through the process discussed to discover the richness of the unit economics of a single outlet, and once robustness is confirmed, you can extend the analysis to a systemwide expansion.

The phenomenon of the whole being greater than the sum of the parts is indicated by the delineation of tasks between the franchisor and the franchisees and is reflected in the value that is created through this cooperative synergy. The principle link between the franchise's proposed financial structure and the principal–agent relationship with the franchisor is the contract. Through the contract, the details of market development, task specification, and investment supply are addressed.

Agency Issues: How to Find the Right Franchise Partner

A key issue raised by any strategic business interdependency is the partner selection process and the ensuing principal-agent relationship. The agent, in most cases the franchisee, agrees to act on behalf of the principal, the franchisor. This symbiotic partnership is one of the key success factors of franchising; it is also one that requires considerable vigilance.

Is This Franchise Right for You?

One of the advantages of franchising is the abundance of information available to the franchisee. Not only do state and federal legislatures mandate the disclosure of pertinent financial information, but there is also a wealth of other current and useful information available. Although considerable due diligence information is available, potential franchisees are sometimes less rigorous about their investigation than they should be. They can quickly fall in love with a concept and forget to do the detailed due diligence on the franchisor that should be done and is readily available.

How Will a Franchisor Select You as a Franchisee?

The selection of franchisees by the franchisor, however, is more problematic. The tendency is for the franchisor to "sell" franchises rather than to cultivate long-term relationships. Yet a franchise agreement is, by definition, a long-term relationship. Moreover, as the franchisor, you rely upon the person you select to deliver the product to standard. You need to be clear about the skills and motivations of the people you select, especially in the early stages of the system's development.

Franchising assumes an urgency to grow. The need to generate capital from franchisees and then to build new outlets can sometimes overwhelm a franchisor's long-term planning concept and deteriorate the working relationships that have been developed with new franchisees. Haste can result in relaxed standards for choosing franchisees, but even when the franchisor is rigorous about franchisee selection, it is impossible to get perfect information about how a person will act as an entrepreneur and partner. To alleviate some of these selection problems, many franchisors have an intensive screening program for prospective entrepreneurs; the largest companies require significant work time in an operating outlet prior to becoming a franchisee. For example, Dunkin' Donuts conducts extensive personality profiling of prospective franchisees to ensure the appropriate match between the demands of the franchise and the skill set of the enthusiastic entrepreneur.

The various agency issues that come up as the partnership develops can only benefit from the free flow of information and open communication. In particular, without communication, two of the biggest hindrances to a successful partnership, free riding and shirking, are liable to rear their destructive heads. A *free riding* franchisee benefits from association with the franchise brand but neglects to pay for this benefit. The franchisee may, for example, agree to accept co-op advertising funds from a vendor in exchange for an endorsement, but then neglect to promote the product as agreed. The weight of the entire franchise system's advertising may still generate incremental customer flow to the individual franchisee even though he or she did not contribute a "fair share" to the advertising effort. Nonparticipating franchisees are said to be getting a "free ride" because they benefit from the system's advertising efforts without contributing their own part. However, in the long run, the system is eventually affected by the omission.

A *shirking* franchisee neglects a specific task or duty as outlined in the franchise agreement. A typical example is substituting less expensive, lower quality ingredients for one of the core ingredients of the franchise's products—such as using slightly less dough in the bagels or a lower grade of beef in hamburgers. Shirking is most prevalent in tourist areas with non-repeat customers, but it has also been known to occur at local franchisees too. For example, a franchisee who uses slightly less beef to make a hamburger still gets the customer's money but is shirking a contractual responsibility. Not only are these individual actions unethical, but they also erode the brand equity of the entire franchise system.

Relational Dynamics: How Are Tasks Best Monitored?

When you shake hands and sign a franchise agreement, what is not being said is this: "If you do everything you're supposed to do, we can conquer the world. If you do something wrong, we are all in trouble." A classic example is what happened to the Jack in the Box franchise in 1993. A franchisee inadvertently served tainted meat to a customer, who died as a result.[5] Brand equity was so severely damaged that it took the entire chain seven years to reach the systemwide revenue it had achieved prior to the incident. These types of unfortunate situations can have far-reaching repercussions not only for the individual franchisee, but also for both the corporate franchisor and other franchisees. If and when such scenarios occur, the depth of the franchisor–franchisee relationship is tested with potential solutions ranging from renegotiating license agreements or contracts to litigation in the worst case scenarios.

The Jack in the Box example is at the extreme. Most conduct detrimental to the franchise is much less significant—slightly slower counter service, dirty restrooms, inventory shortages—but nevertheless gnaw away at brand equity. Franchisors of all sizes and ages can make decisions that prove detrimental to their system. At one point, Ray Krok, the legendary founder of MacDonald's, insisted that a "hula burger" be introduced in MacDonald's restaurants. Franchisees lost a lot of money on the pineapple-covered hamburger that never gained public acceptance. Sten-tel was a burgeoning franchise that used patented technology to offer clients the ability to outsource dictation. They couldn't convince franchisees to make technology changes and eventually abandoned their plans to grow using franchising. Indeed, relational dynamics is the active management of the franchisee–franchisor relationship. The process of managing the relationship is both formal and informal. The reality is that if the franchisee or franchisor insists on a very strict interpretation of the license agreement, then conflict is almost assured, and it will likely result in litigation. So, as expectations are established, the partners need to monitor the activities of each other to make sure they are met.

Often, the franchise relationship is characterized as a principal–agent alliance, with the franchisor as the principal and the franchisee the agent. In reality, however, there is reciprocal interdependence—a dynamic relationship with the roles of principal and agent being filled by both parties under different circumstances. For the franchisor and franchisee to understand their respective roles in any given situation, the parties must conduct a transaction analysis with great care. Remember, transaction analysis is the allocation of tasks in the SDS to the partner best suited to execute them. After the tasks have been allocated, you have to make sure they're accomplished. Relational dynamics is the process of making sure the other parties do their jobs and discussing the implications of both successes and failures of execution. It also deals with communicating changes in the system. The objective is to monitor the activities to ensure compliance and to maintain and enhance the trademark value. The most sophisticated franchise system incorporates both a monitoring and a feedback system. The key is not only to monitor negative behavior but also to examine exceptional performance and feed this performance dynamic back to the rest of the franchise operators. It is incumbent on the aspiring franchisor to design this monitoring and feedback system early.

Of course, it is impossible to monitor all the activities of a partner. Not only is that cost prohibitive, but it would also erode confidence in the relationship. Tasks should be prioritized by franchisors and franchisees according to their potential impact on brand equity. Formal monitoring should also occur according to priority. At the heart of a good franchisee–franchisor relationship is communications. That comes through formal avenues like regional meetings for training and marketing and informal franchisee networks.

Information Systems

The key to building and maintaining a flow of information between franchisee and franchisor is that the flow must adequately police the operational standards of the system and must provide feedback of exceptional performance to the franchisor for review and possible systemwide implementation. Franchise companies provide perfect organizations for accomplishing these objectives. The franchisor must know the sales of the franchisees to collect royalties. Franchisees need access to centralized systems such as supply arrangements, training materials, R&D results, and marketing materials from the franchisor. Many franchises have information systems that monitor franchisee sales and tie them to supply requirements. But a few have learned how to share information among franchisees to solve problems and exploit opportunities as exampled in TIP 2–2.

TIP 2–2 Theory into Practice: Monitoring Tasks:
Technology that Identifies Flaws and Promotes
Winning Practices

In the Jiffy Lube system, point-of-sale computers are integrated with inventory systems. If store A serviced 2,481 cars, the inventory check should reflect that it used 2,655 gallons of motor oil (4.1 quarts per car) and 2,481 oil filters. The flow of information between that store and Jiffy Lube headquarters can show discrepancies. If a franchisee was wiping off oil filters instead of replacing them, it would be picked up by the Jiffy Lube system

Information flow can also uncover innovations that can improve a system. If a franchise headquarters sees that a franchisee is spending 12.5 percent of revenue on labor compared to the 14 percent national average, it may be able to replicate the innovations that the store is using to reduce labor costs across the system. Indeed, that happens at Jiffy Lube all the time. For example, automakers are under heavy pressure to increase gas mileage for their cars. That pressure has led engineers to take weight out of the automobiles (maybe to balance the increased weight of SUVs!). Smaller oil filters in tightly compacted engines makes removal very difficult and excessively time consuming. When a franchisee in Baltimore, Maryland, reported lower labor costs, the franchisor dispatched a team to understand why. The franchisee had invented a strap-like wrench that easily slipped into tight places. The franchisor further engineered the device and made it available to all the franchisees. What had been a problem was converted into a competitive advantage because information flow informed the franchisor.

The integration of control and feedback encourages franchisee participation because it creates the potential for synergy in a franchise system. Simply stated, each franchisee benefit from every other franchisee's effort to solve problems and exploit opportunities.

The Dynamics of the Franchisee–Franchisor Relationship: How Does the Franchise Entrepreneurial Alliance Adjust for Changes in the Market?

The final area of analysis in the FRM relates to the dynamics of the relationship and the mechanisms that help you manage change. The dynamic nature of the FRM is essential for your success. As the market evolves, you must shape your franchise system to efficiently respond. When market changes affect return to either of the parties, the fairness of the economics of the alliance must be reassessed. Pizza Hut franchisees legitimately asked, "Will pizza delivery hurt or enhance my economic position?"

ServiceMaster was founded as a moth-proofing company in 1929 by Marion E. Wade, a former minor league baseball player. ServiceMaster expanded to carpet cleaning in 1952, establishing one of America's first franchise businesses. In 1962 the company took its expertise to the health-care arena and pioneered what is now known as outsourcing. In 1980 it began serving the education market and expanded work offerings to business and industry. Changing with market demand transformed the moth-proofing company into a franchise giant and a Fortune 500 company.

By a fair return we do not necessarily mean an equal return, but rather a subjective perspective on the value of the relationship. When an imbalance is perceived, the two parties should discuss the issue and, if appropriate, make an effort to renegotiate the relationship. There is often "noise" in a franchise system—individual franchisees that have some complaint or other. That is not our focus here. When market dynamics or organizational design cause the majority of the franchisees to lose money, then this dis-equilibrium must be addressed. Problems can be resolved through a formal renegotiation of the license agreement or by making informal adjustments, such as improving supplier relations or instituting greater control over advertising funds. If renegotiation fails, litigation can ensue, although because of the financial and relational cost of litigation, it should be the last recourse of either party.

When you buy a franchise, you are making a 15- to 20-year commitment to a partnership with the franchisor. No relationship of any kind will continue that long without ups and downs. Many of the problems are trivial, some are important, and inevitably a few will test the viability of the company. You have to deal with these issues every day. Usually, the franchisees deal directly with the franchisor's field personnel. They are the people assigned to act as the franchisor's representative with the franchisee. Every franchise has someone in that role. You build a relationship that allows you to interact in a spontaneous and informal way. Building those informal methods of communication creates the credibility to deal with the more important issues. Invariably, the big concerns are centered on changes in the marketplace, competition, changing customer needs, an altered SDS, and inevitably financial implications for the partners. Clearly, the quality of the people in the field positions (their experience, education, training, internal support systems) is a leading indicator of the quality of the franchise organization as a whole.

Conclusion

The Franchise Relationship Model in Figure 2–2 is dynamic—as events affect one aspect of the model, all other aspects must be reviewed in a recurring iterative process. For example, if renegotiation of the license agreement were to result in a reduced royalty, the financial model would be altered. A change in royalty could dictate a change in the services that the franchisor provides. Any change creates a cascading effect throughout the system—a reconstruction of the relationship.

The FRM begins with opportunity recognition and shaping, and then articulates the competitive advantages and costs of the SDS that will extract the demand and create a return on investment. The emergent financial model is the manifestation of the interaction between the primary target customer and the SDS. The competitive sustainability of the franchise is embedded in the delineation of responsibilities between franchisor and franchisee and in the conscious design of the SDS. The franchisor's tasks are centrally executed and focus on economies of scale; the franchisee concentrates on those responsibilities that require local, onsite entrepreneurial intensity. By sharing both the burden of the SDS and the potential for ROI, the franchise entrepreneurial alliance is formed.

Central to the long-term stability of the franchise system is the proper selection of partners and monitoring of key partner responsibilities. However, even in the most stable relationship, a dynamic business environment dictates adjustments in the relationship to assure continued competitive advantage. Understanding the partner's tolerance zone is important. The tolerance zone is an informal interpretation of the rights and responsibilities of each partner; it allows for a margin of error, or tolerance, in the daily activities of the franchise in performance. Reacting to market changes can be standardized by formal review programs and kept unstructured by informal negotiations. As noted, failure to recognize the need for dynamic management of the relationship can often result in litigation.

The FRM illustrates how a concept innovator can construct a franchising company and the pathway for implementing it in the most entrepreneurial way. The model also eliminates those ideas that are best developed using another growth strategy, such as distributorships, licensing, or corporate-owned outlets.

You should now understand that franchising is entrepreneurial and the unique components of franchising that enable this entrepreneurial alliance. It is time to proceed to an in-depth discussion that documents the wealth-creating power of the franchise engine. Chapter 3 cites empirical evidence that franchising can be an effective way to achieve entrepreneurial success and personal wealth.

Endnotes

1. Disruptive technology is a new product or service that disrupts an industry and eventually wins most of the market share.
2. See Clayton Christiansen's article on disruptive technologies such as hard disk drives and steam shovels.
3. *www.iaetc.com*
4. Pro forma is a projection or estimate of what may result in the future from actions in the present. A pro forma financial statement is one that shows how the actual operations of a business will turn out if certain assumptions are achieved.
5. "E-Coli Scare Deals Blow to Seattle Burger Sales," *Restaurant Business,* March 20, 1993; "Fallout of E-Coli Episode Still Troubles Foodmarket," *Nation's Restaurant News,* March 20, 1995.

3 The Wealth-Creating Power of Franchising

Our first two chapters captured and detailed franchising as both an entrepreneurial vehicle and a systematic risk-reduction tool. We clearly established opportunity assessment as the core function of entrepreneurship and then illustrated how franchising must embody this principle. We also defined what a franchise is and how it is best assembled and/or examined using the franchise relationship model (FRM).

Now we discuss several issues that exist in virtually all businesses of scale: administrative efficiency, risk management, and resource constraints. Franchising can overcome such common obstacles. It is an efficient model for significant wealth creation. While making our case that a successful franchise follows from a highly developed franchise service delivery system (SDS), considerable capitalization, and significant growth, we further propose that obtaining public capital as an additional source of funding can be a piece of an overall successful franchise strategy. The most effective way to expand a concept is to launch and grow a small number of company-owned stores, to subsequently sell several franchises, to concurrently obtain public capital to increase the number of company-owned units, and to build an infrastructure for both. Please see TIP 3–1 for key aspects of wealth creation through franchising.

TIP 3–1   Risk Management: Ownership and Wealth[a]

Franchisees

The average franchisee

- owns 1 outlet
- has been in business for 9 years
- spends 8.5 percent of sales on promotions
- has $58,000 in after-tax profit
- has made an average investment of $155,000

Five percent of franchisees own 30 or more outlets.
The largest franchisee owns more than 500 outlets.

Franchisors

The average franchisor

- owns 13 percent of his or her system outlets
- franchises 87 percent of his or her system outlets
- has 75 percent of his or her franchisees owning only one outlet

a. Spinelli, Stephen, Jr. (1995). "A Triangulation of Conflict in the Franchise Inter-Organizational Form." Ph.D. dissertation. Imperial College, University of London, UK.

Understanding the Motivations of an Entrepreneur to Become a Franchisor

There may be no better franchise illustration of the glory and costs of rapid growth than Boston Chicken. Boston Chicken opened its first restaurant in 1985. Eight years later, in November 1993, it was a franchisor and floated an initial public offering. Serving healthy food that actually tasted good in a fast, casual setting was a simple but compelling story. Besides, restaurant sales had shown consistent and impressive growth. But Boston Chicken (which later changed its name to Boston Markets) transformed itself into more of a real estate mortgage company than a restaurant franchise. Until the IPO, Boston Chicken had grown by way of individual franchisees who put up substantial amounts of their own money to open new stores. To accelerate expansion to a dizzying pace, the company signed up financed area developers (FADs). These folks put up 20 percent of the required development costs for a market, and the rest provided by loans from Boston Markets.

The capital market appetite for Boston Chicken seemed insatiable. In 1997 the company raised over $400 million in bond offerings and convertible debt. At the same time, those choice FADs were losing increasing amounts of money—$156.5 million in 1997 alone.

Did Boston Chicken grow too fast, or did it lose sight of the business format that made it a success in the first place? It was probably guilty on both counts. The growth strategy is always dependent on the religious devotion to the business model and store-level economics. Success can be turned into dramatic failure when you forget that.

Historically, an entrepreneur launches a successful single outlet. That success often motivates a desire to add new outlets. If the entrepreneur perceives the opportunity as considerable, the human and financial capital requirement is likely to be bigger than the currently available resources. There are many ways to secure capital for new outlet growth, and as we have discussed, franchising has proven to be a significant method. When a franchisor sells a franchise unit, she is securing both the capital and the talent of the franchise partner—the franchisee. The one-time, upfront franchise fee, ongoing royalties, and franchise management system creates a sharing arrangement between the franchisor and franchisee. Once success has been achieved with the initial rollout of a franchised unit, most franchisors begin to think along the lines of, "If we can have 10 units, why not 25; if 25, why not 50; if 50, why not 150?" and so on. This successive growth logic becomes self-fulfilling as more success leads to more success—but only if you run the stores right and make a profit.

Eventually, Boston Chicken filed for Chapter 11 bankruptcy, reemerging only after being purchased by the MacDonald's Corporation.

Franchise Risk Profile Template: An Introduction

The franchise risk profile template (FRPT), shown in Table 3–1, is a guide in the franchise environment to perform due diligence on a specific franchise. As a prospective franchisee, you can use this tool to evaluate the risk–return scenario. The template allows the franchisee to filter the prospective franchise and the franchisor to construct or modify the franchise so that it scores well and appeals to a larger segment of the prospective franchisee population. This guide has been constructed to help you make an initial assessment of the franchise's strengths and weaknesses that will likely require further investigation. It is by no means meant to assess the overall potential of a franchise. Rather, it offers a perspective on the balance of risk and return that the franchisee requires. The FRTP is a mapping device, not a formula. We have segmented the FRTP by the business model–scaling hurdles that franchising addresses: administrative efficiency, risk management, and resource deconstraining. In the FRTP the level of market performance a franchise has achieved indicates the extent to which it has overcome the given hurdle.

A company that is lower on the risk scale will offer a lower average market return than a company that is higher on the scale. The higher risk franchise will clearly require the promise of an extremely large return to induce investment.

You should consider the criteria in the FRTP before purchasing a franchise. Of course, franchisors should therefore consider these criteria when they make a franchise offering.

Agency Problems and Administrative Efficiency

Even if you run a single store, you can't do everything. But if you want to grow the business, you simply must delegate major responsibilities. The problem is that most entrepreneurs think they do things better than almost anyone else. Simply stated, the concept of *agency* asks, How does the business owner know that delegated tasks are performed exactly as he or she prefers? Once this question can be answered, then the business owner will attain administrative efficiency—a documented process of efficient and effective business operation. Administrative efficiency is the means by which agency problems are managed.

Most businesses grow to the point that the company-owned locations can no longer be managed cost effectively by the corporation. This is the point of zero or negative marginal return. Some additional mechanism for control must be implemented, with additional costs. This can be the trigger for a business to consider franchising.

Monitoring processes implemented through managers or operational and financial system controls are practical ways to monitor quality—but at what cost to the business in dollars, opportunity, or both? One of the biggest cost factors, for instance, occurs when organizations decide to manage and grow their business through the hierarchical use of assistant managers, managers, general managers, district managers, national managers, and so on. When this process of management is used in a corporate-owned chain of outlets, management performance becomes divorced from ownership.[1] The level of performance may become suboptimal because managerial accountability is not directly linked to compensation. Because the outlet managers in a company-owned store do not directly reap the rewards, or suffer the consequences of their actions, the feedback mechanism that could reduce inappropriate management behaviors such as shirking or free riding is, in effect, rusty and relatively less effective.[2] To correct this effect, the entrepreneur and/or the company's management must incur high system-monitoring costs. This may solve the behavioral problems but restrict both the speed and the extent of growth.

TABLE 3–1 Franchise Risk Profile Template

Criteria		Risk/Return Profile			
	Low Risk	**Acceptable Risk**	**High Risk**	**Extreme Risk**	
	Avg. Market Return	**Incremental**	**Marginal**	**Large Return**	
	15–20 Percent Return	**30 Percent Return**	**40–50 Percent Return**	**60–100 Percent Return**	
Agency Concerns:					
Outlet performance disclosed or discerned	Yes, 90 percent + apparently profitable	Yes, 80 percent + apparently profitable	Yes, 70 percent + apparently profitable	No, or less than 70 percent profitable	
Business format	Sophisticated training, documented operations manual, identifiable feedback mechanism with franchisees	Initial training and dynamically documented operations manual, some field support	Training and operations but weak field support	Questionable training and field support and static operations	
Term of the license agreement	20 years with automatic renewal	15 years with renewal	Less than 15 years or no renewal	Less than 10 years	
Site development	Quantifiable criteria clearly documented and tied to market specifics	Markets prioritized with general site development criteria	General market development criteria outlined	Business format not tied to identifiable market segment(s)	

TABLE 3–1 Franchise Risk Profile Template (Continued)

Criteria	Risk/Return Profile			
	Low Risk	**Acceptable Risk**	**High Risk**	**Extreme Risk**
	Avg. Market Return	**Incremental**	**Marginal**	**Large Return**
	15–20 Percent Return	**30 Percent Return**	**40–50 Percent Return**	**60–100 Percent Return**
Franchise fee and royalties	Present discounted value (PDV)[a] of the fees are less than the demonstrated economic advantages (reduced costs or increased revenue) of the franchise versus standalone	PDV of the fees are equal to but projected to be less than the economic advantages of the franchise versus standalone.	PDV of the fees are projected to be less than the expected economic advantages (reduced costs or increased revenue) of the franchise versus standalone	PDV of the fees are not discernibly less than the expected value of the franchise
SIZE/RISK MANAGEMENT:				
Multiple market presence	National	Regional	State	Local
Market share	#1 and dominant	#1 or #2 with a strong competitor	Lower than #2	Lower than #3 with a dominant player

TABLE 3–1 Franchise Risk Profile Template (Continued)

Criteria	Risk/Return Profile			
	Low Risk	Acceptable Risk	High Risk	Extreme Risk
	Avg. Market Return	Incremental	Marginal	Large Return
	15–20 Percent Return	30 Percent Return	40–50 Percent Return	60–100 Percent Return
Number of company owned outlets	Cluster of company owned outlets near headquarters and or regional franchisor offices	Some company owned outlets used for R&D	No company owned outlets or a large number of company outlets purchased from former franchisees	No company outlets and no strategic plan to develop such outlets
RESOURCE CONSTRAINTS:				
National marketing program	Historically successful creative process, national media buys in place	Creative plus regional media buys	Creative plus local media buys	Local media buys only

a. The present discounted value of an income stream evaluates the income stream of an opportunity and the discount rate that incorporates a measure of risk into the equation.

Let's refer back to the FRPT in Table 3–1 for a moment. Under Agency Concerns, we list outlet performance disclosed or discerned—the economics of the individual unit as a key indicator of an efficient system. In plain language, if the stores are profitable, then the franchisor system has, generally speaking, overcome agency issues. The second criteria, business format, allows you to understand whether profitability is a result of overcoming agency issues through a well-documented system or simply a case of the "rising tide" phenomenon. When a franchise offers something new to an accepting customer base, it may gain success because it was the first and maybe only such offering. Inefficiencies that become more apparent as the market develops and competition increases will deteriorate store-level economics. Boston Chicken is a prime example. In either case you would like to understand whether the system is moving in the right direction toward documentation and monitoring of the mechanisms that generate profits. The best way to discover the truth is to study the revenue growth in existing stores from quarter to quarter and examine how fast new stores reach and exceed breakeven. Asking the franchisor and existing franchisees direct questions is always a good idea!

The next criteria, franchise fee and royalty, is the mechanism that franchising uses to share the productive benefits of the relationship and therefore create the economic motivation for both parties to "act like owners." The franchise fee and royalties are payments from the franchisee to the franchisor. The profit or loss from operating a store is the incentive for the franchisee. The partners share responsibilities and feel better that their goals are aligned through the profit incentive. Ownership induces behavior that is directly linked to the bottom line—positively or negatively. In order to better understand how franchise fees and royalties are determined, it is helpful to first look at the framework franchisees use in evaluating whether to buy a franchise or open their own business.

Buy a franchise, or launch a standalone?

We can begin to manage the decision process surrounding a franchise opportunity by using the PDV exercise in Figure 3–1; this will help us understand the reality of pursuing a franchise by considering the income streams and discounted value of both franchise and standalone opportunities.

We are often asked, "Should I buy a franchise or develop my own store?" While PDV is a pretty straightforward formula, greater nuance is necessary to tease out the issues that affect the calculation.

"The present discounted value of an income stream" contains two key concepts—discount and income. The discount rate is the reduction in the future income based on the chance (expressed as a percentage) that we will not achieve expected results. A new business idea is often "discounted" up to 70 percent in pro forma financial statement analysis. The greater probability of success of a

A franchise should be bought instead of an independent operation started when the PDV of the income stream from the franchised outlet is greater than the present discounted value of the income stream from the standalone operation. While our experience is that few franchisors or prospective franchisees actually do the math, they all think through the exercise by reviewing the options. Why not be more rigorous and apply numbers? The market rate of franchisee fees and royalties should be set at the point where the calculation is favorable to the franchise instead of the standalone.

FIGURE 3–1 PDV exercise.

franchise lowers the discount rate for the franchise operation because a "proven" business model has less risk than a new concept (i.e., a new standalone operation). Because the success of a franchise rests, to some degree, on the development and beta testing of a business model, positive market response to this business model is what the franchisor is really "selling" when a franchise is sold. The discount rate could be half that of a standalone operation.

An additional benefit to franchising is economies of scale in marketing, purchasing, and property, plant, and equipment (PP&E), which translates into more efficient growth and faster solidification of the brand. In most cases, having a recognized franchise brand versus a new standalone brand results in greater income sooner.

How Do Franchisors Determine the Amount of Franchisee Fees and Royalties?

Similar to the analysis franchisees conduct in assessing whether to pursue a franchise or standalone model, franchisors often ask, What should I charge for franchisee fee and royalty? The franchise fee is the one-time, upfront payment, and the royalty is paid as a percentage of sales as they occur over the term of the license agreement. The answer is to make the same PDV calculation as in Figure 3–1, but to interpret the results from a slightly differently perspective. If the PDV of the franchisee's income stream is not greater than the PDV of the standalone operation, the concept is weak. If the PDV is greater, then we have a monetary value, which is essentially the difference between PDVs, to begin with and then to alter according to current market conditions. Hypothetically, if the franchise PDV is $1 million and the standalone PDV is $700,000, then the franchisor can reasonably charge a franchise fee plus royalty of $299,999 or *less*, depending on current market conditions. In the marketplace of franchise business opportunities there are presently approximately 4,200 franchises. The perceived strengths of the franchise and the respective costs of other business opportunities create the adjustments to the $299,999 difference between the franchise's income stream and the outlet's income stream.

Current market forces will of course naturally control how high a figure will be tolerated. The stronger the franchise is perceived to be, the closer to $299,999 can be charged. What part of the theoretical $299,999 should be franchise fee and what part should be royalty is generally the next question on the franchisor's mind. Because the market does not supply perfect information, the prospective franchisee cannot know everything about a franchisor. However, in general, a higher franchise fee is a signal to the potential franchisee that the franchise is of high quality. For example, many home-cleaning franchises have a franchise fee of under $20,000, and Merry Maids is $32,500. Why? Such a difference in cost would signal the differentiated and higher quality aspects of the Merry Maids franchise. Which is better, a $10 bottle of wine or the $20 bottle? In reality, we don't know which wine is better. But for many people, the price signals one as better than the other.

Some franchisors might attempt to charge a very high franchise fee to send a false signal of quality. The reality is that the market won't sustain that fee if stores aren't profitable.

The franchisee and franchisor are making the same bet that the franchise outlets will generate a faster-growing and more stable income stream than a chain of independent outlets. In general, although the perceived or actual strength of the operation will increase the royalty and franchise fee for the franchisor, it will also reduce the risk for the franchisee. You must remember that the marketplace is dynamic, and the PDV calculation must be reassessed often to monitor the marketplace. There are several risks to consider in pursuing a franchise as a business opportunity, but with the PDV exercise, you can gain a great deal of insight into the actual financial opportunity.

Size and Risk Management

The next section of the FRPT relates size of the system to risk. Generally, the larger the system becomes, the larger are the economies of scale, the lower the costs, the higher the profits, and therefore the less risky is a franchise opportunity. For example, when a system has only four units, the media exposure and brand awareness that are generated—and that subsequently reinforce themselves over time—are entirely different from the exposure and brand strength of a system that has reached 1,000 units. When a significant size is reached, signals of strength and consequently reduced risk are sent to the market. These are real factors of lowered risk for the franchisee. As the next exercise demonstrates, these lowered risk factors not only increase the income but will also lower the discount rate for the franchisee. Total number and market placement of outlets is indicative of consumer acceptance and power in the marketplace. Profitability drives the need and motivation to grow a system, and growth makes profitability more feasible because of economies of scale. It is a virtuous economic cycle.

The FRPT links multiple market presence and market share as defining criteria for measuring market size. For example, a system that has 100 units spread across the country does not have the same market presence as a system that has 100 units in one geographic region. The concentration of outlets tends to create marketing economies of scale and increases administrative efficiency. Therefore, the system with dominant market share in a number of markets is the least risky.

Most franchisors make an attempt to operate stores. Some have proven to be quite good store operators. Radio Shack has 2.5 times as many company-owned stores as franchised stores.[3] It pushes out geographically from its headquarters until the monitoring costs become too high or until it simply wants to grow faster than its available capital allows, and then it sells more franchises. Keeping in mind that the per-unit development cost for each new unit is identical for franchisor and franchisee, you must consider the capital requirements of the franchisor. For example, developing four corporate-owned units could be capital-prohibitive in comparison to developing one corporate unit and franchising the other three. In the former case, the required investment for development could be so high as to retard growth, whereas in the latter, the increase in cash flow may very well enable further expansion more quickly. Therefore, the franchisor seeks to implement franchises as a means of leveraging the concept and franchisee capital—a fundamental underpinning of franchising. TIP 3–3 illustrates the principle of balancing capital needs in a growing franchise system.

TIP 3–2   Theory into Practice: Risk Management—An Intelligent
                Growth Strategy[a]

Panera Bread is an interesting, relatively new franchise. Originally based in Saint Louis and called Saint Louis Bread Company, it expanded to 20 company-owned stores between 1987 and 1993. Panera used St. Louis to discover the nature and extent of its economies of scale, to create brand awareness in a large, single market, and to refine its service delivery system. After making numerous enhancements to the concept, the company began to franchise. By early 2003, Panera had over 400 stores and $350 million in revenue. It currently has franchisee commitment for over 700 new outlets.

Panera's is executing a classic franchise strategy. It used its capital to build out the market surrounding its headquarters, perfected the concept, then used franchisee capital to create explosive growth. Panera has balanced its ability to grow company-operated restaurants with its available capital. But by using franchising, it has been able to accelerate growth 250 percent, as shown in the table below.

a.   *http://www.panera.com*

Year	U.S. Franchises	Canadian Franchises	Foreign Franchises	Company-Owned
2002	291	0	0	123
2001	212	0	0	100
2000	134	0	0	87
1999	73	0	0	79
1998	31	0	0	63

Balancing Company and Franchised Outlets

Thirteen percent of all outlets in franchise companies are company-owned stores. For every store that a franchisor develops, seven more franchised stores are built—a finding supported by our discussion of capital allocation. Refer to Figure 3–1 for the number of outlets criteria. The average franchise system's investment capital (including franchisor and franchisee) can produce seven times the number of stores that a wholly owned independent chain can by leveraging the franchisor's concept with the prospective franchisee's capital. The franchisor has expanded the brand system by four units but has incurred direct investment costs for only one unit.

Once a company begins to expand in size, the principal administrative requirements shift to the *franchisees*. At what size, in terms of number of outlets owned, does the franchisee exceed her management capacity? Clearly, this is different for each system and indeed for each franchisee. But the smart franchisor is aware of the issue and monitors management capacity. Franchisees often invest a significant portion of their net worth in a single outlet. By doing so, they are not taking full advantage of the diversification benefits that can accrue through a diversified portfolio of outlets in different franchise systems. That diversification can occur by simply using the investment you would make in purchasing a franchise to instead purchase a portfolio of franchise company stocks. These franchisees leave themselves potentially exposed to a high level of franchisor-specific risk, just as an investor that holds only one sector of investments, or only one stock, faces similar risks of overspecification. In a frictionless market in which information sharing is seamless and instantaneous, no additional returns would be expected to compensate for what is, in effect, the self-inflicted pain of not diversifying when perfect information is possible.

However, the franchise market is far from frictionless, with limited buyers and sellers, large degrees of informational asymmetries, and constrained capital. Under these circumstances, it is conceivable that above-market rates of return need to be provided to franchisees to entice them to join the franchisor's system. Therefore, franchisees are more likely to invest in those franchises that outperform the general corporate market. This suggests that younger systems may have to adjust their franchise fee and royalty down. In and of itself, this conclusion begs the question of which needs to come first: the chicken or the egg—quality franchisees or high-performance franchisors? The reality is that most systems are dynamic. Early franchisees are taking a bigger risk. If performance is exceptional, they attract high-quality people to the system.

Resource Constraints

Any organization's attempt to grow will inevitably be hindered by a lack of capital. Franchising can meet the need to conserve capital while continuing to achieve growth.[4] In a franchise context the capital influx from franchise fees reduces the need for the franchisor to raise money to grow,[5] conserves the franchisor's capital,[6] and establishes a distribution network more quickly than does a chain of company-owned outlets.[7] Franchisee capital is specifically earmarked by the franchisor for implementation of a rapid growth strategy.[8] Entrepreneurs clearly perceive the opportunity for rapid growth and the acquisition of franchisee capital as important reasons to pursue franchising.[9] The FRPT tracks the general use of franchisee capital contributions to the growth of the system and the financial health of the franchisor. The franchisor's health is due in part to the health of the stores and in part to good management of resources.

The FRPT is our guide to franchisor-specific due diligence. Industry-standard documentation in franchising contains much of the information for due diligence and reveals extensive financial data. The Uniform Franchise Offering Circular (UFOC) and the license agreement can answer many of the questions raised by the FRPT. The first is government-mandated franchise disclosure. The second document is the contract between the franchisee and the franchisor, which is typically standardized within a franchise system.

Franchise Disclosure: An Insight into Individual Franchisor Health and Wealth

The franchise relationship is characterized by a high degree of informational asymmetry. This means that the franchisor and the franchisee do not have access to the same knowledge about the strengths and weaknesses of the franchise. The Federal Trade Commission (FTC) does not require franchisors to disclose franchisee earnings, which tends to reinforce the franchisor's ability to camouflage poor performance and to maintain a financial advantage (higher franchise fees and royalties) far longer than might prevail under more stringent disclosure rules. The FTC argues that a disclosure of average earnings would be as misleading as no disclosure at all, because such a wide range of earnings exists among franchisees that the average is relatively meaningless.[10] Limited disclosure does not benefit all franchisors either, but it generates a "lemons" problem[11] wherein good firms are pooled with bad firms and, unable to attract capital at reasonable rates, progressively disappear from the market. Franchisors can signal their superior quality, however, by building their brand through successful stores. By constructing the franchise concept with the FRM in mind, the franchisor will extract the most efficient system and highest returns and will stand out in the crowd of those who have chosen not to perform such due diligence in the shaping of their opportunity.

License Agreement: How the Franchise Shares Responsibilities and Wealth

One of the key operating features of the franchise partnership is the license agreement, a document that codifies the relationship between franchisor and franchisee. Six sections of this document are relatively consistent throughout franchising and represent the core of the operating arrangement. Table 3–2 is a chart that describes the license agreement item, its overall impact, and the effect of that impact on your perception of the return potential as a franchisee (called a *marketplace signal*).

TABLE 3–2 **License Agreement Key Provision Impact Analysis**

License Agreement Item	Impact	Marketplace Signal
TERM: Details the length of the contract between the franchisor and franchisee in years.	This defines the number of years used in the calculation of the PDV of the income stream.	Longer = positive
RENEWAL: This defines the ability of the franchisee to add additional years to the license agreement.	This increases the number of years of potential income stream.	Renewal = positive
FRANCHISE FEE: The one-time, upfront fee the franchisee pays the franchisor when the license agreement is signed.	Impacts the initial investment and signals relative quality of the franchise.	Higher = positive

TABLE 3–2 **License Agreement Key Provision Impact Analysis** (Continued)

License Agreement Item	Impact	Marketplace Signal
ROYALTY: This is a percentage of the outlet revenue that is paid to the franchisor throughout the term of the license agreement.	Establishes the linkage between the success of the franchisee and the franchisor.	Higher = positive
MARKETING FEE: This is usually a percentage of revenue (sometimes a flat fee) that the franchisee must commit to marketing expenditures.	Signals the firm's commitment to building the brand and driving economies of scale in marketing.	Higher = positive
SUPPLY REQUIREMENTS: Outlines the rights and responsibilities of the franchisee in purchasing.	Some franchisors attempt to make money by selling goods to their franchisees. Others act as a negotiating agent for the franchisee to obtain national contracts. This section of the license agreement is key to understanding the potential for economies of scale in supply.	National contracts with third-party vendors = positive

These license agreement features offer a realistic context in which to consider the specifics of the concept. They codify the economic relationship between the franchisor and franchisee and therefore affect the income stream that is used in the PDV calculation. They are also tools to differentiate a given franchise from another. For example, when the average advertising fee is $20,000 and yours is $100,000, the difference screams, "Why?" Your higher fee should correspond to higher quality, and you should be ready to communicate that advantage to franchisees.

Franchising Benchmarks

Remember our discussion regarding the franchise fee and royalty rate that the franchisor can charge? Although we focused on the Present Discounted Value calculation, we were careful to discuss the adjustments to the calculated amount brought on by market forces. What are the other 4,199 franchisors charging for their franchises? Table 3–3 reflects some of the essential variables that define market conditions. Remember, not only are you making a decision to buy a franchise or start a stand alone business, you are also making a decision among franchises. When you assess a particular franchise this data provides a benchmark to make a comparison.

TABLE 3–3   Key Factors in the Franchise Relationship[a]

	Average	Range
Percent outlets owned	26.4 percent	0–88.1 percent
Percent outlets franchised	74.25 percent	12.1–100 percent
Franchise fee	$28,559	$5,000–$122,500
Royalty rate	5.58 percent	2–12 percent
Advertising fee	3.84 percent	0–15 percent
Term of the contract	13.79 years	5–20 years
Total number of outlets	2,652	104–13,604

a. Spinelli, Stephen, Benoit Leleux, and Sue Birley, (2003). "An Analysis of Shareholder Return in Public Franchisor Companies," Journal of Private Equity, Summer 2003.

Key Factors in the Franchise Relationship

These franchise dimensions are taken from 91 publicly traded franchisors that, as a cohort, have outperformed the S&P 500 over 10 of the last 11 years. They help us understand what to look for from existing franchisors and also provide a template for aspiring franchisors to reshape their opportunities. Some important interpretations include the following:

- The top-performing franchisors have a mix of company-owned and franchised outlets. Some franchisors expand their store ownership through accessing public capital. These franchisors have the best of both worlds: rapid growth and store ownership. Owning company stores also signals the franchisor's ability to do point-of-sale research and development.

- The calculation of the franchise fee and royalty is affected by what other franchisors are charging. Table 3–3 establishes the high-performer standards for the fees paid to the franchisor.

- The average marketing fee, in combination with the total number of outlets, explains the firm's marketing power.

- The term of the contract not only helps in the PDV calculation but also establishes the time frame required to provide a return on investment in line with the top-performing franchises.

Franchisor wealth creation results from an intricate combination of key characteristics. Traditionally, this combination has centered on rich unit economics, an ability to transfer excellence, and the potential for economies of scale. However, the bond between franchisors and franchisees, as embodied in the license agreement and in the parties' informal relationship, is of equal importance. Potential franchisors should understand that the details in the license agreement will shape the relationship with the franchisees. Franchisees in turn should use these details as a clear pathway to choosing a potential franchise.

Our general assumption has been growth through internally funded sources or through the introduction of franchisee capital. But public capital can serve as a supercharged catalyst for systemwide growth. Let's explore the notion of public capitalization in further detail.

Public Capitalization: An Expanded View of the Franchise Company

Because rapid growth is the goal, most franchise systems are continually seeking additional capital. When scale is achieved, the amount of acquired capital becomes increasingly important. Accessing capital through the public stock markets is a faster, if not the fastest, means of obtaining large amounts of capital. Some franchisors have not limited their capital to franchise fees and royalties. Many have used private equity, and approximately 250 of the total 4,200 franchisors have acquired public capital.

Our research compared the total shareholder return for public franchisors to the S&P 500 index for an 11-year period from January 1990 through December 2001. For 10 of those years, excluding 1999's "irrational Internet exuberance," public franchisors outperformed the S&P 500 in total return to shareholders.[12] The wealth created by these "public" franchisors makes it apparent they're doing something right. It is also clear that the public markets are an additional source of capital that can enable the explosive launch and growth that franchise entrepreneurs crave.

Public capital might allow the franchisor to lower the franchise fee. The effect is to accelerate growth because lower startup costs attract more franchisees. The franchisor can then back-load her income stream with a higher royalty. Royalties on sales directly tie success of the franchisor to the success of the franchisee. While this seems obvious to most of us, franchisors can lose sight of it. Boston Chicken got so caught up in growth that it forgot about its franchisees' success. It actually derived more of its income from financing franchisee development and receiving interest on the loans than from royalties.

Conclusion

The sheer size of franchising in terms of number of stores, revenue generated in the United States, and its significant portion of the U.S. GDP is evidence enough of its success. Franchising accounts for more than a third of the annual retail sales in the United States; clearly, it is a successful wealth-creating vehicle.[13] The capital marketplace would simply not support this pathway to entrepreneurship if return on investment did not warrant it. This chapter is the first clear documentation of both franchisee and franchisor wealth creation. The debate is advanced in favor of our argument that franchising, for all the stakeholders, is entrepreneurial in nature and fact.

Although the potential for wealth creation is clear, the road to success is fraught with details that can derail great opportunities. Here, we've provided substantial evidence that franchising as an entrepreneurial alliance can fulfill the promise of wealth creation. By examining the major components of the SDS in later chapters, we also show how the combination of these components can create sustainable competitive advantages for the franchise company.

Endnotes

1. Carney and Gedajlovic, 1991; Kruegger, 1991; Castrogiovanni, Bennet, and Combs, 1995

2. Holstromm, 1979

3. Martin, 1998

4. Oxenfeldt and Kelly, 1969

5. Fladmor-Lindquist, 1996

6. Martin and Justis, 1993

7. McGuire and Staelin, 1983

8. Fladmoe-Lindquist et al., 1996

9. McGuire and Staelin, 1983

10. Tannenbaum, 1997

11. Alkerhof, 1970

12. Return to shareholders is defined as dividends plus capital gains.

13. *www.de.state.az.us/links/economic/webpage/eaweb/gdp.html* shows retail sales in the United States for 1999 as $858,364,000,000.

4   Service Delivery System and Real Estate

Anyone reading this book will learn my real estate secrets. I'm not sure I'm happy about that.

—David Townsend, Real Estate Developer

MacDonald's is one of the largest *real estate* companies in the world. Boston Markets' problems discussed in Chapter 3 were rooted in its real estate strategy. At the International Council of Shopping Centers convention in Las Vegas, Radio Shack is a major player.

In this chapter we revisit the subject of the franchise's Service Delivery System (SDS), first introduced in Chapter 2 as part of the franchise relationship model (FRM) and explore the role of real estate. The SDS is the core of a franchise system, just as the "kernel"[1] is the core of a software program's written code. Chapters 4 through 6 cover three of the major aspects of the SDS: real estate and construction, monitoring and control, and marketing. Although each subject is looked at in turn, they are interwoven and interdependent.

We first concentrate on the most tangible aspects of the franchise SDS—real estate, buildings, construction, and operations—essentially, the customer-facing front end of the franchise's operation. This is not simply a discussion of building stores; rather, it is about building your brand in your market. Also, the links between real estate and business format franchising can help you increase wealth.

We investigate the SDS's real estate from a developer's perspective and then weave in the monitoring and control needs of a franchise. They are integrated to create a competitive advantage that becomes a highly efficient wealth-creating platform. Well-developed real estate processes enable the business format franchise to transfer excellence in a more standardized fashion. The extent to which a system can integrate its real estate and operational aspects determines the robustness of the resulting SDS.

Let's begin with a review of the major definition of an SDS.

In its most narrow sense, the SDS could be the way in which a building is set up, how a cooking area is designed, how a mobile fleet is dispatched and routed, or the manner in which customer service representatives are trained. TIP 4–1 offers some insight into a well-known franchise that relies heavily on its service delivery system to achieve success.

TIP 4–1 Theory into Practice: Service Delivery System

Kinko's[a] primary target audience (PTA) is the college student. Because of this focus, Kinko's locates its real estate acquisitions as close to a major college or university as possible. Easy access by the PTA is an essential element of its SDS. The delivery of services to students is prioritized by the amount of demand. For example, the wide counter area nearest the front entrance is essentially a triage system, which evaluates the nature of the specific customer's demand and then funnels the DIY (do-it-yourself) traffic to self-serve computers or copiers, or serves the DIFM (do-it-for-me) job requirements. Location, flow of internal customer traffic, and an understanding of detailed customer demand are all intimate and essential aspects of the Kinko's SDS.

a. Kinko's is 30-year-old photocopy business that caters primarily to businesses and students. Kinko's has also included rental computers into its product mix. Please see *www.kinkos.com* for complete information.

Just as the aspects of the SDS are derived and designed based on the needs and characteristics of the PTA, the characteristics of the SDS dictate the parameters of real estate development. The real estate is often the point-of-sale, the deciding factor for making a retail sale. Of course, the building, either existing or new construction, is important also, but the building can be altered—the land cannot.

Our discussion covers how to select and value real estate properties and some of the financial and operational issues regarding how franchisors and franchisees can best maximize property value.

The Basics of Real Estate

Real estate has long been a vehicle for the creation of wealth for both individuals and businesses. For example, when an individual pays down a mortgage, he receives a return on his investment through mortgage reduction. This investment eventually leads to full ownership of an asset and an overall increased net worth. In addition, some businesses also create wealth through the development of real estate for sale or lease to other businesses. In the past, real estate has played a primary role in wealth creation for some of the nation's wealthiest people. In the 1990s the role of real estate as a driver of wealth diminished in the United States. In 1984, approximately 33 percent of the people on the *Forbes* 400 list of the nation's wealthiest people acquired their wealth from the real estate and the oil and gas industry. This number dropped to approximately 20 percent in 1994 and 17 percent in 1997. However, with the bear market early in the 21st century, money is again pouring into real estate. A majority of the list has significant assets in real estate. Real estate still plays a critical "indirect" role by driving the success of several businesses, which directly drives wealth creation in the United States.

However significant these statistics may seem, they belie the fact that the underlying real estate is only valuable if it provides a platform to deliver a product or service in fulfillment of market demand. The value of the services you provide on the real estate validates real estate investment.

Platform for Service Delivery System and Influence of Buyer Behavior

Purchasing behavior is the aspect of the PTA research that drives the real estate sourcing process. Specifically, buyer behavior varies according to the product being sold. Retail purchasing behavior is often categorized in three general ways: spontaneous, semi-planned, and planned. The building is in essence the physical platform through which the franchise delivers its value to the customer. The phrases "location, location, location" and "a B location guarantees you a failure in profitability" are not to be ignored. However, the premise that location is key to success holds to varying degrees according to the type of customer that is being targeted by the franchise. We address some of the customer behaviors that guide the type of real estate that should be acquired.

- *Spontaneous Purchase Behavior:* A spontaneous purchase is a purchase in which the time between deciding to make the purchase and the actual purchase are nearly simultaneous. Essentially, no planning is involved in such purchases. The items purchased are often low-commitment items.

The convenience of the purchase is a paramount factor in deciding where to make this purchase. Examples of spontaneous purchases include one's morning coffee, gasoline, or a daily newspaper from a newsstand. Because convenience is critical for purchase, prime real estate is also critical for success of these retail businesses. Even a well-known brand such as Dunkin' Donuts located in a class B site can fail.

- *Semi-Planned Purchase Behavior:* A semi-planned purchase consists of two stages. First, there's a triggering event that initiates the actual decision to make a purchase. For example, when three months have passed, or 3,000 miles have been driven in your car, you recognize it is time to have an oil change. Second, there's a time gap between the times at which the "problem" is identified, the decision to make a purchase has been made, and the purchase transaction occurs. The Moto Photo franchise exists on the premise that customers want to shorten the time from taking a picture to having a high-quality print. The nature of the purchase allows for a period of delay because the need is not perceived as immediate. The time period can be extended for two reasons: The actual execution of the purchase will take some time and therefore must be fit into the customer's schedule, and/or the purchase itself requires some consideration and more planning time is required.

Another example of a semi-planned purchase is the dry cleaning services of Zoots, a fairly new entrant in the laundry and dry cleaning landscape. The franchisor observed people and determined frequency with which customers need regular dry cleaning services. Also in question are larger ticket cleaning items, such as formal wear and even fur garments. Because individuals may be able to forgo dry cleaning for a few days at any given time, the need for this service is not as acute as for other products. But timing of the dry cleaning need is generally calculable.

The real estate associated with a semi-planned business purchase is often the most difficult behavior to preselect because it is not clear exactly how "prime" the real estate needs to be for success. Prime real estate is that which will most likely produce retail revenue and which market forces will naturally price at the highest levels. But when a retailer is assessing where to locate her business, real estate should be selected relative to what is optimal regarding cost and benefit. Remember, the retailer's goal is to minimize real estate cost while optimizing the location benefits required by the customer. This is usually an iterative process that a franchisor and franchisee deal with every day. Collecting the appropriate data and experience allows the franchisor to pass on the key elements of location that best deliver value to the customer. If you purchase prime real estate and business is not profitable enough to support the high expense, then unit economics will not be robust enough to merit operation. Prime real estate is, by definition, the most expensive and therefore imposes high fixed overhead. However, the richness of the unit economics is paramount in defining the occupancy cost of the property as a percentage of the revenue generated at the site. Conversely, attempts to cut corners with a poor site will also prove fruitless because the losses from the operation's lower revenues will absorb any real estate cost savings. The nature of consumer buying behavior affects the real estate decision. In the semiplanned purchase discussed in the previous example, the consumer takes some time to contemplate the purchase. This "thought time" relaxes the requirement to have a location convenient to the immediacy of the spontaneous purchase decision. TIP 4–2 illustrates the significance that location choice has on the profitability of a franchised unit.

- *Planned Purchase Behavior:* A planned purchase is one in which the time between deciding to make the purchase and actually making it is relatively long. There is a great deal of consideration involved in this purchase behavior, which might necessitate visiting several stores regarding a possible single purchase. These items tend to be more costly and can often be classified as either capital necessities or luxuries. Examples include the purchase of an automobile, furniture, home appliances, electronics, or a personal computer. Luxury items might include a diamond engagement ring. By definition, convenience is not a primary factor in the purchase, and therefore prime retail real estate may not be critical for the success of the business. However, alternative variables such as price, quality, and overall brand perception may have significant impact.

TIP 4–2 Theory into Practice: Location Choice

Pizza Hut originally employed a strategy of family style eat-in dining. But when Domino's' delivery-only model began to impact its business volume, Pizza Hut had to react. The original Pizza Hut locations were situated on prime real estate. However, when it began to change its overall model to incorporate a delivery aspect, Pizza Hut understood that the "delivery-only" locations could not and should not be located on expensive real estate, but had to be relatively well placed in regard to access roads to make delivery to customers time- and cost-effective. Pizza Hut clearly understood the distinction between consumer purchasing behavior and how to modify its cost requirements regarding its physical locations.

Purchase Behavior Quick Screen

Figure 4–1 depicts the relationships between the types of purchasing behavior exhibited and the level of consideration given to a particular purchase in the context of the required real estate. In most cases high and low consideration is interchangeable with high and low price. McDonald's would be at point 1 on the graph. The average ticket or amount spent per person or the average bill at McDonald's is under $10. Point 2 is an example of a quick oil change that has an average ticket of $30 to $35. Point 3 is the purchase of a refrigerator or an automobile with price points in the hundreds or thousands of dollars. As the price or consideration increases with the movement from a spontaneous to a planned purchase, the importance of the real estate decreases.

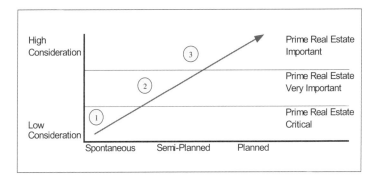

FIGURE 4–1 Purchase behavior quick screen.

As the purchasing behavior associated with the product or service moves with the direction of the arrow, the the impact that prime real estate has on the success of the business decreases. Benchmarking existing franchise companies can be an excellent way to gage the kind of real estate required for your opportunity.

How to Select Real Estate

A study by Ernst & Young published in *Chain Store Age Magazine* highlighted common practices in assessing retail markets and site selection.[2] A major theme was that retailers should change their emphasis from the quantity of stores they open to the quality of stores they open. Although several factors are considered, the top three criteria for selecting a trade area are projected sales potential, population, and geographic location, according to the survey. In terms of site selection, 71 percent of respondents use statistical models to develop sales forecasts for sites, and the vast majority has minimum criteria for usable square feet, demographics, and traffic levels. Yet, more than 30 percent do not have minimum standards for income levels or competitive indexes. The strides in new location selection technology help the franchisor develop models designed to rank markets, rank locations within markets, and predict sales plus or minus 10 percent, 90 percent of the time.

The real estate process is essentially comprised of three steps: selecting the site profile based on primary target audience demographics, finding the trade area that best matches this profile, and then assessing the attractiveness of both the trade area and the actual site. We consider each of these aspects in turn as well as how much weight to assign to each.

A *trade area* is a geographic area within which, by rule of thumb, approximately 70 percent to 80 percent of the total customers will originate. Although this area, when drawn on a map, is identified in miles, the trade area is actually defined in minutes traveled to the site. Most franchisors do continuing research to assess how long a customer is willing to travel for a product or service. For example, if customers are willing to travel 15 minutes to the site, then in congested areas the actual trade areas will be much smaller than in noncongested areas. Also, people will tend to enter a trade area less frequently if there is a natural boundary present; therefore, trade areas often border natural phenomenon such as lakes and rivers or constructed obstacles like major highways.

Trade areas may be more attractive if there are other businesses that act as "anchors" to the trade area, such as shopping malls or convention centers, which attract incremental traffic that would not otherwise flow into the trade area. Just as shopping malls have one or two anchors stores—well-known brand-name destination businesses that act as a magnet for the mall's consumers—so too do geographic trade areas have such anchor businesses to attract traffic.

Let's now consider assessing quantitatively the viability of a particular site within a trade area. Typically, as mentioned, the most important criteria in site selection is analyzing population demographics that lie at the core of the FRM. This calculation is usually comprised of four components:

1. Identify the percentage of people in the trade area that are in the PTA.

2. Determine the estimated market share that is expected as a percent of the PTA.

3. Estimate the number of visits per year and multiply that by the expected market share to calculate the total number of customers per year. (Please note that the number of visits per year is influenced by foot and vehicle traffic patterns and traffic volume.)

4. Estimate the average ticket price (ATP) and multiply it by the total customers to arrive at the estimated revenue for the year. If this is sufficient to support the franchise, and the site is favorable from a demographic perspective, then proceed to the next stage. If the revenue is not sufficient, then the issues that inhibit this must be addressed with the franchisor.

This specific calculation used to derive revenue projections from population demographics is less important than the identification of a link between the trade area demographics, the PTA, and the expected revenue stream. The reason for the use of the calculation is to instill the discipline of consistent use of metrics in your decision-making process. But the overriding importance of the identification of the PTA, its density in the trade area, and the potential for revenue is to understand the greater connection among these variables.

During the refinement process of PTA demographics, an important statistic that is often overlooked when analyzing demographics is daytime versus nighttime populations, also known as bedroom and commuter communities. In many cities the daytime population is significantly greater than the nighttime population. This is often an overriding factor for some franchises. For example, McDonald's franchises want a high daytime population to support its orientation towards lunch, whereas a Blockbuster Video requires large nighttime populations to support the high percentage of video rental business conducted at night.

1. *Identification of density of the Primary Target Audience:* As seen in Chapter 2, population demographics and psychographics[3] provide a solid base to project revenue and profit. For example, successfully attracting the PTA will build the brand equity for the first year, and then, by the second and third years, the franchise will begin to expand business into the secondary and tertiary target audiences, capturing a greater share of the total trade area. Market segmentation into primary, secondary, and tertiary audiences occurs within the geographic trade area of the franchise. There are at least two ways to think about secondary and tertiary market segments. First, as the outlet gains greater recognition, it generally increases the reach of its geographic area for profiled customers. There is also a greater likelihood that over time other nonprofiled customers will be attracted to your offering. Remember Boston Chicken, the fast, "home-cooked" meal concept? Boston Chicken defined the PTA as families. Over time, it expanded its reach to elderly individuals who sought a healthier diet with a time-sensitive delivery.

   Remember, the PTA is the profile of the most likely customer to need and use your service or product. Secondary and tertiary audiences have less perceived need and are therefore less likely to patronize your franchise. Although secondary markets provide less revenue, they are likely to enhance profitability substantially once attracted by the success of the brand. This analysis is very important for two reasons. First, it provides a framework for building reasonable base-case, worst-case, and best-case scenarios for business and financial planning. Second, tracking and documenting the actual results of a site's successes and/or failures can provide the foundation for future growth within the current trade area and into new trade areas. A better understanding of the nature of a particular franchise's trade area enhances the entire franchise system. The ease with which future sites are developed is greatly enhanced by your local entrepreneurial knowledge and by the accumulation of such local knowledge across similar markets.

2. *Traffic volume:* A second element in determining the attractiveness of a site is the traffic volume that passes the site. This is often measured in terms of pedestrians and vehicles traveling past the site on a 12-hour and 24-hour basis. Also, the data should be segmented between weekday and weekend volume levels. This data is usually available from a state or local municipality. If the data is not available, then you may have to measure the pedestrian and auto traffic manually.

3. *Traffic patterns:* A third important element in assessing the viability of a particular site is traffic patterns: inbound and outbound sides of the street. Examples include corner locations, often perceived as a positive aspect of the site. Also, a site on the homebound side of the street could be a positive or negative aspect, depending on the nature of the franchise. For example, a Dunkin' Donuts is far more successful when located on the work bound side of the street. However, a convenience store franchise such as 7-Eleven is generally more successful when located on the homebound side of the street. Moreover, if there are periods of traffic congestion near the site, this is generally a negative aspect, because it dramatically reduces retail volume.

4. *Site visibility:* Visibility of key aspects of the store's location (e.g., sign, entrance, and building) measured in both feet and seconds before the potential customer is aware of the site is important. Convenience is important to retail semi-planned and planned purchases and crucial for spontaneous buying behavior. You must allow ample time for oncoming traffic to identify your franchise and to be able to safely enter the site. Be aware that when you determine visibility (time to view), it is critical that the actual speed of automobiles rather than posted speed limit is considered. It's important a site's visibility be considered from the perspective of all seasons, especially in four-season climates that experience foliage and inclement weather such as snow. Consider a site in New England during the fall and winter months when all the leaves fall off trees, compared to that same site in spring and summer months. The visibility could be high during fall and winter but poor during spring and summer.

5. *Zoning:* A fifth area of consideration is governmental ordinances, sometimes called zoning and permitting. Several elements of the site selection process may stay relatively constant from town to town and even state to state. However, zoning and permitting changes have a great impact particular to each municipality and may require a host of professionals, such as a land use attorney, architect, surveyor, civil engineer, and environmental and traffic specialist, to assist in each step of the pro-

cess. Either directly or indirectly, the franchisee always pays this cost. If the franchisee owns the real estate, then he pays the costs directly. If the franchisor or third party owns the real estate, then the cost is included in the calculation of the lease payment. The cost can be significant, in some cases an additional 5 percent to 10 percent of the land cost. Before committing to a property, add 10 percent to the purchase price and make sure the economics of the business still work.

6. *Traffic flow to the site:* Ingress and egress are real estate terms for the entrance to and exit from a site. The overall flow of traffic, which can be largely determined by placement of entrances and exits on the site, should be viewed as part of the SDS. Properly managed site flow can maximize volume and throughput in and around the building, which will maximize revenue inside the building. As you might expect, this factor has the greatest impact in spontaneous purchase behavior situations. Drive-through facilities in fast food and in dry cleaning add a level of complexity to this exercise. The flow of in-store customer and drive-through customers is difficult and important.

7. *Complementary versus contradictory neighbors:* This is the issue of whether like businesses are more successful when clustered together or when clustered among unrelated businesses. There are certain franchises that may actually perform better if located next to a complementary competitor. For example, Wendy's always wants to be close to McDonald's. The same goes for automobile franchises. Conversely, there are franchises that perform worse if located next to a competitor, in which case the competitor would be considered a contradictory neighbor. It does not bode well if a Blockbuster Video moves next to another major video franchise. So, the question remains, what makes some competitive franchises complementary neighbors and others contradictory neighbors? The answer lies primarily in the discussion of the nature of trade areas and the group dynamics that can occur. Franchises that are complementary neighbors tend to create mini-trade areas among themselves, which draw more customers to the area than each franchise could otherwise do individually. This generally occurs within franchises that fill a specific need through a variety of different products options. The Massachusetts Turnpike remodeled all of its service areas to create multiple franchise food offerings in food mini malls.

In the example above a customer who decides that she wants a quick lunch can drive to a mini trade area with a Sbarro's, McDonald's, and Taco Bell, and then decide what to eat. The decision is essentially postponed until she arrives in the mini trade area, but the variety of choices enhances the spontaneity of driving to that area impulsively. A "bundle" of purchase options caters to the consumer need for variety in diet. A number of restaurants located in a general area attracts a wider audience. Once in the area, the customer looks around and decides what to eat based on the variety available. Such a scenario is especially true when discussing automobile dealers and service franchises. These types of businesses often display the characteristics of a planned behavior in which location importance falls with the increase in purchase preparation. For example, a consumer decides that he would like to purchase a new Nissan Maxima. While at the Nissan dealership, he glances across the street and sees a Toyota dealership that offers the Camry, and next to it a Honda dealership offering the Accord. The consumer originally visited the Nissan dealership, but will shop at the other dealerships due to their close proximity. A geography that clusters dealerships gains market awareness and draws customers. This concept also works in the context of the other two dealerships. The volume at all three dealerships in the cluster will be higher than it otherwise would be had they individually been several miles apart.

Conversely, if a consumer wants to rent a specific movie and she approaches two video stores that are next to each other, it is a zero-sum game—one store will win and the other will lose. The *Star Wars* at one store is the same as the *Star Wars* at another. If you place 10 video stores next to each other, they do not offer any incremental value-add for the customer and therefore will not create a mini trade. Each store might attempt to differentiate itself, but the competitors will likely copy any differentiating actions if they prove successful in acquiring market share. For example, one video store may begin to feature DVDs. If customer behavior begins to favor DVDs, then the other nine stores will follow.

Understanding these elements and incorporating them into the site selection decision-making process adds the structure and objectivity required to compare and contrast different sites. The summation of all these factors manifests in the form of a site selection template. The template is a one-page worksheet that captures the critical elements of the site selection process and weighs them to derive an overall score for a particular site. This score can then be used to compare different sites. From a franchising perspective, it allows for the standardization of the process so that it can be transferred and duplicated throughout your franchise system. In addition, as the experience builds within a franchise system, the template is enhanced to incorporate the results of past franchisees, the added experience of new franchisees, and changing characteristics of the PTA. This becomes operational in terms of adding new elements to the site selection template and shifting weights among elements.

Although it is advantageous to do the site evaluation on your own, it is also time-intensive. There are companies that can be hired to perform the work, such as Pannell Kerr Forster, chartered accountants and managerial advisors. An example of a site selection template is shown Table 4–1. Be aware that the actual template employed should be tailored to the specific franchise and therefore will vary among franchises; this however, provides a basic framework to consider.

TABLE 4–1 Site Selection Template

Excellent	Good	Fair	Poor	The Market
_____	_____	_____	__X__	Total Population
_____	_____	__X__	_____	Growth Projection
_____	_____	__X__	_____	Income per Capita
_____	__X__	_____	_____	Disposable Income
_____	__X__	_____	_____	Avg. Customer Expenditure By Concept
0	2	2	1	Overall Market Assessment
				Trade Area Definition
__X__	_____	_____	_____	Clearly Bounded Trade Area
_____	_____	__X__	_____	Commercial Development
_____	_____	__X__	_____	Retail Development
_____	__N/A__	_____	_____	Future Development Plans
_____	__X__	_____	_____	Competition
_____	__X__	_____	_____	Traffic Count
1	2	2	0	Overall Trade Area Assessment
				Site Location
_____	__X__	_____	_____	Siting of Property (Corner, Main Street, Non-Corner, Side Street, Ill-Defined)
_____	__X__	_____	_____	Visibility of Signage
_____	__X__	_____	_____	Adequate Parking
__X__	_____	_____	_____	Visibility Of Store
_____	__X__	_____	_____	Complementary Retail Activity
_____	_____	__X__	_____	Other Commercial Activity

TABLE 4-1 Site Selection Template (Continued)

Excellent	Good	Fair	Poor	The Market
_____	__X__	_____	_____	High Pedestrian Traffic
_____	__X__	_____	_____	High Automobile Traffic
_____	__X__	_____	_____	Speed of Automobile Traffic
_____	__X__	_____	_____	Entry—Ingress
_____	__X__	_____	_____	Exit—Egress
3	8	2	1	Overall Site Location Assessment

The X Factors of Site Selection

Although several elements of site selection have been highlighted, some factors are often overlooked. These factors are not so obvious and therefore have been titled the X factors of site selection.[4] The three X factors are the employee base, the "green acre" syndrome, and the transportation systems.

1. *Employee base:* Sometimes, if a particular franchise is in a prime location in terms of potential customers, it may be in a poor location in terms of potential employees. An upscale marketplace may be so upscale that there are very few people in close proximity who would be promising employees. These markets tend to have a comparatively larger supply of younger workers who live at home and do not need a significant income. Their threshold is lower for unappealing work, and staffing these retail outlets becomes difficult.

2. *Green acre syndrome:* The green acre syndrome is applicable to a site that has a rich population in terms of residential, office workers, and retail patrons but very few retail (franchise or otherwise) establishments. If this area is on the fringe of a development and a lot of undeveloped land (hence the term "green acres") surrounds the site, this may be a short-lived opportunity. The potential problem is that you think you are entering a market that is underserved, resulting in a disproportionately high demand for your product or service, and as a result you acquire real estate to support that demand. As the trade area becomes more developed, competition moves in, and you could find yourself in an overserved market. This could result in a business that cannot support the significant overhead costs from the real estate. When looking in a market that is sparse, be sure to factor in the idea that the available land may well turn out to attract numerous competing franchises. State and local municipalities should be able to provide data regarding future development.

3. *Current and future traffic patterns:* As previously noted, traffic patterns are an important element of site selection. However, what are often overlooked are the future traffic pattern changes and their potential impact on the franchise. For example, a new road through a trade area could alter the traffic patterns such that the current main intersection in the area could become significantly less traveled. If you were valuing the location based on the traffic through the intersection, the quality of the site you bought could change for the worse.

How to Value Real Estate

There are three common methods used to value real estate:[5] the cost approach, the sales comparison approach, and the income capitalization approach.[6] Regardless of whether the property is to be leased or purchased, the actual occupancy cost (i.e., monthly payment) directly correlates to the value of the property. In a purchase scenario, the correlation is quite clear. If the value of the property is $100,000, then the seller will be compensated $100,000. But in a lease scenario, the calculation of value is slightly more involved. For a lease, the monthly or annual rent equals some percentage of the total valuation. If, for example, the value of the leased property is $100,000, then the rental amount will generally be approximately 8 percent to 12 percent annually, or $8,000 to $12,000. Several examples of these scenarios follow to further illustrate the point. However, it is important to remember that, especially during times of depressed economic markets that see little or no sales of existing properties or new building activity, both the cost and sales methodologies will have marginal utility. We briefly describe each in the following:

- *Cost approach:* The cost approach is most often used when you want to buy property that has an existing building on it. Estimating the current cost to construct a replacement for the existing structure and adding the estimated land value plus an entrepreneurial profit derives an indication of value. The cost approach is useful for financing construction projects only to the degree that it tests the reasonableness of the project's cost, not its true value.

- *Sales comparison approach:* Compare the property being appraised with similar properties that have been sold recently. Be careful that the comparison properties are truly comparable. Size of the lot, square footage of existing structures, and quality of infrastructure and construction are important variables. The sales comparison approach assumes that the market is efficient (or accurate) and sets the value of the real estate based on a view of supply and demand. This approach is feasible in situations in which there is a sufficient turnover volume, such as in most consumer goods, and if the different motivations of buyers and sellers are statistically reliable. The commercial real estate market may not fit this description because it is composed of a large number of submarkets with low turnover rates and a limited number of buyers and sellers.

- *Income capitalization approach:* Ask the question, How much money can I make operating my franchise on this property? Convert anticipated benefits—that is, cash flows—into property value by using a market-derived capitalization rate[7] or a capitalization rate reflecting a specific income pattern. The income capitalization approach is the best and most commonly used method of the three valuation types. However, this approach is only an estimate of value because the methods to ascertain the capitalization rates are unstructured, the proven cyclical nature of the real estate market is hard to anticipate, and only one value is calculated.

From your perspective as an operator, the income capitalization approach helps you determine the highest amount of money that should be spent on a piece of real estate in support of a franchise.

In the previous section, "How to Select Real Estate," a framework was presented that outlined how to estimate revenue for a particular site within a trade area. With the revenue estimates derived from that analysis, you can apply the projected revenue and operating expenses in the business plan to arrive at projected pro forma income statements for a particular site. Next, you should run various rental cost scenarios to determine a range of annualized lease expense that the business can afford and still provide a durable return. A durable return is simply a return that is market or better for a given level of risk over the life of the investment. Once the annual lease expense range is determined, divide it by a market capitalization rate to determine a high and low range of prices for real estate that can support your franchise. The market capitalization rate will be "given" by the market. This is generally an applied rate that is understood by local real estate agents, commercial developers, and bankers.

For example, a franchisee has used our methodology to determine that a particular site can generate between $2.5 million and $3.0 million in pro forma annual sales. That revenue determines the acceptable range of occupancy costs that the business can support. Let's say that the business can afford between $125,000 and $180,000 of lease expense and still generate a durable profit. The next step is to understand the market capitalization rate. If the market rate is, for example, 10 percent, then this franchisee should be looking to purchase real estate that costs between $1.25 million and $1.8 million.[8] If any additional money is paid, there is increased risk that a durable return will not be provided. When the cost of real estate exceeds that prescribed by pro forma modeling, there should be a thorough review of the revenue-generating potential of the location. Beware. We have seen zealous development overwhelm rational pro forma projections.

One caveat that must be made before proceeding is the notion of "highest and best use." This commonly used term describes a theoretical valuation technique for real estate. The definition is *a legal use that is reasonable, probable, physically possible, feasible, and yields the highest net value to the land.*[9] Practically speaking, this means that the value of the real estate is equal to what the highest bidder will pay and still make economically viable use of the real estate. For example, if a Midas Muffler were to replace an office building in Manhattan, the pro forma income projection would not yield a value of the property near that which could be generated by a skyscraper. That is because an automotive service retailer is not "the highest and best" use of the property. In the income capitalization method of valuation, the property must be used for its most financially beneficial activity. You should not get caught in a bidding war for a piece of real estate because the other party may have a better use for the property that generates a greater return and therefore can afford to pay more. Stay with what the business plan supports. Also, keep in mind highest and best use is a dynamic measure of value. This is because the elements that determine the highest and best use of land (and sometimes buildings) are ever changing. For example, over time as cities and towns grow and develop zoning laws, traffic patterns and occupants change. This may alter the highest and best uses for the available property and thus change the value.

As the entrepreneur develops an SDS from the data presented by the demographics studies of the target customer market, the concept of what sort of "box," or building, will most effectively house the SDS develops as well. In many fast food restaurants the target customer requirements dictate that a drive-through be constructed. However, O'Naturals, a health food restaurant, requires a small "farmers' market" within the restaurant. Remember, the ideal location and arraying of physical assets are first designed in theory, then in a company-owned operation, then with a small number of franchisees. Refinements of the ideal "package" occur along the way and are documented within the franchisor's intellectual property and transferred (via building plans, policies and procedures manuals, etc.) Once the physical business model has been designed inside of the box, then the search begins for the real estate regarding its size, configuration, and location. This is a logical step-by step process that cannot be circumvented for a successful design and development of the physical franchise.

The building is a semi-fixed constraint that defines the physical boundaries within which your franchise operates. During the process of franchise concept development and *beta* testing, the franchisor will have defined the "ideal" architectural framework that suits the business format. As the franchisor begins to expand its system and duplicate units, it must consider both the constraints of the real estate if a standalone construction and the limitations of modifying an existing structure. Just as the customer sets the stage for the SDS, and the SDS for the real estate property, so too do the constraints of the real estate set the tone for the construction process.

Construction

The realities of space constraints and market conditions that often influence a franchisor to change the physical layout of an outlet must earnestly be considered before rushing into changing "one small aspect here, another there, and maybe one more over there." Once the ideal building/space has been articulated, designed, and constructed or modified, it is important to understand that changes can be made to the structure only as long as they are understood in terms of two distinct categories.

The first is that changes to the ideal structure need to be rationalized in the spirit of research and development for new markets or new product offerings. Ad hoc changes should be avoided. Typically, the "standard" design is provided to you by the franchisor. Your local unit development entails many variables that simply cannot be anticipated. Specific land configuration, environmental restrictions, and local zoning laws are examples of an ever-changing commercial landscape. Second, changes can be made only when market conditions dictate making relevant modifications to the existing format. For example, consider the addition of a salad bar to a restaurant franchise. Roy Rogers struggled for many years whether or not to offer a salad bar. There are multiple effects that need to be considered, such as customer flow in a restaurant, the reduction in seating, and an expanded floor plan. Roy Rogers eventually installed the salad bar, but the debate raged on. Over time, Roy Rogers ended up selling off many of its sites. Changes need to occur at the franchisor level after testing that includes investment analysis and revenue and cost implications. How important is the additional offering, and how much revenue can be generated? In other words, "revisions" must be reconciled with your unit economics. Furthermore, contingency plans clearly must be made in the event that the projected results don't happen. Standardization is the very essence of franchising as a risk-reduction tool for a successful entrepreneurial venture. Your success ratio generally increases when each successive unit is similar to the prior one, and decreases the greater the variance in each successive unit. Can changes to the SDS be reconciled in the context of the entire franchise system? Will franchisees be prepared to make changes to existing facilities and operating systems? TIP 4–3 illustrates further of the necessary considerations when modifying a standardized physical structure.

Financing Alternatives

Although there are numerous real estate financing alternatives available today, we focus on some of the common forms from a franchising perspective.

TIP 4–3 Theory into Practice: SDS and Construction

The Pizza Hut franchise began as a sit-down, family style restaurant. However, customer demand, as demonstrated by competitive pressures, appeared to be strong for take-out and delivery. Pizza Hut began research and development for altering the SDS. Just think of the implications. Take-out customers have different parking expectations than do eat-in customers. Then, the waiting area could become crowded with a mix of eat-in customers waiting for a table and take-out customers waiting for an order. Would that hurt eat-in business as prospective customers falsely estimate a long delay for seating? Other problems included delivery cars parked (close to the building for quicker service or far from the building to reserve premier parking for eat-in customers?). Ultimately, Pizza Hut redesigned the SDS to accommodate both take-out and delivery after considerable consultation with franchisees and significant systemwide investment. The dynamism of the SDS's growth should be clear, as it originates from the target customer and then itself induces a particular real estate plan, which in turn necessitates a respective construction methodology. All aspects bend back into the other, blending together to meet the needs of customers and to extract the maximum value for the franchise.

Generally, financing for franchise development of commercial real estate takes the form of some kind of lease agreement. Understanding that each lease/buy decision requires specific analysis, in general, it is cheaper over the long term to own than to lease (if you plan to occupy a building over a long period of time). In the case of real estate, this is because developers include in the lease payments incremental profit for financing in addition to the base profit. So, if owning is on average cheaper, why do so many franchisees lease? The answer in two words is—leverage and cash flow. Most entrepreneurs, standalone or franchisee, are in need of cash to launch the business. And as the franchise becomes profitable, leasing provides the leverage required to grow at a much faster rate than would be possible if you purchased the real estate. In most cases the advantages of cash flow and leverage outweigh the additional financing expense of leasing.

Some of the common forms of leasing agreements that franchisees utilize are fee simple, land lease, subordinated land lease, wraparound mortgage, and build to suit.

- *Fee simple:* A fee simple agreement is a standard lease in which the franchisee pays a fee on a periodic basis to the owner of the land and as a result gets use of the land for a specific period of time.

- *Land lease:* A land lease is when the franchisee leases the land from an owner and secures a mortgage from a bank for the building. This puts the bank in an unfavorable position because if the franchisee goes bankrupt, the bank has rights to the building but not to the land. Payment of the land lease supercedes bank rights, so the landowner can take title to the building. Therefore, a bank often requests a subordinated land lease. With subordination, the landowner agrees to grant the bank first claim on assets if the business can't pay the mortgage.

- *Wraparound mortgage:* A wraparound mortgage is a situation in which a bank already holds debt on the land and you request combining it with new debt for the building. This works only if the initial debt on the land is minimal, usually less than 60 percent.

- *Build to suit:* Build to suit is an arrangement in which the owner is willing to construct a new building on his or her property, and the total cost of both the land and building is capitalized into a single lease.

Lease Agreement: The Contract Between Property Owner and Occupant

Once you decide on the lease agreement, there are several specifics to the actual lease structure that can significantly impact the ongoing value of the franchise and your ability to extract wealth from the franchise. Five of the most important considerations follow:

1. Determine the cap rate (market capitalization rate), then calculate the rent. Will the rent be fixed, or will it vary? Sometimes, you can negotiate that the rent varies with the revenues of the business. This may be attractive in the early stages of the franchise when there is slow growth; however, as the franchise becomes more successful, the lease expense could grow excessive, essentially placing a ceiling on future profitability. This element of the lease can place a heavy burden on a planned exit strategy. A fixed rent is typically higher than a variable rent in the beginning years. This creates a longer time to breakeven. Another option is a hybrid of the two that will better fit your goals. This hybrid lease may begin with a minimum rent, which is slightly below market rate. Then, when either a specified time passes or a specific revenue level is achieved, the rent increases by a percentage of the outlet's total revenue. This arrangement gives the lessor the incentive to collect a smaller payment during the early years of the lease in the hope of achieving a higher rent over the long run.

2. Who pays for the fitting-out costs (i.e., leasehold improvements)? Ultimately, you will pay directly for leasehold improvements, or, if the lessor agrees to pay for enhancements to the property, it will be included in the calculation of the lease payment. When negotiating a lease agree-

ment, there is a tendency for entrepreneurs to gravitate towards a short lease term with numerous renewal options. There is a logical cost/benefit tradeoff between duration, flexibility, and cost. All else being equal, the shorter the lease term, the greater your flexibility and the higher your cost. The landlord wants compensation for the additional risk associated with finding a new tenant if you leave after a short term. For example, a 10-year lease with a renewal option at the end of 5 years will have a higher cap rate than the same lease with a renewal option at the end of 10 years. Furthermore, a 10-year lease with a renewal option each year will have a much higher cap rate than the two leases previously listed.

3. Escalation clauses are included in most leases and provide specifics regarding the ability of the lessor to raise the rent over the term of the lease. Take the time to determine what the potential cost actually is before committing to the lease agreement. It can be easy to dismiss 2 percent a year; however, compute this over 15 years, and the impact to profits could be significant.

4. Single, double, or triple net leases mean that the lessee pays for the insurance, taxes, and utilities respectively. You'll likely be responsible for any required maintenance costs and common area maintenance (CAM) charges if you share property with other tenants. This typically happens when the property is located among other outlets that share common driveways and parking facilities.

5. Clauses regarding eminent domain define the rights of the lessee in the event the government takes the property.[10] Eminent domain is a situation in which the local or state government forces a closure of the franchise because the land is needed for a municipal function, which in turn leads to a buyout of the business. The issue here is who has the rights to the money from the buyout. Leases vary dramatically on this subject, and while eminent domain is fairly rare, why take the chance of losing your business with no compensation?

Other items to consider and negotiate are, for example, who is the beneficiary of any insurance policies in the event of fire or other natural disaster. As well, the question arises whether or not you'll have a right of first refusal on the sale of the property. Also, does the lessor have right of first refusal (or any input) regarding the sale of the franchise? It's almost always better to negotiate these issues at the inception of the lease.

Differentiating Between a Capital Lease and an Operating Lease

Holding real estate on the balance sheet through a capital lease is always more expensive (in absolute dollars) than holding the real estate off the balance sheet with an operating lease. This is because you are paying for the entire useful life of the real estate with a capital lease rather than for a portion of the useful life with an operating lease.

A lease should be capitalized if it satisfies any of the following criteria:

1. If ownership automatically transfers to the lessee at the end of the lease term.

2. If the lease contains a bargain purchase option at the end of the lease (i.e., the lessee can purchase real estate that is valued at $1,000,000 for $1).

3. If the lease term is more than 75 percent of the useful life of the asset.

4. If the present value of the lease payments is greater than 90 percent of the purchase price.

If any of the four above criteria are met, then the lease is considered a capital lease per generally accepted accounting principles (GAAP). In essence, the government taxing authority is saying that the transaction is more a purchase than a lease. Therefore, you have a long-term asset (the lease) and a long-term liability (required payments for the lease). The risk is that while negotiating a lease, the franchisee may inadvertently commit to a capital lease and not realize it until it is too late. It should be noted that the details of this topic go beyond the scope of this chapter. We recommend pursuing a relationship with the appropriate legal and financial experts before proceeding into such complex matters.

Leasing Issues and Potential Traps

Eric H. Karp, a prominent franchisee attorney, recently published and presented a paper focusing on leasing issues for franchisees.[11] Adapted excerpts from that paper are included in the following text, which focus on issues within the context of franchisor and/or franchisee as lessee and a third party as lessor.

Common Traps to Avoid When Leasing

- *Relocation issues for franchises in shopping centers:* It is not unusual for a lease to give a landlord, sometimes but not always near the beginning or end of the lease, the ability to force a tenant to relocate to another area

within the same shopping center. This may run afoul of a franchise agreement, which is often granted only for a specific site. You may have to
choose between violating your lease or your franchise agreement if the
franchisor is unwilling to consent to the move.

- *Purposes clause:* Many franchise agreements provide that the franchisor
  can make major changes in the nature and operation of the business,
  including the kinds of goods and/or services offered for sale. This right
  may run afoul with the purpose clause of the lease, which may restrict the
  occupant to a highly restrictive and well-defined purpose.

- *Alterations:* Many leases allow landlords to make minor alterations to
  leased premises and to make even major renovations and changes to the
  shopping center itself. At the same time, franchise agreements often
  restrict the ability of a franchisee to make any changes, even cosmetic, to
  the franchised premises.

- *Use of trade name:* Often, the lease restricts the tenant to the use of a specific trade name. If the franchisor changes the trade name, this can create
  a violation of the base lease. It can also create a problem if you leave the
  franchise system and go independent. If you change the name, you lose
  the lease.

Advantages of Real Estate Ownership

Ownership of real estate does have some advantages. Although it can slow development, it can also hedge risk. By and large, the rationale for owning real estate
is to accumulate equity in the real estate while the business is able to service the
mortgage. You build equity in real estate in two ways: The first is by paying down
the mortgage and thereby reducing the debt on the property. The second is when
a property appreciates in value as a result of market forces. Investing in the property with equity is often a necessary component of obtaining a mortgage. Paying
a long-term mortgage will clearly restrict the business's ability to grow with any
speed, but it also creates a downside floor for you should the business fail. In this
case you would fold the business and be able to sell the real estate at (hopefully)
an appreciated rate. Although the income stream of the business failed to bear
ample fruit, the security of the real estate provided some financial safety net. On
the other hand, if leasing is the preferred choice of real estate financing, then the
business may in fact be able to grow more quickly because less of the capital is
tied up in the real estate. But in this case, should the business fail, no equity will
have been accumulated in the real estate, and no "salvage" value can be obtained
as a last resort.

Lowering the Cost of Capital

In addition to being used as the platform for the SDS, real estate can also be used to lower the total cost of the capital for starting your franchise. This is accomplished because debt is cheaper to obtain than is equity, and real estate is most often financed with a mortgage. Because the debt is asset-based (i.e., the debt is collateralized by the real estate), it is often at a more favorable interest rate than a nonasset-based loan because the risk is lower for the bank. A potential opportunity to lower the bank's risk and perhaps the cost of debt is to show several alternative uses for the property should the business go into default. The easier it is for the bank to sell the property to someone else if you fail, the lower the perceived risk and the lower the interest rate charged. If the bank is reluctant to grant a lower interest rate, then, at least this will help to increase the probability of getting capital. For example, when attempting to get financing, Jiffy Lube franchisees were given a handbook from the franchisor that outlined 100 alternative uses for Jiffy Lube real estate in the event that a unit failed, and they were encouraged to share it with the bank during financing negotiations.

Real estate can also be used to a great extent as a means of "engineering" financial strength through off-balance-sheet leasing. Owning real estate off the balance sheet is achieved by establishing an entity like a real estate partnership to buy the real estate and lease it back to your operating company. Some advantages include the ability to separate the real estate from the business upon sale, added protection from legal liability, and the option for you to extract wealth through aggressive lease rates when the business does well.

If real estate is held on the balance sheet, the real estate can be depreciated for tax purposes and can be explicitly linked to the sale of the business. Under circumstances in which the building is specific to the franchise and "fitting-up costs"[12] would be extremely high for other business formats, it may be prudent to sell the real estate with the business. For example, a colleague of ours has a physical therapy practice and wants to sell. A Health Maintenance Organization (HMO) wants to purchase the business without the real estate. Under normal circumstances, this might be an ideal situation. However, if the HMO decides to buy and then after a year decides to move the practice to a different site, our colleague will be stuck with a highly specific piece of real estate with limited potential buyers. Therefore, it is not always suitable or a guarantee that real estate is an easily liquidated asset.

Real estate held off the balance sheet provides greater flexibility. When you sell the franchise, you can keep the real estate and receive rental income. However, remember that a long-term lease might have balance sheet implications that a bank or other debt holder may consider. Holding real estate off the balance sheet with operating leases does not lower the debt-to-equity ratio, because the amount of the annual lease expense is simply multiplied approximately five to seven times and then added back to the balance sheet as debt.

Another consideration in holding real estate off the balance sheet is that it can be used to extract wealth out of a business at a favorable tax rate to the entrepreneur. To accomplish this, the real estate is owned by the entrepreneur and then leased back to the business. The lease expense is tax deductible for the business, and the rental income that the entrepreneur receives is taxed at the entrepreneur's rate instead of at the higher corporate tax rate. In addition, this wealth can be allocated to other individuals (such as family members) at the same or lower tax rate as the entrepreneur, while the franchise maintains control over the real estate.

There are several forms of off-balance-sheet ownership structures:

- *Sole proprietorship:* This structure is very simple to set up and operate. An individual can manage this structure without the need for partners or a board of directors. Income taxes pass through the sole proprietor as an individual, meaning there is no double taxation as an individual or a corporation. The major disadvantage to this structure is that there is unlimited personal liability.

- *General partnership:* This structure is relatively simple to set up and operate. The tax implications are essentially the same as for the sole proprietorship. Disadvantages include unlimited and equal liability for all partners, regardless of the ownership percentage within the partnership. Partners also have equal voice unless otherwise arranged in the partnership contract.

- *Limited partnership:* The same rules that apply to a limited partnership apply to a general partnership except that the general partners are fully liable, whereas the limited partners are only liable for the cash they invest. The exception is if the limited partners sign personal guarantees, which is very rare and defeats much of the purpose of the limited partnership structure. Another advantage is that only the general partners have a voice in the decision-making process.

- *Real estate trust:* The trust holds the real estate for a third party. This structure is often used to shield the identity of the true owner of the real estate. Otherwise, the advantages and disadvantages are the same as for a limited partnership in that there is limited liability.

- *Limited liability partnership:* This structure reduces risk for all partners by eliminating the general partners and transforming all partners into limited partners; this is the S corporation of real estate. This structure is the most favorable form for holding real estate in the United States today.

- *Limited liability corporation (LLC):* This structure has become the most popular form of business incorporation. It has all the advantages of both the C corporation and the subchapter S company but without any of the disadvantages. Individual states place legal nuances on most organizational forms, and local attorneys should be consulted in reference to all of these structures.

Allocating Risk

Franchising provides a unique opportunity to manage risk through the use of real estate. The additional risk and return associated with the ownership of real estate can be allocated either to the franchisee or the franchisor based on the specific goals of either party to grow more rapidly or hedge operating risk. Some franchise companies share real estate ownership between partners.

If the franchisor owns the real estate and leases it to you, then the franchisor has the additional risk/return generated by the real estate. If the franchisor owns the real estate, it makes money by getting royalty and lease payments. So, if something happens and you feel that the relationship with the franchisor is going badly, the first consequence is that the royalty is not paid. The second ramification is that the lease expense (to the extent that the real estate is held by the franchisor) is not paid. However, control is another element in the equation of ownership. The entity that owns the real estate has increased control. If there is a breach in the relationship between you and the franchisor, and the real estate is owned by the franchisor, then the franchisor could more easily replace you with someone else and continue doing business as usual. Conversely, if you own the real estate and the same situation occurs, then you might change the sign and continue doing business under another name. Although there are terms written into the franchise agreement that make these situations more complicated than presented here, the basic points are valid.

Conclusion

Real estate can make you a lot of money or be an anchor around your financial neck. Most franchise companies constantly reevaluate their real estate requirements and strategies. The consequences of poor decisions are simply too dramatic. Some of the elements included in the best-in-class franchise real estate strategies are standardized formats, standard lease and ownership policies, and standardized requirements for location and site selection. Additional elements include a centralized real estate department, sharpened analysis of sites and markets, planned exit strategies, and performance measures and incentives. An overwhelming majority of franchisors use performance measures to ensure that sites are opened on time and within budget. However, incentives need to be linked to ongoing performance of the site after it is opened. There is no authoritative in-depth analysis regarding the extent of real estate investment in franchising. However, with over 600,000 outlets in the United States alone, and most of those outlets situated on prime retail real estate, one could estimate franchise real estate holdings at about one half trillion dollars. Pay attention to the real estate or fail.

Endnotes

1. Kernel: An essential subset of a programming language, in terms of which other constructs are (or could be) defined. Also known as a core language.

2. Ernst & Young Retail Real Estate Survey. (June 1997). "Maximizing Real Estate Decisions." *Chain Store Age.*

3. The behavioral mindset of a customer related to product purchases.

4. Miller, Bill. (March 3, 1997). "The X Factors of Site Selection." *Restaurant Digest.*

5. Larr, Peter, and Andrew Riebe. (May 1995). "Real Estate Appraisals Recommendations to Reduce Risk." *Journal of Commercial Lending.*

6. Definitions of the three methodologies have been adopted from the *Dictionary of Real Estate Appraisal,* 2nd edition (Chicago: American Institute of Real Estate, 1989).

7. Capitalization rate: The discount rate used to determine the present value of a stream of future earnings. Equals normalized earnings after taxes divided by present value, expressed as a percentage.

8. $125,000 / 10% = $1,250,000; $180,000 / 10% = $1,800,000.

9. Warren, Charles B. (Winter 1997). "Some Perspectives on Highest and Best Use." *Real Estate Appraisal in the 1990s.*

10. The right of a government to appropriate private property for public use, usually with compensation to the owner.

11. Karp, Eric H., Esq. (February 1994). "Leasing Issues for Franchisees, Pitfalls for the Unwary," presented to an MBA class at Babson College, February, 2003.

12. Leasehold improvements.

5 Selecting and Monitoring Franchisees

The average franchise license agreement term is almost 15 years.[1] Choosing the right franchise and choosing the right franchisee are very difficult. Clearly, creating the best business format with the highest potential, as described in earlier chapters, is an important start. But there are no perfect selection methods, and monitoring behavior and performance for both franchisor and franchisee becomes a high priority. But, because of the need to make sure partners are meeting each other's expectations, they sometimes miss superior performance. The most astute franchisor monitoring, control, and feedback loops are important aspects of a high-quality and evolving SDS. Remember that both you and the franchisor will be creating and refining the physical aspects of the SDS while also working out the appropriate business operations and control mechanisms. With tangible and intangible assets working in concert, you greatly increase the chance of success for your franchise.

Selection and Monitoring: Franchising's Dual Challenge

An employee or partner could misrepresent his or her true abilities or simply be misunderstood by the employer. Also, you cannot know for certain if an employee, agent, or partner is working effectively and productively or is shirking.

The same dynamic can be at work when the potential franchisee is investigating the purchase and operation of a franchise. The pervasive but unsophisticated view of franchising is that the franchisor alone bears the risk of choosing the wrong franchisee and monitoring a franchisee to prevent shirking. There is also substantial risk of the franchisor misrepresenting itself or being less than responsible. Selection and monitoring of your partner are particularly important problems in franchising because system growth almost certainly forces roles to evolve. If you are the right franchisee to own and operate one store, it doesn't mean you are the right person for two or three stores. Furthermore, even the finest franchisee operator is imperfect and can benefit from the kinds of monitoring systems that go beyond policing and that share information. Again, the same is true for a franchisor. A franchise system of 100 stores is much more personal and much less complex than a system with 1,000 stores. Therefore, selection and monitoring challenges are conjoined in franchising.[1]

Designing a system of internal controls to promote desired behavior, establishing a means of monitoring behavior, and creating both formal and informal feedback loops between the entrepreneur and agents are key elements in minimizing the impact of imperfect choices of partners and shirking operators. The reality is that there are no perfect partners and therefore no perfect franchisors or franchisees. Most franchisors put monitoring systems in place to make sure the franchisees perform according to the business format and then pay the correct amount of royalties. The larger and possibly more important question is, Can the system of monitoring provide a positive benefit to a franchise system? By the same token, if a well-designed monitoring system detects underperformance, can it also identify superior performance?

Many companies choose franchising as a growth vehicle because of its ability to minimize the risks of poorly chosen and underperforming managers. Franchising minimizes these risks, among others, because the goals of the franchisor and franchisee are more congruent than those found in an employer/employee relationship. Because franchisees share the wealth with franchisors through the profits of the business, there is less incentive for them to shirk in the same manner as an employee might. For example, if an employee steals $1.00 by putting payment from a customer in her or his pocket instead of ringing it up on the cash register, the employer loses the entire $1.00. The same action by a franchisee results in the franchisor losing only the royalty percentage of the $1.00, usually between 5 percent and 8 percent. In other words, some element of ownership is transferred from the franchisor to franchisees. Furthermore, because franchisees usually invest a significant portion of their personal wealth into the franchise relationship, they generally have more to lose than the franchisor if their individual unit should fail. So, franchisees have less incentive to misrepresent their abilities to the franchisor than do prospective employees.

---

1.   Special thanks to Alexis Parent for her assistance in articulating this point.

While incentives are better aligned between franchisee and franchisor than between employee and employer, they are still not exact. For example, consider the financial goals of the two parties: Franchisors earn their profits primarily through royalty payments and therefore have an incentive to maximize system-wide sales. Franchisees are motivated by net profits and therefore have incentive to maximize profit through both revenue enhancing and cost-saving measures. The classic example of this franchisor–franchisee incongruity occurs when the franchisor wants to promote a discount while franchisees are concerned that the discount will erode profits. As a consequence, even in a well-established franchise system, all advertisements are qualified with the small print, "Only at participating stores." Therefore, franchising does not eliminate the need for monitoring and controlling operational systems. Internal controls and monitoring are essential to protect the interests of the franchisee, the franchisor, and the system as a whole.

The inconsistency between the financial goals of the franchisor and the franchisee leads to two specific behaviors that require monitoring and control: free riding and shirking. Free riding happens when a franchisee takes advantage of a lack of monitoring by gaining benefits from the system without paying his fair share. This can be a big problem in franchise system advertising. If a franchisee doesn't spend his locally required advertising, he "rides free" on the brand. Classic shirking is using a lower quality of beef in a hamburger to save cost. Both free riding and shirking insidiously deteriorate the brand.

The Tolerance Zone

Franchising is a negotiated relationship in which franchisors and franchisees must live with some degree of flexibility regarding each other's performance. In essence, the franchisee and franchisor create a "tolerance zone" unique to their relationship, an informal performance standard on many dimensions. No party to any relationship behaves perfectly all the time, so strict interpretation of the license agreement is usually a prelude to legal action. In our experience an hour spent in almost any franchisee outlet will uncover numerous breaches of the license agreement that could result in legal action. By the same token, a franchisee who strictly interprets the license agreement can easily highlight franchisor breaches. The result is a litigious environment that serves no one.

The tolerance zone is defined by a series of services that franchisors provide franchisees. In our professional lives as franchisors and franchisees, we have spent much time understanding the nature of the dealings between franchisor and franchisee that are most important to maximizing the relationship. The following list represents the franchisee's perception of dealings with the franchisor that constitute the tolerance zone.[2] Many people make the mistake of thinking all they need to do is watch sales and profits, and they can rest assured the system is healthy.

- Access to franchisor management
- Accounting systems
- Credit policies of the franchisor and in franchisor negotiated contracts
- Equipment
- Fair dealings in the relationship
- Financial management assistance
- Inventory assistance
- Local advertising
- Management systems
- Market information
- National advertising
- New store development
- New product development
- Support in operations
- Problem-solving assistance
- Promotions
- Purchasing
- Training

From this pool of services, franchisees prioritize two major categories of interaction with the franchisor: operations and marketing. Within each of the operations and marketing umbrella categories, franchisees further articulate which individual interactions have the least tolerance from franchisees. See Table 5–1 for specific interactions on which you should focus your monitoring systems.

The franchisor monitors franchisees in a number of ways. Franchisees have high expectations of franchisors in dealings regarding the support of their store operations and support of franchisee marketing of the franchise. The message to franchisors is to prioritize your efforts in these categories, and franchisees will be forgiving when you perform less well in other areas.

Understanding what is most important to franchisees, franchisors should work towards building their monitoring systems with operations and marketing parameters in mind. Concentrating on these issues will build a monitoring and control system that engenders a tolerant and sharing long-term relationship. Ultimately, franchisees and franchisor begin to understand their own tolerance zone that will create goodwill from both sides.

TABLE 5–1 The Tolerance Zone and Prioritizing Operations and Marketing

Highly Sensitive Tolerance Zone Services
Operations Interaction
• Field personnel visits to outlets • Formal outlet inspections • Field personnel hours in outlets • Field personnel response and documentation of franchisee concerns • Field personnel response to emergencies • Overall field personnel impact on franchisees success
Marketing Interaction
• Value of marketing materials • Overall helpfulness of field marketer • Timeliness of response to needs • Collection and sharing marketing data/information • Days per month franchisee spends with field marketing personnel • Overall impact of field marketing personnel as perceived by the franchisee

More on the Components of Internal Control

Internal controls are a system of checks and balances put into place by the franchisor to promote specific appropriate behaviors and to discourage inappropriate ones. Effective internal controls are often expensive to design and implement, but are normally a one-time investment that provide significant return to the organization over its lifetime. Entrepreneurs who are considering becoming a franchisor to grow their business must consider the types of internal controls they wish to implement, because the decision will affect the way the franchise agreement is drafted. Eric Karp, a noted franchisee attorney, believes, "The content of the franchise contract will greatly influence the control the franchisor has over which monitoring methods are to be used and the degree to which franchisees must adhere to recommendations made by the franchisor."[3] The franchise contract is the place for the franchisor to articulate exactly what is expected of the franchisee and how the franchisor intends to ensure that its expectations are met. These expectations generally fall into one of two categories: execution of the SDS and financial reporting.

Monitoring and Controlling
Execution of the SDS

Companies work to build brands and trademarks because they communicate to potential customers the promise of a certain level of product or service quality. Customers come to rely on these promises, and failure to fulfill them erodes brand equity. Accordingly, ensuring that the SDS is executed properly is a means of protecting brand equity (see TIP 5–1).

TIP 5–1 Theory into Practice:
             Monitoring and Control: Supporting the Brand

Jiffy Lube's existence was made possible because of consumers' pain—it took too much time and was too complicated to purchase basic automotive preventive maintenance. The solution was to package preventive maintenance services in an understandable format and a prescribed time period. Although that sounds easy, the SDS necessary to execute this strategy was extremely detailed and required precise operations. The threat to the brand was significant if franchisees didn't perform to basic standards of a 14-point service in 10 minutes. Monitoring and control systems were designed to ensure these key strategic elements were executed consistently. Field personnel brought stopwatches into the stores, and point-of-sale computers timed entry into and exit from the service bays. Timing complaints from customers were quantified and shared within the Jiffy Lube franchise system. In the marketing plan, promoting the 10-minute, 14-point service message dominated advertising. Although it is essential that the franchisor monitor franchisees to protect the brand, franchisees are equally at risk because brand value affects all outlets.

There are several different schools of thought about how to choose the right franchisee. Some franchisors maintain that they are not interested in franchisees with related prior experience because they might bring the bad habits from other organizations to their own business. Other franchisors maintain that prior related business experience is essential to ensuring that the franchisees can be successful in the business. Allied Domecq vice president for retailing states, "While there is not universal agreement on whether a franchisee must have experience in the field of the franchise, franchisors generally look for overall business experience."[4]

For the new franchise, the place to start in choosing franchisees is by recruiting would-be entrepreneurs who are comfortable in an operating role and who have some experience in marketing. Established franchisors should analyze the most successful franchisees in the system and use the data to develop a prospective franchisee profile. The startup franchisor can discuss franchisee selection with existing successful franchisors, but ultimately they begin by *being* selected by those drawn to their offering. Frankly, most new franchisors are resource starved, and a "hot prospect" with a franchisee fee can be most alluring. Still, franchisors can immediately establish a process for collection and review of profile data. Eventually, a successful operation becomes more selective. Then, you can consider the potential franchisee's ability to execute the SDS relative to the requirements of the franchisee profile you've developed. Asking the right questions beforehand can save a considerable amount of trouble later, because a failing franchisee needs a significant amount of time and attention.

An initial control for addressing issues related to the execution of the SDS is requiring that franchisees, per the franchise contract, follow the current operations manuals and subsequently updated manuals. These updated manuals are the result of recurring feedback loops consisting of regular interactions between franchisees and the franchisor, and then between the franchisor and the entire system of franchisees. In the best franchise systems this interaction is a formal process. Both positive and negative information is evaluated and integrated, with constant iterative feedback, between the field and the franchisor. This is the most effective and fluid mechanism for ensuring that realistic and real-time changes are created and executed into the system. This iterative process creates a responsibility for the franchisor to painstakingly document all of the procedures required for properly running the operation. Furthermore, the franchisor must communicate to the franchisee, in the franchise contract, that updates to existing operations manuals may be required at the discretion of the franchisor. Failure to adequately document the franchise operations as they develop will make preparing effective operations manuals that can protect the SDS a monumental task. Additionally, the franchisor who pays attention to the development of the system and meticulously documents that development will have a far easier time transferring excellence than will the less diligent franchisor. When your system's SDS is documented in such a fashion, achieving scale becomes a significantly more manageable process. The result is more successful franchisees, a more stable franchise system, and enhanced shareholder value.

Developing the Operations Manual.   The operations manual captures the fundamental tasks of the SDS. It serves as both an information resource and a training tool. It must be well organized and written in clear terms, and the information it provides must be kept up to date and accurate.

- When you are developing your SDS, document all functions, changes, and reasons for changes.
- Write a manual for executing the SDS in the first location, detailing the actions required to deliver the goods and services.

- Keep in mind that the franchisor will have to train new franchisees and that the manual is an extension of that training.

- Use professional trainers and writers to work together to produce the operations manual.

- Produce the operations manual in a binder that allows for frequent and rugged use and easy page changes.

Monitoring Methods

Multiple tools exist for monitoring store operations. They include, but are not limited to,

1. Field support
2. External service audits
3. Peer review
4. Analytical tools
5. Customer feedback

Typically, these techniques are used together to monitor franchisee behavior. These are tools to execute the monitoring and feedback requirements. The tolerance zone tells us to focus the attention of these techniques in marketing and operations areas. We cannot stress enough that monitoring includes rewarding superior performance as well as controlling underperformance.

Field Support

Many franchised organizations use field support personnel to act as a liaison between the franchisor and franchisee. Their main responsibilities include communicating the needs of the franchisees to the company and ensuring that company policies are upheld by franchisees. Franchise field support personnel often function like district or regional managers in a non-franchise company, but with less direct enforcement authority. Acting in this capacity, field personnel are responsible for evaluating franchisees, identifying potential problems, and implementing any necessary corrective actions. Alternatively, field support personnel may serve an internal audit function, regularly inspecting individual store operations against a set of specified criteria. When the field support function is designed in this manner, franchises usually operate with a rating system designed to communicate to franchisees how they are performing relative to company standards. These standards usually start with revenue comparisons in detailed segments. General Nutrition Centers offers product category comparisons. Friendly's Restaurants helps franchisees compare day part revenue. Expense standards focus on variable cost-line items, especially labor cost. At Jiffy Lube, each location's labor hours per car are shared nationally. A franchisee whose comparables fall below minimum requirements is given time and support to improve performance. A franchisee who fails to improve risks having his or her franchise agreement terminated.

Regardless of the capacity in which they serve, field support personnel are most effective in monitoring franchisee activities when there is a high ratio of personnel to franchised stores. However, the greater the number of field support personnel on the payroll, the more expensive this monitoring technique becomes. There needs to be a balance of people and policies and formal and informal governance structures. The quality of the relationship between the franchisee and the field support personnel, as measured by the franchisee, dramatically enhances the functioning of operational synergy in the system. Not surprisingly, franchisees rate franchisors more favorably when they perceive a high degree of communications with field support personnel.

External Service Audits and Peer Review

To address the rising expense of monitoring, franchisors can also use external audit services or peer review methods, contracting with an outside agency to evaluate franchisee operations. Organizations offering such services can generally achieve economies of scale, making them less expensive on a contractual basis than they would be if performed by the franchisor. An example of such a service is "mystery shopping." With mystery shoppers, the company with whom you have contracted the service is briefed on the criteria upon which the franchisee is to be evaluated and given a description of what is expected for each criteria. A representative of the company then visits a franchised unit posing as a customer, typically without the franchisee's prior knowledge. After the visit is completed, an evaluation of the visit is prepared and submitted to the franchisor. Although mystery shopping can be an effective means of evaluating a typical customer experience, it is limited as an overall monitoring tool. Its limitations relate to the subjective nature of the mystery shopper's opinion and the limited view he or she has of the operations as a whole. A complete evaluation would require access to back-end operations like inventory control and production, which is not feasible.

A more thorough and cost-effective means of evaluating franchisee operations is a system of peer review. A peer review is conducted by and between franchisees in the same franchise system. Results are confidential and not shared with the franchisor. Franchisees visit locations, work in the operation, review the back office, and interview employees and customers. Consider the Jack in the Box incident in which a breakout of *e. coli* bacteria sickened several customers. The entire system suffered as a result of the incident, not just the individual franchisee, because customers rely on the brand name, not the local entrepreneur, for assurances of quality. This incident highlights that a single franchisee's peers will in fact be affected by such negative events. Because franchisees have a vested interest in each other's performance, a program of peer review can be an effective means for monitoring franchise behavior. This method also eliminates the problem of limited access afforded to the mystery shopper, who is not able to evaluate back-end operations.

The franchise contract can be used to defer some of the monitoring costs. Many franchisors do this. As a matter of course the International Franchise Association recommends that franchisors support the establishment of a "franchise advisory council" (FAC). The franchisee association helps build a line of communication with the franchisor. Many FACs help establish the criteria for both minimum and exceptional performance.

Analytical Tools

Franchisor performance expectations are a powerful and relatively inexpensive monitoring tool. Franchisors can develop a set of performance expectations based on the performance of their own company stores. For example, in the fast-food restaurant industry the franchising company has a complete understanding of what food costs and labor costs should be as a percentage of sales. Franchise company personnel can compare actual franchisee results to these expectations and develop "exception" reports. Any store falling outside the parameters set for expected performance is highlighted for further investigation. Using analytical tools in combination with field support can be a means for stretching a franchise company's monitoring budget and ensuring that it is addressing problem areas rather than policing stores that show no evidence of performance issues.

However, managing (or monitoring) by exception also means investigating the franchise operation that appears to be a superior performer. For example, why might a franchisee report lower than normal labor expense? At MacDonald's a franchisee did just that. Investigation revealed a specialized intercom system for the drive-through that increased productivity. Eventually, this new intercom system became standard operating procedure in all restaurants, and labor cost was reduced for the entire system, saving millions of dollars. In the ideal system, innovative work flow, specialized tools, and incentives systems developed by a franchisee can be analyzed by the franchisor and exported to the rest of the franchise system. The performance model is then modified to establish an enhanced standard.

Customers

Probably the best way to monitor a franchisee's performance is to ask customers whether they are being well served. Current customers can provide a wealth of information regarding how well a store is meeting expectations and reasons for their satisfaction or dissatisfaction. Quantitative customer ratings are an excellent tool for tracking how well a franchisee is serving the needs of the customer and where opportunities for increasing service levels might lie.

In addition to soliciting feedback from existing customers, you should also contact potential customers, that is, secondary and tertiary markets. Surveying customers who fit the description of the primary target audience, but who do not currently frequent the franchise in their local area, may provide useful information regarding franchises performance. If the feedback results in the identification of actionable issues, then communicating to potential customers that their concerns have been addressed may help increase the customer base for franchisees in the area. In addition to monitoring and control development, customer surveys are an important marketing and advertising tool, because the customer is the heart of all SDSs.

Monitoring and Controlling Financial Reporting

Financial controls are typically designed to protect the financial interests of the franchisor. Because franchisor compensation is usually based on a percentage of sales, ensuring that all sales are reported is a key element to protecting the company's financial interest. The most basic concern of franchisors is therefore efficient reporting of sales. The process of collecting financial data enables you to establish a more thorough monitoring and control system.

One advantage of having a broad-based information technology monitoring system is that with it you can capture every aspect of the business, from sales to inventory, to marketing, to labor hours, in an easily aggregated, understandable, and transferable form. The best way for you to capitalize on such an information system is to set parameters both positive and negative, above and below which the controller will organize an exceptions list of variances that will help focus the auditing process on the line items or stores that fall outside the accepted parameters.

Several means for controlling financial reporting by franchisees exists. They include but are not limited to

1. Centralized point-of-sale systems

2. Financial reporting

3. Financial audits

Point-of-Sale Systems

The most basic function of the point-of-sale system is to capture sales data. Ancillary functions may include collecting inventory data as well as numerous other inputs, such as employee information and customer and marketing data. For example, at Jiffy Lube the customer's name and address plus vehicle-specific information (year, make, model, and mileage) are all captured when the service is rendered and recorded. At the same time, the employees who worked on the vehicle can be tracked and productivity can be measured. Inventory controls include calculating the correlation of oil filters used and gallons of used oil extracted from the vehicle.

Point-of-sale systems can range in sophistication from wide area network (WAN)-based systems to manual cash registers with a journal tape. The more sophisticated the system, the more difficult it is for franchisees to misreport sales information. Electronic data capture that sends information to the franchisor is likely to minimize both unintentional and intentional reporting errors by the franchisee. If the franchise grows to the point where this complex type of system is required, this is a sign of success and value. When you draft the franchise contract, you should plan for the use and modification of such a system in the future. If the need for a more sophisticated system should arise, what type of power will you have to force franchisees to adopt it, and who will pay for its implementation? Another consideration when drafting the franchise contract is what access you have to franchisee financial data. You'll want to consider the following questions:

1. How often do franchisees have to report sales?
2. In what format must the reports be?
3. What type of supporting documentation must franchisees provide?
4. Does the franchisor have the right to perform sales audits?

Financial Reporting

Using analytical tools, such as budgets and forecasts, to monitor franchisees' financial reporting is a highly cost-effective monitoring tool. Budgets and forecasts make a good benchmark against which you can compare actual financial results. Significant deviations between the budget and actual results can identify stores that may warrant closer attention and investigation.

Franchisors must bear in mind, however, that comparing actual results to expectations is a worthwhile exercise only when those expectations are realistic. Just as company stores are an incubator for developing the SDS, they can also serve as a laboratory for developing expectations for financial performance (see TIP 5–2). Company stores can serve as a baseline for expectations, but differences between the baseline and the franchise in terms of the markets served, size of store, labor markets, and so on must be included in the forecasts developed; excluding these variables will clearly cause any forecasts to be unrealistic and relatively useless as a monitoring tool.

Financial Audits

Another way to ensure that franchisees accurately report their financial performance is to reserve the right to conduct an external audit. Hiring external auditors to audit the financial statements of each individual franchisee is too expensive to be used as the sole monitoring tool for financial reporting. However, it is a highly effective means of investigating a franchisee that you expect is inaccurately reporting his or her financial results. When drafting the franchise contract, include the right to require an audit and require that franchisees comply with the requests for information made by the external auditors.

TIP 5–2 Theory into Practice:
        SDS and Monitoring and Control:
        Reconciling Local and National Forecasts

At Dunkin' Donuts, franchisees prepare sales and development plans. Regional managers compile the data that is then merged into a master document. The franchisor develops a similar national forecast. The two documents are compared and eventually reconciled. Franchisor and franchisee goals are aligned. This process often creates stress but seldom engenders conflict. When there is a disagreement, the franchisor has the contractual upper hand in development, and the franchisees dominate regarding individual store forecasts. In contrast, many franchisors build annual business plans and report them "down" through the system from field support personnel to individual franchisees. The Dunkin' system creates a strategic plan authored in partnership with the franchisees. Financial reporting becomes a better management information mechanism because actuals are compared to budgets. The growth of the system is more realistically assessed based on the apparent variances. Reconciling national goals with actual local capabilities has enabled Dunkin' Donuts to expand in a more effective manner.

Creating a Feedback Loop

Monitoring and controlling franchisee behavior emphasizes the aspects of the franchisor–franchisee relationship in which the goals of the two parties are seemingly inconsistent. However, these inconsistencies are minor in comparison to what the two parties have in common. The best interests of both the franchisor and franchisee are served when brand equity is built and the end customer is better served. As a result, it is important for both parties to abandon the "us against them" mentality and instead work together to strengthen the system. Communication between the two parties is essential to create a strong working relationship; this seemingly simple mechanism will often separate great success from immediate failure.

Franchisors such as the Great American Cookie Company (GACC) and Kampgrounds of America (KOA) recognize that franchisees know customers in a way that the franchisor never could. These franchisors have tried to understand and integrate into the system the ideas provided by franchisees by working closely with franchisee groups. For example, the franchise association for KOA for years had been requesting that the company adopt a central reservations system supported by a toll-free telephone number and had consistently been denied by the franchisor. When rival camps implemented such systems, KOA was in a position of playing catch up. When the toll-free telephone system was finally implemented, it was an immediate success. An August 1997 *Success Magazine* article states that, "KOA is one of a growing number of franchisors that are giving serious attention to franchisee groups, turning to them for ideas on everything from packaging to rewriting their franchise agreement."

In another example of listening to franchisees, the Great American Cookie Company was able to substantially increase its brownie sales. Franchisees alerted the home office that there was a packaging problem. The brownies, which are topped with a thick layer of frosting, were served in bags. Customers complained that the bags made the brownies too messy to eat. When the company switched to serving the brownies in boxes, sales increased.

Some franchisors won't assist franchisees in forming an association. They're afraid of a union mentality. In both situations the key feedback came from a franchisee association. The CEO of the Great American Cookie Company FAC indicated, "There is a perceived threat to the franchisor that the association has a bank account and money that can be used as a war chest (to sue the franchisor in a dispute). We keep reassuring each other. If you look at what we have in the bank and what they have, there is not even a comparison." The CEO of the franchise association agrees. The biggest benefit of the FAC is the teamwork and being able to work with franchisees towards a common goal. By helping franchisees organize a franchise advisory council and taking it seriously, franchisors can tap into a great resource. Furthermore, by creating an atmosphere of cooperation, franchisors can prevent the potential lawsuits that can result when the relationship is adversarial.

Conclusion

The relationship between the franchisor and franchisee is a delicate one. As a result, franchisors must strike a balance between policing franchisee behavior to protect their own interests and partnering with franchisees to improve the system as a whole. The more that franchisees are treated as true partners, the less likely behaviors such as shirking and free riding will exist. The infrastructure implemented to manage the franchise relationship should be one that promotes desired behavior and facilitates communication, thereby minimizing the need for monitoring and control. Before proceeding onto the next aspect of an SDS—marketing—we'd like to leave you with some pearls of wisdom (see TIP 5–3) that mirror the ground covered in this chapter on how to maintain a strong franchisor–franchisee relationship.

TIP 5–3 Theory into Practice:
Seven Ways to Build and Maintain
a Lasting Franchise Relationship

Based on the experience of Bob Rosenberg, former CEO of Dunkin' Donuts

1. Franchisee attitudes are directly proportional to ROI and to the growth of profitability at the unit level.
2. Many franchisees need to participate and self-actualize beyond store management. The best franchisees learn and grow as business leaders in their franchise systems and in their communities.
3. Involvement in governance (e.g., advisory councils) can be beneficial, but it is very difficult for the franchisor to achieve the right balance between listening and leading.
4. Transparency in contract and ongoing relationships is essential.
5. Expectations must be set up front. Franchisor and franchisee should share a common objective with regard to unit profitability.
6. New products and programs should be tested and meet financial tests before being rolled out.
7. Franchising is a relationship business that takes continuity, face time, and delivering on promises to build trust.

Endnotes

1. Spinelli, S. and S. Birley. (December 1998). "An Empirical Evaluation of Conflict in the Franchise System." *British Journal of Management, 9*(4): 301–325.

2. For a thorough discussion of the franchise tolerance zone, please see Steve Spinelli, Jr., and Sue Birley (1995) "An Empirically Supported

Model of Tolerance in a Franchise Inter-Organizational Form," *Frontiers of Entrepreneurship.*

3. Attorney Eric Karp in a speech to MBA students, February 1999.
4. In an telephone discussion with Steve Spinelli, January 2003.

6 The Service Delivery System and Marketing

Three of the top six companies in United States in terms of marketing expenditures are auto giants—General Motors, Ford and DaimlerChrysler—*and* their franchised dealers. Total annual advertising budgets of the combined companies were $7.7 billion dollars in 2002. During the same year Yum Brands (Pizza Hut, KFC, and Taco Bell) spent almost $1 billion in advertising. One of the reasons entrepreneurs use franchising to grow rapidly is to generate the marketing dollars that these companies use to create a national brand and to build a barrier to entry that keeps would-be competitors out of the market.

The scope of marketing within franchised organizations is vast, and a full understanding of the potential benefits and pitfalls can make the difference between a company remaining a moderate success or growing into a national or even global firm. There are over 600,000 franchised outlets in the United States, with revenues estimated at more than $1 trillion.[1] The central production of marketing materials by the franchisor allows local units to concentrate their activities predominantly on media purchases—specifically radio, television, newspaper, and direct mail. The marketing expenditures for franchised organizations across the United States are estimated to be $60 billion for 2002. On what is all of this money spent? Approximately $8 billion is spent on creative and production-related activities, $20-plus billion on national advertising, $22 billion on regional efforts, and $6 billion on local activities. Collateral material such as point-of-sale signage and flyers is a smaller yet equally important component.

Why is Marketing Important in a Franchise?

Marketing States the System's Promise to the Customer

If you know who most needs and wants your product and have a pretty good idea where those folks live and work, then you have to convince them to make a purchase. Marketing drives a process that stems from an understanding of the demographics, geographics, and psychographics of the PTA (primary target audience). You use this understanding to make a promise to customers that their needs will be met in a consistent fashion across all points of contact, often a store, an office, or a vehicle. When the point-of-sale validates that promise through your SDS, a brand is built. The larger the franchise system, the more marketing dollars get generated. Eventually, only a small percentage of the marketing budget is needed to produce first-class marketing material, and the rest goes into buying advertising time and space.

Marketing Sells Franchises and Raises Capital

A strong, well-known brand is not only important in attracting customers, but also helps in both selling franchises and obtaining additional financing for growth. From a debt-financing perspective, a successful franchise brand carries the preexisting recognition that promotes a level of comfort in creditors. Banks like brand names! For example, the United States Small Business Administration has a special lending program for franchises.[2] The benefit of having a recognized brand in terms of financing also holds true from an equity perspective, especially in the case of an initial public offering (IPO). During the weeks leading up to an IPO, franchised offerings often use significant marketing expenditures to further leverage their existing brand awareness. This practice has been credited with increased multiples on the stock and greater growth capacity.[3]

Marketing Leverages Brand Awareness as the System Grows

The franchise layered approach to marketing, using local, regional, and national programs and campaigns, allows a system to grow into its marketing capabilities over time and at a speed that is consistent with the system's growth. As new outlets are developed, the marketing budget grows and generates sales. A carefully designed and executed marketing program reduces your time to breakeven and significantly enhances the steady-state level of profitability. Ultimately, this creates greater value for your franchise and a "virtuous cycle"[1] of growth and enhanced valuation.

---

1.   A "virtuous cycle" occurs when the reaction to an event is a positive introduction to the reoccurrence of the event. In this example growth enhances value of the franchise system which again encourages growth.

What are the Forms of Marketing in Franchising?

Marketing within a franchised organization takes on several forms and combinations:

- **Franchisor marketing:** The franchisor is normally responsible for centralized marketing and materials production, and development of national advertising campaigns. Once this function is fulfilled, the franchisor is principally responsible for the purchase of media on a national level. It also is responsible for providing advice and approving local and regional advertising done by the franchisee.

- **Franchisee marketing:** Franchisees are often responsible for regional and local advertising to promote their individual store. The franchisor provides informational support regarding buying behavior, media costs, and market trends. As a franchisee, you have a contractual obligation to spend marketing dollars in your local market on promotions and public relations. Then, if the franchise is large enough, regional advertising is accomplished through the cooperative efforts of franchisees in a "region" that is served by a common media, often defined by the reach of the largest network television affiliate. Clearly, regional cooperatives create increased buying power for your franchise. For example, the New York regional cooperative for most franchises includes New York City, Long Island, southern Connecticut, and northern New Jersey. Therefore, with one store in southern Connecticut, you can advertise on "Imus in the Morning" or on the broadcast of the New York Yankees if there is substantial store penetration in New York and New Jersey. Franchisees of any given system in this geography pool a (sometimes contractually obligated) portion of their marketing budget in a regional cooperative fund. The franchisor builds on the informational support system with direct governance impact through its seat on the regional board of cooperative directors.

You have to remember that although national advertising execution is a franchisor responsibility, it is funded through a contractually obligated contribution of all franchisees to a franchisor-administered fund.

- **Supplier advertising cooperatives:** Supplier cooperatives in which franchisees and suppliers team up and share advertising expenses are a common practice in franchising. An example of this is when Pennzoil shares advertising expenses with Jiffy Lube. Jiffy Lube agrees to feature Pennzoil's motor oil in each advertisement for a specific percentage of time or space, and in return Pennzoil subsidizes the advertising expense. You'll see Pepsi in most Burger King ads. Not only do supplier cooperatives provide franchisors with additional financial resources, but they can also be extremely valuable in helping you leverage the brand support of a nationally recognized supplier.

- **Joint advertising:** Joint advertising occurs when, for example, Dunkin' Donuts and Baskin Robbins, which are both owned by Allied Domecq, find ways to promote each other's products within their respective franchise systems. Franchisors have recently developed dual or triple branded outlets, with joint signage linking the two or three brands. A few years ago Allied Domecq added Togo's Eatery, a high-end sandwich offering, to its franchise brands. Of course, in addition to joint marketing, franchises are seeking operational synergy from combining brands.

- **Cross-promotion:** Cross-promotion is a local promotion between you and another local firm that induces purchase for both entities. The product being promoted in your franchise is often completely unrelated to your product. Jerry Houle, cofounder of the Licensing Association of America and president of Bliss House, a license consulting firm, loves franchising. "If you're licensing a property like Curious George, McDonald's provides you with 30,000 distribution points to get that furry little guy in the hands of kids. How about Match Box cars in a Midas Muffler?" Dinner at Pizza Hut might include tickets to the professional sports franchise. Another example occurs when the back of your receipt from the supermarket is a coupon for a free Taco Supreme at Taco Bell. Creative marketing is a hallmark of cross-promotion.

Local Marketing

Local marketing in franchise organizations most often manifests in the form of promotional activities. As a result, you'll be responsible as a franchisee to drive activity, because it requires a high degree of knowledge of the local market dynamics. A colleague of ours owns and operates a Subaru dealership and must contribute a certain percentage of sales to the regional and national Subaru marketing funds as well as satisfy his local level of marketing expenditures. At the local level, he uses a great deal of promotional activities, such as sponsoring local youth sports teams, rather than advertising to increase revenue. The franchisor provides detailed target customer and buyer behavior information that is then combined with the franchisee's in-depth local knowledge to deliver highly targeted and effective promotional campaigns. This builds both the Subaru brand and our friend's specific location.

Regional Advertising

A key achievement in the life of a franchise occurs when it gets big enough to pool advertising funds for regional[4] media purchases. In regional advertising, all franchisees within a defined geographic region are obligated to participate by contributing as much as 4 or 5 percent of their revenue to an advertising fund. Television reach has traditionally defined the region, but there are a variety of methods. Krispy Kreme is the extreme and maybe classic example of a focused, regional market strategy. The goal was to build a sufficient number of restaurants in the southeast to create a critical mass of outlets. The company was formed in 1937, began franchising in the 1970s, and didn't reach New York until 1996. Along the way it filled in most of the southeast and dominated the market. The focus on radio and television as the principle measure of marketing efficiency underpinned direct-marketing campaigns and other guerilla marketing tactics. The advantage of this program is that these tactics provide a higher level of flexibility on the part of the regional co-op because there is so much money for marketing. Most franchises use a combination of many marketing tools. The key issue is to understand that regional differences will affect the marketing mix. Therefore, contractual obligations have to be flexible enough to meet local needs, yet they must also be measurable by the franchisor. Dunkin' Donuts dominates fast-food advertising expenditures in New England with a formal regional program called "4-walls marketing." Again, the regional co-ops (greater Boston, Hartford, and Worcester, Massachusetts, for example) focus on local events like sponsorship of the "slam dunk" exhibit in the Basketball Hall of Fame or the Dunkin' Donuts night at the American Hockey League's Hartford Wolf Pack. These events leverage the franchise's television and radio coverage.

From an operational perspective, regional co-ops utilize nationally produced materials and implement them at a regional level. This usually translates into buying economies initially for radio and newspaper, and eventually for television as well. When television economies are achieved at the regional level, it begins with cable television and then moves to network television. Network television spans the nation, and a purchase at one network can satisfy several regional markets. However, the cable television industry tends to be more fragmented. National cable purchases are cumbersome. To deliver a national spot in cable, a franchisor would have to purchase advertising spots from several cable operators, which would diminish the potential economies. The same holds for newspaper and radio. In addition, radio and newspaper efficiencies at the national level are low (and sometimes negative) due to the differences in listening audiences in regional markets. With radio, cable television, and many newspapers, the optimal economies of scale can be achieved at the regional level.

Regional advertising is governed by the advertising cooperative bylaws outlined in the franchise license agreement and summarized in the UFOC (Uniform Franchise Offering Circular). Multiple outlet owners often dominate the decision-making process of the co-op because they contribute the most money to the fund. However, single-unit owners gain a disproportionate benefit, because they contribute the least amount of money and receive the same marketing benefits as the others. This dynamic tends to be less of an issue in situations where area development agreements or trade area franchises are in place, because all of the participants are approximately the same size, thus reducing the amount of conflict.

The franchisor often participates in the governance of the regional co-op through a seat on the board. Although the franchisor seldom has veto rights, its role is to offer assistance and, more importantly, to ensure that there is consistency between the regional and the national advertising strategies. Bylaws of the co-op are explicit and include voting rights for both the franchisees and the franchisor. Achieving the appropriate size to implement regional advertising cooperatives tells you that a franchise system has gained scale and should continue its growth on a national level.

National Advertising

A franchisor generally spends the money needed to produce highly professional production materials and distribute them on a local level to franchisees. This separates the franchise from its their mom-and-pop competitors in the community early in the game in an attempt to build brand equity. As the number of outlets in a franchise system grows, the contributions by franchisees to the national advertising fund will exceed the amount needed to produce marketing materials. The balance that is left represents the dollars that the franchisor will spend on national advertising. National advertising is the holy grail of marketing economies. As the total national advertising budget expands, franchisees usually want a formal voice in the way the national money is spent. Many franchisors form an advisory council to solicit the perspective of franchisees. As a franchisee, you will need to press the franchisor to include your marketing perspective and local market knowledge. Remember, one of the important values of a franchise relationship is your direct understanding of consumer needs and requirements, as you are the closest link to the consumer. Bringing that knowledge to the marketing decision-making process is a key franchise synergy.

The concept of a national advertising council was initially derived from a study by the International Franchise Association (IFA) during the 1970s. The study noted that if a franchisor did not take a leadership role in organizing a formal council that could listen to issues and offer guidance, feedback, and action, then the franchisees would form an informal association to meet the need. We agree with the IFA's findings and recommend that franchisors preempt this activity by forming a formal governance structure. This action displays a leadership role on the part of the franchisor and ensures that the franchisor and franchisee communicate with each other, focusing on key marketing issues.

The advertising council consists of single unit and multiunit franchisees. The role of the council is to manage the relationship with the advertising or marketing agency (including hiring and firing), to administer funds, to determine the pricing and timing issues around promotion, and to introduce new products. This council is often considered the most significant franchisee organization within a franchise system and therefore there is great demand by franchisees to participate. Often, the national advertising fund is held in a separate escrow account and protected with a third-party certified audit and reviewed by this council. While council review of the fund is optional, an audit is a requirement. Beware of the franchise that doesn't audit their national advertising fund.

Supplier Cooperative Advertising

Supplier cooperatives are most common in branded supplies, such as Coca-Cola and Pennzoil. The agreement is usually initiated by setting up a fund account based on purchases between Coca-Cola and the branded retailer, such as McDonald's. For example, if McDonald's purchases a certain number of containers of syrup from Coca-Cola, then Coca-Cola will contribute a certain amount of money per container to the pool. That money can then be used to fund a certain percentage of a media purchase. Usually, there are three criteria to get supplier money: physical space in a print ad, electronic time, and brand mentions.

For example, let's suppose that Mail Boxes, Etc. has a supplier agreement with Weyerhaeuser for corrugated packaging. Weyerhaeuser might contribute six or even seven figures to the national advertising fund. In addition, the agreement might have the supplier contribute up to 20 percent for any ad that contains the Weyerhaeuser brand. If McDonald's places a full-page ad in the New York Times that costs $100,000, Weyerhaeuser will pay for $20,000 provided that 20 percent of the ad represents Weyerhaeuser in an acceptable form. In a 30-second ad on television, the Weyerhaeuser product would need to appear in the ad for about 6 seconds for Weyerhaeuser to contribute to the ad. There are, of course, risks in using supplier cooperative advertising. For example, you might have to give up some flexibility in your advertising decisions. The supplier's concern is that it has to be sure that any representation of its product is consistent with the existing brand image; otherwise, brand equity could be eroded rather than built. Suppliers may want to review and potentially veto the ad before it goes public.

There is a downside to supplier cooperative advertising. The franchised brand can become inextricably linked to the supplier's product, and if the supplier is involved in a crisis, the customer might identify both brands with the problem of the supplier. Please see TIP 6–1 for a scenario in which this occurred.

TIP 6–1 Theory into Practice: Ford and Firestone—
the Ultimate Brand Marriage

There are not many companies that have had as long and fruit-ful an industrial history together or become sewn into the fabric of American society as cultural icons as the Ford Motor Com-pany and the Firestone Tire & Rubber Company. In 1906 Henry Ford and Harry Firestone formed a friendship and a corporate alliance that not many thought would last almost a century. Even the families themselves became interwoven through marriage; Ford's current chairman, William Ford, Jr., is the son of heiress Martha Firestone. For 94 years these companies have pros-pered together, with Ford automobiles being equipped with Fire-stone tires. Over time, the brand association of each company with the other became commonplace, almost automatic—embedded in the American consumers' subconscious aware-ness—always spoken about in the same sentence. Each com-pany's share price tracked along steadily with the other, through both the ups and downs.

This situation of course changed drastically starting in August 2000 when the first news broke about a recall of what would eventually be 6.5 million Firestone Wilderness tires that had been original equipment on Ford's popular SUV, the Ford Explorer. Months were spent passing blame back and forth between the companies—neither one wanting to accept blame for its potential role in the injuries that occurred. Eventually, after a federal investigation, blame would come to rest with Firestone, now an American subsidiary of Japan's Bridgestone Tire Com-pany. The dispute spurred the removal of both firms' CEOs. Once the announcement of the tire recall was made, the images of both companies, Ford and Firestone, became tarnished, as reflected by public anecdotal opinion as well as by the perfor-mance of the company's share prices. As illustrated in the fol-lowing graph, Ford's and Firestone's stock prices tracked in a fairly parallel fashion. Then, with the August 2000 announce-ment, both stocks fell. While Ford's share price slipped slightly with the August announcement, Firestone's fell drastically and continued to do so.

TIP 6–1　Theory into Practice: Ford and Firestone—
the Ultimate Brand Marriage (Continued)

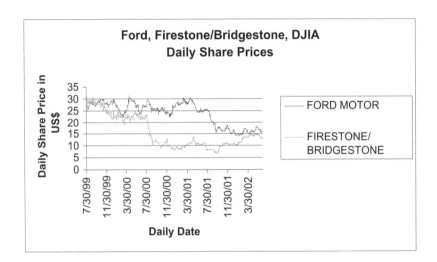

By 2002, with a revamped and revitalized version of the Ford Explorer, Ford seemed to have stabilized. Ford now relies more heavily on other tire manufacturers for original t-equipment tires for its vehicles. Firestone's share price has recovered only slightly from this disaster, but not nearly to the level of August 2000. However, a turnaround is in sight, with Firestone giving much of the credit to its dealers and distributors (franchisees), according to Michael Gorey, chief financial officer of Bridgestone/Firestone's American operations.

Production of Marketing Materials

While building a strong brand, it is critical to deliver consistent messages about the promise you are making. It's the franchisor's responsibility to develop that message. The starting point for this is ensuring that all of the material is built from and remains linked to the initial concept. Remember "Where's the beef?"[5] Enter that phrase into Google today and you'll get 1,200 hits. Most are titles of articles criticizing the substance of something. A franchise slogan used 20 years ago has become a part of Americana. To facilitate the process of marketing material development, the marketing department of the franchisor typically engages an advertising and public relations agency. Then, working with a representative group of franchisees, the franchisor develops a marketing theme. This theme is manifested in the production materials. You pay for this activity through contributions to the national advertising fund. The amount contributed is stipulated in the license agreement; it is often a minimum fixed expenditure in addition to a certain percentage of revenues. The production function includes the design and development of print, radio, and television material. The print material includes all newspaper and magazine layouts as well as direct mail materials. With the emergence of the Internet as a viable tool for business development, web media are also classified under the print media umbrella.

Understanding the elements of the media production function can also be used as a tool to evaluate franchises. As a prospective franchisee, you need to do your homework to make sure the franchisor does the necessary production activities and can describe the links between concept development and each form of media and its execution. This kind of due diligence isn't rocket science. Look at and listen to the advertising, and ask questions of the franchisor.

An Overview of Marketing and the License Agreement

When the franchise relationship becomes litigious, marketing always seems to have some role in the breach, so it makes sense to see how marketing is handled in the license agreement. It should explicitly outline all fees and expenditures mandated by the franchisor. Some franchisors require payments that go beyond the advertising fee for such things as printing collateral material like point-of-sale posters. The market penetration (in number of outlets) that must be achieved to form a regional cooperative also should be detailed in the agreement. Finally, the agreement should clearly outline the governance of the national advertising mechanisms. As previously mentioned, a large amount of your dollars flows through the fund. The proper checks and balances should be in place to ensure the proper allocation of those funds. Please refer to Chapter 10 for a more complete discussion of the franchise license agreement.

Potential Marketing Problems

Distribution of Benefits

One problem in marketing a franchise system is that there will not be an even distribution of the benefits of the advertising. This discrepancy should be stipulated in the license agreement and understood by the franchisees. By that, we mean you must not get in the way of good media purchases because there is an unequal distribution of the benefits. An example of this potential problem would be if Alpha Graphics decided to run an ad during the Super Bowl and the New England Patriots were representing the American Football Conference. New England-based franchisees would clearly receive more benefit than franchisees based in Texas or Michigan. As a result, some advertising councils have gone as far as to stipulate that there will be an attempt to balance the benefit going forward based on the results of past media buys. Franchisees who receive disproportionate benefit from one campaign will either contribute more to the fund or receive a lower benefit on a future campaign. While this is theoretically possible, it is impractical to execute.

Franchise Marketing and Pricing Issues

Some of the pricing issues that can emerge as a result of the franchise marketing relationship include promotional campaigns, antitrust issues, and regional disputes. Promotional campaign problems occur when the franchisor wants to boost revenues without regard for the short-term effect on your profitability. The franchisor constructs a promotional campaign that often includes a price discount. The promotion is designed to drive more traffic into stores. While this might result in increased revenue, the price decrease reduces the franchisees' operating margin and might negatively affect profitability (again, at least in the short run). However, the franchisor derives its income from a percentage of total revenue in the form of a royalty, not franchisee profitability. So, some promotions may benefit one party at the other's expense, resulting in the franchisor making more money and the franchisee making less. For example, when Midas Muffler runs a 2-for-1 special for two weeks, the franchisees have to bear the extra cost of such a promotion. In this case, the phrase "at participating stores" is always part of the promotion; however, it is difficult for a franchisee not to participate when customers are coming in expecting the special deal from every dealer. The franchisor is happy because the system will sell more mufflers and therefore enhance royalty revenue. The Midas example also highlights issues regarding tying agreements and antitrust issues if Midas (the franchisor) also manufactures the muffler and exhaust components that its North American franchisees sell to the public. There must be careful language written into the license agreement regarding the pricing, limitations, and franchisee purchasing options.

Marketing and the Free Riding Risk

Free riding can be pervasive throughout the franchise relationship, but it is most evident in marketing. Local marketing expenditures are fertile ground for the franchisee abuse of free riding to occur. Because a little less money spent by any individual franchisee will not likely affect the brand or revenue of the entire system, franchisees may be tempted to restrict their share of the spending. By holding back local dollars, the individual franchise gets a free ride on the system's brand. This problem is vexing because the expenditures in the area of local marketing are difficult to monitor. As initially discussed in Chapter 2 regarding unethical franchisee behaviors, the franchisor has limited knowledge of the use of dollars spent on local marketing. For example, a franchisee could take his or her family out to dinner and charge it to the local marketing account. The franchisor would have no way of knowing. Remember, local advertising is typically a contractual requirement. The franchise system uses this requirement to increase marketing impressions and create brand equity for all outlets. Anytime the allocations of marketing funds are withheld or misused, the marketing impact is diminished for the entire franchise system. Imagine if McDonald's did not monitor contractual requirements. If each franchise misallocated only a small amount of the required local advertising expenditure (e.g., $100/month) the systemwide impact would be over $30 million annually in reduced advertising.

Conclusion

Ralph Waldo Emerson said, "If a man can write a better book, preach a better sermon, or make a better mouse-trap than his neighbor, though he build his house in the woods, the world will make a beaten path to his door." Emerson was a talented writer, but we believe his business insight was fundamentally flawed. If you build a better mousetrap, you had better make sure the world understands why it is better and where they can get it.

Franchise marketing is the communication tool that promises the customer, "We have what you need, and you can count on us to fill that need no matter which of our locations you go to." There is usually a simple message at the core of marketing and a consistency in delivering on that message that embeds in the consumer's mind as a brand. Examples include "We'll change your oil in ten minutes," "It's time to make the donuts," "Billions and billions served," "We'll do it your way," "The Pepsi Generation," and "Just do it!" Clearly, once a product's marketing becomes part of a culture's daily vernacular, spectacular success has been achieved.

If the franchise has indeed identified a need and has an operating system that fills that need better than the competition does, the SDS must be located conveniently, and then people must be told about it often. Franchise marketing combines the advantages of local knowledge with the buying economies of a large company and multiple locations. One reason franchising has grown so much over the last 40 years is that it integrates the value proposition for both customer and operator. Simply stated, by building more stores, the system has more marketing dollars. The increased marketing attracts more customers, more revenue, and ultimately a continued ability to open more stores. But as a system grows, so does the size and complexity of the marketing program. Well-defined governance with open and frequent communication among the franchise players is a necessity.

Endnotes

1. International Franchise Association, *http://www.franchise.org*.
2. Appendix 3e of SBA's Standard Operating Procedure 70-50(3).
3. Spinelli, Stephen, Jr., Benoit Leleux, and Sue Birley. (2003). An Analysis of Shareholder Return in Public Franchisor Companies, Journal of Private Equity, Summer 2003.
4. A *region* is defined as an area reached by the local network television affiliate and the largest radio stations.
5. Wendy's Old-Fashioned Hamburger advertising theme in the 1980s.

7 Transaction Analysis

Transaction analysis, financial analysis, and the dynamics of the franchise relationship are particularly complex issues that need deeper context to make them come to life. Therefore, the next three chapters illustrate the execution realities of developing a franchise operation through several full-length case studies. Each chapter consists of an explanatory note followed by a case study that illustrates the key points of the chapter.

No business succeeds in the long run without competitive advantage, a fact that is especially true in franchising. One of the enticing aspects of franchising is that it enhances competitive advantages as the system grows. In fact, with foresight the franchisor can and should plan the expansion of stores and advantages simultaneously. By that we mean the competitive advantages driving a franchise's initial success intensify as the system grows in number of units. The impact and long-term sustainability of the competitive advantage(s) franchisee and franchisor share result from two major principles: the operational synergies and cost advantages due to ever-increasing economies of scale.

In chapters 4 through 6 we explored the development of the SDS. In this chapter we outline the ways that franchising can enhance the SDS by segmenting the functions, or transactions, in a system and assigning them to the franchise partner/party best suited to carry them out. Taking a close look at transaction analysis is like peeling several layers from the proverbial business model onion. This analysis allows us to examine the innards of a franchise to determine the exact source of a system's competitive advantage. Once you dissect the franchise into its individual transactions, the system advantages are identified and the tasks allocated to the party who does them best, you or the franchisor. When this is done, the transfer of excellence across a system becomes significantly easier. When it is clear which partner is responsible for each function, then training becomes more focused and efficiency increases. Also, a clear understanding of responsibility makes analysis and changes easier. This means that the franchise can grow better and faster.

Our first step is to deconstruct the SDS into the series of transactions. We then assign those transactions to either the franchisee or franchisor. These assignments should have cost and execution advantages. A cost advantage is typified by the enhanced purchasing power of a number of franchisees compared to the purchasing power of an individual. For example, Jiffy Lube negotiated multimillion-gallon motor oil purchases and had individual deliveries of 3,000 to 6,000 gallons of oil made to franchisees. The standalone competitors were buying oil in 55-gallon drums. The cost advantage to Jiffy Lube is significant. The execution advantages are derived from a networked group of stores sharing knowledge and best practices. The combination of these two economy-of-scale principles enhances the competitive advantages of the brand.

Using Transaction Analysis to Improve the Service Delivery System

As a franchisee, you work in your stores and offices every day to meet customer needs. No one knows your business like you do. In the transaction analysis you use that knowledge to define the distinct functions of the business. Of course, the issue is how finely transactions should be defined. Our experience tells us that we should start with the bigger tasks and then refine each task into smaller and more refined experiences. The way a franchise organization combines the tasks from the gross to the refined and allocates them to the partners defines the company's proprietary knowledge. Let's begin with a look at a typical franchise's SDS in Table 7–1. The Transaction column lists many tasks typical in outlet development. Then, we allocate the tasks involved in completing these transactions to the Franchisor and Franchisee. The desired result is to create the franchise SDS of synergy and efficiency between the franchisees and franchisor.

When the franchisor is developing the SDS and simultaneously performing a transaction analysis, it's important to maintain close communications with the franchisee to set the proper expectations. In a dynamic market, as the system evolves and changes, execution requirements will also change. An organization that has clear understanding of principle responsibilities will adjust more smoothly.

TABLE 7–1 Transaction Analysis for the Generic Franchise SDS

Transaction	Franchisor	Franchisee
Site criteria	Define the key elements of a location that best serve the target customer.	Apply the site criteria to the specific local market.
Site acquisition	Advise the franchisee and offer lease and purchase agreement templates.	Negotiate and execute the lease or purchase agreement.
Zoning and permitting	Advise the franchisee regarding zoning laws and professional contacts such as lawyers and engineers.	Manage the local zoning process by meeting with local boards and hiring professional consultants.
Construction	Prepare blueprints. Create standardized contract and PERT chart. Provide management support.	Obtain local government approvals. Solicit bids from local contractors. Handle day-to-day management of the contractor relationship.
Equipment purchase	Negotiate national contracts.	Establish purchase timing and installation, and make payments.
Building or leasehold improvement	Create standardized plans and blueprints, and manage contractor.	Modify plans for local building codes and monitor contractor relationship.
Inventory purchase	Establish efficient inventory levels and order quantities; negotiate national contracts.	Place local orders and manage unit level inventory.
Employee training	Establish training programs and deliver franchisee and founding employees' training.	Deliver ongoing training for initial staff and training for new/replacement employees.
Grand opening advertising	Design a grand opening marketing template and advise the franchisee on local customization.	Customize and execute the marketing plan and develop local promotions.
Ongoing advertising	Creative development and national advertising brand support.	Local media purchase and promotional execution.

Support Systems and the Franchisor-Franchisee Relationship

A significant advantage of a franchise is the creation and expansion of the brand. By brand we mean an SDS with competitive advantages that, by definition, provides consistent value to a customer. The underlying concept of a brand is that the promise made by the franchise can be fulfilled at any of the locations in as exact a manner as possible. Franchises are fond of calling this the "transfer of excellence." That is how a brand is expanded!

To ensure excellence, most franchisors establish a support system that interacts with the franchisees. It is in this interaction that the brand is maintained and the transfer of knowledge occurs. Let's look at the transaction analysis of the basic franchise support systems once the franchise is established; see tables 7–2, 7–3, and 7–4.

TABLE 7–2 Transaction Analysis for Ongoing Outlet Operations

Transaction	Franchisor	Franchisee
Operating manual	Develop the business model and document it in a manual for use by the franchisees.	Adhere to the business model and maintain its confidentiality.
Training manual	Create a training department for operations R&D and the development of training material like manuals and videos.	Train employees.
Advertising manual	Create an advertising department to develop a national advertising program working with an advertising and public relations firm.	Purchase local media and execute through media purchase and local promotions.
Location inspection/monitoring	Write evaluation criteria based on the operations manual. Field support personnel visit stores and consult with the franchisees.	Cooperate and communicate with the franchisor. Discuss operational problems and solutions.

TABLE 7–2 Transaction Analysis for Ongoing Outlet Operations (Continued)

Transaction	Franchisor	Franchisee
Research and development	Operate company-owned outlets and share knowledge with the franchisees.	Problem solving and communication. Sometimes acts as a test location for new products or procedures.
Inventory	Establish, review, and approve product specifications and manage national contracts.	Develop local vendors for non-national contract supplies and manage the inventory.

TABLE 7–3 Transaction Analysis for Advertising and Public Relations

Transaction	Franchisor	Franchisee
Brand definition or message	Develop the advertising theme or message.	Provide advice and feedback.
Material development (electronic and print)	Manage marketing material production by managing the advertising agency.	Contribute the contractually agreed-upon amount to the national advertising fund.
Regional marketing	Provide input to and exercise voting rights in regional advertising councils.	Contribute to regional advertising fund and participate in cooperative governance.
Media placement	Make the national advertising (TV and radio) purchases utilizing the national advertising fund.	Make regional media purchases through the cooperative and local media purchases individually. Use franchisor-developed creative materials.
Promotions	Develop national promotional events and provide advice on local promotions.	Evaluate "participating store" consent for national promos. Create local promotions.

TABLE 7–4 Transaction Analysis for Product Supply

Transaction	Franchisor	Franchisee
Product specification	Prioritize product usage and detail specification.	Provide feedback on product performance.
Approved suppliers	Investigate vendors who meet specification criteria.	Introduce new suppliers for franchisor approval.
Supply contract development	Negotiate national buying contracts.	Purchase for local needs and make payment.
Research and development	Field test new products, report of new product introductions, and make the appropriate changes to the operations manual.	Field test new products, communicate product success and failure, and recommend product needs and changes.

If centralizing the function lowers the overall or unit cost of the transaction, then the franchisor is likely to be the best-suited player to execute it. If the transaction needs intense or focused management to be executed, or if local knowledge affects the level of execution, then the franchisee is best suited for that function. It is the combination of economies of scale and local entrepreneurial capacity that drives competitive advantage for the franchise company.

Introduction to Case Study: Bagelz[1]

This case study tracks the development of a bagel franchise from its beginning as a company-owned system to its partnership with a well-known franchisor. This case covers six years. The case is jam packed with insight and lessons to apply to your own business. We recommend keeping the notion of transaction analysis in mind to notice which transactions comprise Bagelz's competitive advantage and which party is better suited to execute which task. We revisit the case at its conclusion to highlight the points most relevant for gaining a complete understanding of the transaction analysis process and the links between task segmentation and execution, competitive advantage, and cost efficiencies. Although some of the dates and names of people and companies have been changed, the events are a true depiction of the vastly complicated human and organizational interactions.

---

1. This case is used to illustrate complex franchise decision-making, not to judge the adequacy of those decisions.

Bagelz

Mike Bellobuono[2] knew he had a lot to consider. It was an exciting time for the bagel industry. Industry-wide sales had exploded, and his company, Bagelz, a Connecticut-based bagel chain, had established seven retail locations in just three years. There was tremendous opportunity for growth, but Mike knew that the company needed to achieve this growth quickly or risk an inability to compete against larger existing competitors.

The company's four-member management team had to decide whether to begin selling franchises or to remain a wholly company-owned operation. There was a great deal at stake in this decision for president Joe Amodio, vice president Wes Becher, territory development manager Jamie Whalen, and director of operations Mike Bellobuono. Originally, they had planned to remain a company-owned operation, but then they met Fred DeLuca, who suggested franchising and offered financing. Fred, cofounder of Subway, a multimillion-dollar sandwich franchise, had the potential to be a tremendous asset for Bagelz. He had access to large amounts of capital, an array of resources such as advertising and legal support, and most of all, experience: His company had more locations in the United States than any other franchisor. However, Mike knew that Joe and the team did not want Bagelz to simply become an extension of Fred's empire. The four were accustomed to operating as members of a small, closely knit team, and they were unsure whether partnering with Fred would result in the loss of control of Bagelz.

If they decided to franchise, Mike wondered if they would be able to find franchisees who had the finances, motivation, and ability to successfully run a Bagelz store. He had also heard many stories about conflicts arising out of franchisor–franchisee relationships. True, some of these conflicts were preventable, but inevitably there would be some difficulties that could end in legal challenges. This aspect of the franchisor–franchisee relationship greatly concerned him; he knew that disgruntled franchisees could damage the company's reputation, and he was worried about maintaining the high standard of operations in that Bagelz had put into place in its seven company-owned stores. He knew how difficult it was to build a name and how one bad incident could destroy the brand beyond repair.

If Mike and his teammates decided not to franchise, however, they ran the risk of missing a major opportunity. They also risked being locked out of certain geographical areas by the competition. Bruegger's Bagels was opening units throughout New England (See Figure 7–1 for growth statistics), and Manhattan Bagel, a new industry player, had gone public, giving the company access to

---

2.   All quotes are by Mike Bellobuono unless otherwise noted.

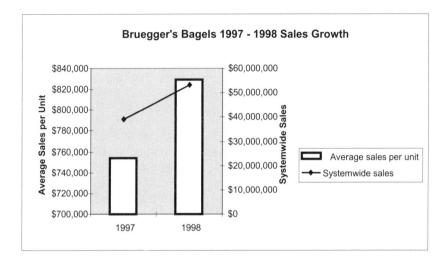

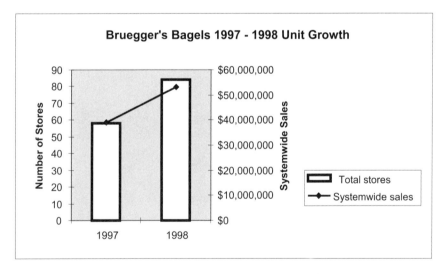

FIGURE 7–1 Bruegger's Bagels growth statistics. Source: *Restaurant Business,* July 1999.

large amounts of capital for expansion. (See Figure 7–2 for company comparison.) Operating as a chain store, as Bagelz was currently doing, constrained the company's potential growth rate. If the company decided against franchising, the team wondered if Bagelz would be able to withstand the onslaught of competition that was sure to come. They wanted to make the right decision, but there was so much to consider, and the offer to partner with DeLuca would not stay on the table for long. The bagel wars were heating up, and Mike knew that they had to develop a superior growth strategy to become an industry "player."

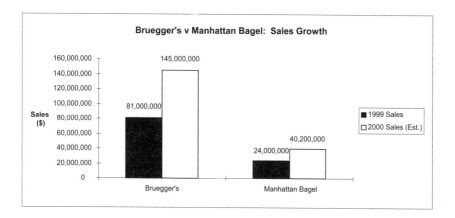

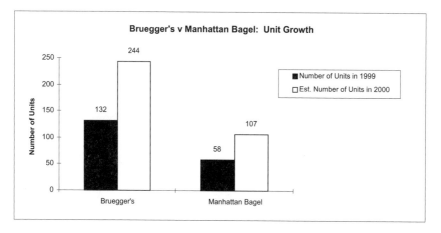

FIGURE 7–2 Comparison of Bruegger's Bagel Bakery and Manhattan Bagel. Sources: *Nation's Restaurant News,* July 1999; *Restaurant Business* July 2000; and *Business Week,* May 2001.

Mike's Background

Mike graduated from Babson College with a Bachelor of Science degree in May 1996. While he was working for a lawn service, he and his college friend, Jamie Whalen, were looking to establish careers in the next hot market. Specifically, the two were looking at bagels and chicken franchises. Although neither of them had any previous food-franchise experience, as part of a class project during Mike's senior year, they had done an in-depth study of the food-service industry. Based on this research, they believed that the industry would experience continued growth and that bagels and chicken would be the next high-growth segments.

It was then that Mike first met Wes Becher and Joe Amodio. The two had opened a bagel store called Bagelz a year earlier; business had gone so well that they opened a second store and set their sights on developing additional locations in the near future. (See Figure 7–3 and Figure 7–4 for Bagelz's 1998 and 1999 income statements.) Mike was impressed with Bagelz's operations and the possi-

	Weekly	Annually	Percent of Total Revenue per Store
TOTAL REVENUE PER STORE	$8,000.00	$416,000.00	100%
COST OF GOODS SOLD			
Salaries & Wages	2,000.00	104,000.00	25%
Food	1,680.00	87,360.00	21%
Beverages	800.00	41,600.00	10%
Paper Supplies	320.00	16,640.00	4%
TOTAL C.O.G.S.	**$4,800.00**	**$249,600.00**	**60%**
GROSS PROFIT ON SALES	**$3,200.00**	**$166,400.00**	**40%**
OPERATING EXPENSES			
Payroll Tax	136.00	7,072.00	1.70%
Payroll Service	20.00	1,040.00	0.25%
Rent	480.00	24,960.00	6.00%
Connecticut Light & Power	200.00	10,400.00	2.50%
Connecticut Natural Gas	120.00	6,240.00	1.50%
Telephone	24.00	1,248.00	0.30%
Advertising	200.00	10,400.00	2.50%
Local Advertising	80.00	4,160.00	1.00%
Insurance	80.00	4,160.00	1.00%
Linen & Laundry	16.00	832.00	0.20%
Repairs & Maintenance	80.00	4,160.00	1.00%
Rubbish Removal	40.00	2,080.00	0.50%
Office Supplies	40.00	2,080.00	0.50%
Uniforms	16.00	832.00	0.20%
Professional Fees	40.00	2,080.00	0.50%
Miscellaneous	20.00	1,040.00	0.25%
TOTAL OPERATING EXPENSES	**$1,596.00**	**$82,992.00**	**19.95%**
TOTAL INCOME FROM OPERATIONS	**$1,604.00**	**$83,408.00**	**20.05%**

* All figures have been estimated based on industry data and do not necessarily represent the actual financial performance of a Bagelz store operation.

FIGURE 7–3 Bagelz 1998 per-store earnings (estimated).

bility of getting in on the ground floor of their expansion opportunity. After considering alternatives such as Cajun Joe's, Boston Chicken, and Manhattan Bagel, Mike decided that he liked both the company and the taste of Bagelz's bagels best. He also decided he wanted to be more than just an employee. He looked at Bagelz as an investment opportunity.

Due Diligence

Mike first approached Bruegger's about opening bagel stores in Connecticut, but the company believed that there was no market potential there. Mike then considered Manhattan Bagel. He liked Manhattan's analysis of the bagel market, which agreed with Mike's conclusion that Connecticut was a viable market. However, in the end, Mike decided to invest in Bagelz because he believed that Bagelz had

	Weekly	Annually	% of Total Revenue per Store
TOTAL REVENUE PER STORE			
Sales	$8,000.00	$416,000.00	100%
Total Revenue	$8,000.00	$416,000.00	100%
COST OF GOODS SOLD			
Salaries & Wages	1,760.00	91,520.00	22%
Food	1,520.00	79,040.00	19%
Beverages	720.00	37,440.00	9%
Paper Supplies	320.00	16,640.00	4%
TOTAL C.O.G.S.	$4,320.00	$224,640.00	54%
GROSS PROFIT ON SALES	$3,680.00	$191,360.00	46%
OPERATING EXPENSES			
Royalties	640.00	33,280.00	8%
Payroll Tax	136.00	7,072.00	1.70%
Payroll Service	20.00	1,040.00	0.25%
Rent	480.00	24,960.00	6.00%
Electric	200.00	10,400.00	2.50%
Gas	120.00	6,240.00	1.50%
Telephone	24.00	1,248.00	0.30%
Advertising	200.00	10,400.00	2.50%
Local Advertising	80.00	4,160.00	1.00%
Promotions	4.00	208.00	0.05%
Insurance	80.00	4,160.00	1.00%
Linen & Laundry	16.00	832.00	0.20%
Repairs & Maintenance	80.00	4,160.00	1.00%
Rubbish Removal	40.00	2,080.00	0.50%
Office Supplies	40.00	2,080.00	0.50%
Uniforms	16.00	832.00	0.20%
Professional Fees	40.00	2,080.00	0.50%
Misc.	20.00	1,040.00	0.25%
TOTAL OPERATING EXPENSES	$2,236.00	$116,272.00	27.95%
TOTAL INCOME FROM OPERATIONS	$1,444.00	$75,088.00	18.05%

FIGURE 7–4 Bagelz 1999 per-store earnings (estimated).

several distinct competitive advantages. First there was Irving Stearns. Irv, Bagelz's chief bagel-maker, had been in the business for more than 20 years and knew everything there was to know about bagels. He baked a product that tasted better than any Mike had ever eaten, and he could quickly develop new products. There simply was not anyone else like Irv. Mike also liked the flexibility of Bagelz's management. It were quick to spot and react to new market trends and directions. For example, Bagelz offered customers five different kinds of flavored coffees before flavored coffees became popular—at a time when all of its competitors offered only regular and decaffeinated. Finally, with Bagelz, he was in on the ground floor.

Bagelz

Mike and Jamie persisted until Joe and Wes agreed to sell them a store as a limited partnership.[3]

> I looked at a partnership as giving me greater control over my own destiny. If we didn't form a partnership, and I just opened up stores for them, I would have no control over any changes they decided to make; having this control was extremely important to me.

Mike and Jamie opened the Manchester, Connecticut, store in December 1996. Then Wes, impressed by Mike and Jamie's dedication, approached the two about becoming full partners in the company. Wes explained to Mike that although he had several prospective investors, he was interested in offering the two a partnership because he and Joe were looking for investors who would work for the company, not simply finance it. To buy into the company, Jamie and Mike arranged financing through their fathers, and the two became full partners the next year. Mike, Wes, Jamie, and Joe handled all aspects of the partnership. Each store was visited by one of the four members of the team on a daily basis to ensure that operations were running smoothly and to solve any difficulties that arose. Wes, Jamie, and Mike focused on the day-to-day operations, and Joe on growing the company. By 1998, Bagelz had seven stores with the goal of saturating the entire state of Connecticut by the year 2005. Bruegger's was not in the state yet, and Manhattan had only a few locations, but Mike knew they were coming:

> We were Bagelz, and we wanted to make Connecticut our turf, so that you knew that if you were going to go into Connecticut, you would have to fight us.

The Bagel Industry

Although the exact origin of the bagel is not fully known, legend maintains that the first bagel was created for the king of Poland, as celebratory bread when the king's army repelled a 1683 Turkish invasion. Many years later, Jewish immigrants introduced the bagel in the United States, and for decades bagels were perceived as a strictly ethnic food with limited mass-market appeal.

Traditionally, bagels were made from water, flour, yeast, and salt, combined and formed into a ring shape. These rings were boiled in water to create the crust and shiny appearance, and then baked in brick ovens to produce a crispy outside

---

3. A limited partnership is a business organization with one or more general partners, who manage the business and assume legal debts and obligations, and one or more limited partners, who do not participate in day-to-day operations and are liable only to the extent of their investments.

and soft, chewy inside, which was considerably denser than most breads. As bagels gained mass-market acceptance across the country, the industry grew at an accelerating rate. Modern-day bakers often use machine-formed bagels and large stainless steel ovens, complete with rotating racks for faster, more uniform baking. As competition between bagel shops has increased in the United States, the traditional bagel recipe has been adapted to increase the variety of flavors (e.g., egg, salt, garlic, onion, poppy seed, sesame seed, blueberry, chocolate chip, corn, and cheddar cheese). Lender's, now a division of Kraft General Foods, first successfully marketed a mass-produced, frozen, supermarket bagel in 1962. Before this time, only fresh bagels had been sold. By 1996, Lender's had grown to sales of $203 million, and Sara Lee, Lender's closest competitor, who had entered the frozen bagel market in 1990, had sales of $22.4 million.

During the 1980s, Lender's and Bagel Nosh opened bagel shops nationally, but both companies failed because they were never able to attract enough customers. By the early 1990s, however, bagels were gaining mass-market acceptance across the country. Most notably, the industry was growing on the east coast where, as of mid-1997, more than half of all bagel sales in the United States (51 percent) came from 15 east-coast cities. Frozen supermarket bagels achieved sales of $211.9 million in 1997, an increase of 4 percent over the previous year, but fresh bagels, the most rapidly growing segment, increased sales to $95 million, up 28 percent from 1996. For 1998, sales of frozen bagels were projected to increase 6 percent to $224.4 million, and sales of fresh bagels were projected to increase 17 percent to $111 million. Consumer awareness and consumption of bagels had increased steadily, but most dramatically throughout the past six years. Breakfast accounted for 65 percent of all bagel sales, and with the trend toward increased consumer-health awareness, bagels had become a natural, low-fat, high-carbohydrate alternative to other menu items, such as doughnuts and muffins.

Fred DeLuca

In the spring of 1998, the Bagelz team was contacted by Fred DeLuca, the founder of the Subway sandwich franchise. A vendor that sold luncheon-meat slicers to both Bagelz and Subway had told Fred about Bagelz's operation, and Fred decided that he wanted to tour the plant and meet the team. Fred was well known in the franchise industry. While still in college, he had opened his first Subway location in 1965. Nine years later, he began franchising, and by 2000, Subway had grown to more than 10,000 locations. In addition, *Entrepreneur Magazine* rated Subway the number-one franchise in its annual franchising 500 six times between 1993 and 1998.

> We never thought that he wanted to do business with us. We were just excited to meet him. When we realized he was interested in making a deal, we were astonished.

It was then that the team first seriously considered franchising.

To Franchise or Not to Franchise?

Fred had offered to buy into Bagelz and turn it into a world-class franchise, but first he wanted to be sure that the bagel team was fully aware of, and ready to meet, all of the potential difficulties involved with franchising:

> Fred wanted to know why we wanted to franchise. He said, "Do you know what you are getting yourself into? Are you sure you really want to deal with all the problems that arise from franchising?"

The team weighed both the pros and cons of becoming a franchisor. They evaluated two basic strategies: either to grow rapidly throughout Connecticut as a chain or to franchise and grow nationally. How many stores is the right number for Connecticut? Did they have the management talent, the money, and the time?

A Decision Is Made

Mike recalled that for six months he and his team discussed with Fred the possibility of forming an alliance:

> We met with Fred numerous times during this period. It gave us the chance to really get to know him and gave him the opportunity to get to know us just as well. This was an important time for us because based on these meetings, Joe, Wes, Jamie, and I decided that we really liked Fred and, more importantly, that wanted to align with him and with Subway. Fred felt the same way about us; he thought that together we would make a great team.

In late 1998 an agreement was reached and each party defined its role in the new organization. Fred DeLuca and Peter Buck (Fred's Subway partner) purchased a 50-percent stake in the franchise company. Mike, Jamie, Joe, and Wes retained the other 50 percent, and 100 percent of the commissary—a separate company founded by the four that supplied Bagelz franchisees with bagel dough and cream cheese.

Aligning with Fred offered numerous competitive advantages as a franchisor. Franchising offered Bagelz a high-growth vehicle—essential to compete against other industry players such as Bruegger's and Manhattan Bagel. But the team was concerned because as the company expanded, the likelihood of franchisee problems also increased. They wondered how they could best defend against this and thought that perhaps some changes were in order. The team thought they needed to fully assess at least two factors: the way they selected franchisees and the company's internal management structure. With the goal of rapid expansion set, they needed to reevaluate their plan to determine how to best support this growth.

Franchising Operations

Bagelz was registered as a franchise company in December 1998 and began selling franchises in the summer of 1999. Mike recalled,

> When we began to franchise, many people thought we were already doing it because a lot of people didn't know the difference between a chain and a franchise. We had gotten dozens of letters from people asking to buy a franchise. That was where we got our first franchisees.

A charismatic and a natural-born salesman, Joe assumed responsibility for selling stores—a critical position. Jamie, Wes, and Mike concentrated on the operational aspects of the company, consulting with Fred often:

> Fred was the one who really made it all happen. Without him, we would have never franchised; we simply felt that we didn't know enough about it to do it on our own.

Franchising and the Bagelz Business Format

Franchising had become increasingly popular throughout the U.S. restaurant industry as a growth method. But franchising was an expensive growth method, and based on financial projections, Bagelz needed to open a minimum of 50 locations before there was the potential to obtain a profit as a franchisor. By 1999, 12 Bagelz franchised locations were operating and six other franchised sites were under development. So, the Bagelz team knew that it had to grow faster to get to the 50-store profit point.

In addition, one franchisee was planning to open a variation of the traditional Bagelz franchise format, multiple nonbake satellite units. A nonbake location was one in which there is no oven on the premises and bagels must be supplied from another Bagelz store. The first nonbake location had been opened in Saybrook, Connecticut, in 1998, in response to a bet: A landlord challenged Mike and his team to build a store in three weeks' time to meet the start of the summer tourist season. They accomplished this feat in exchange for lower rent, and the store became an instant success. Sales revenues were comparable to those of traditional stores, but rent, labor, and equipment costs were significantly less—as was the population needed to support the unit. Additional nonbake units would enable Bagelz to grow while minimizing costs.

Developing stores was a cash-intensive process, and it often took as long as two years to build a steady customer base. (See figures 7–5, 7–6, and 7–7 for Bagelz Franchising Corporation's financial statements.) Additionally, Bagelz asked for a lower franchise fee than its competitors. Mike limited this fee to $10,000 because although it meant less income for Bagelz in the short term, he wanted to attract mom-and-pop franchisees. He felt that they were the most motivated to make a Bagelz store succeed.

To help minimize corporate costs, Mike used Subway's legal department to write the Uniform Franchise Offering Circular (UFOC) and Subway's architects for designing new stores. Because of this, Bagelz's corporate franchise-development costs were significantly lower than they otherwise would have been.

BAGELZ FRANCHISING CORPORATION

(An S Corporation)

BALANCE SHEET

December 31, 2000 and 1999

ASSETS

	2000	1999
Current assets		
Cash	$3,230	$2,590
Accounts and other receivables	11,916	3,450
Other current assets	1,210	2,281
	16,356	8,321
Property & equipment	95,412	95,412
Less accumulated depreciation	(14,964)	(3,230)
	80,448	92,182
Other assets		
Due from affiliates	88,318	44,091
Other assets	12,853	16,991
	101,171	61,082
	$197,975	$161,585

LIABILITIES AND STOCKHOLDERS' EQUITY (DEFICIT)

	2000	1999
Current liabilities		
Accounts payable and accrued expenses	$44,425	58,824
Due to affiliates	42,855	96,679
Other current liabilities	1,210	2,281
Income taxes payable	500	250
	$88,990	$158,034
Loans payable - stockholders	87,976	38,217
Deferred franchise fee revenue	13,000	28,700
Stockholders' equity (deficit)		
Common stock, no par value, 20,000 shares authorized, 200 shares issued and outstanding	1,000	1,000
Additional paid-in capital	194,217	56,000
Accumulated deficit	(187,208)	(120,366)
	8,009	(63,366)
	$197,975	$161,585

FIGURE 7–5 Bagelz balance sheet.

BAGELZ FRANCHISING CORPORATION

(An S Corporation)

STATEMENT OF LOSS

For the Years Ended December 31, 2000 and 1999

	2000	1999
Revenue		
Royalties	$ 265,313	$ 57,144
Initial franchise fees	76,700	86,300
Other revenue	16,902	6,499
	358,915	149,943
Selling, general and administrative expenses	(409,393)	(262,496)
Loss before depreciation and amortization	(50,478)	(112,553)
Depreciation and amortization	(14,372)	(5,857)
Loss from operations	(64,850)	(118,410)
Other income (expenses)		
Interest income	5,350	-
Interest expense	(7,092)	(1,306)
Penalties	-	(150)
	(1,742)	(1,456)
Loss before state income tax	(66,592)	(119,866)
State income tax	(250)	(500)
Net loss	(66,842)	(120,366)

FIGURE 7–6 Bagelz income statement.

Mike and his team sold only site-specific locations:

We didn't sell territories or give assurances that we wouldn't open a store next door. The problem was different population densities. For example, a mile radius in New York City could have supported many locations, but in much of Kansas, a mile just wouldn't be large enough to support even one store. Also, if there was one store on the Massachusetts Turnpike and one in the nearest town, although located in close proximity to each other, they would clearly serve two different markets of customers. We looked very carefully at each individual situation when we developed stores near each other. We weren't looking to annoy franchisees—we knew they were the key to successful development.

BAGELZ FRANCHISING CORPORATION

(An S Corporation)

STATEMENT OF CASH FLOWS

For the Years Ended December 31, 2000 and 1999

	2000	1999
CASH FLOWS FROM OPERATING ACTIVITIES		
Net loss	$ (66,842)	$ (120,366)
Adjustments to reconcile net loss to net cash used in		
operating activities:		
Depreciation and amortization	14,372	5,857
(Increase) decrease in		
Accounts and other receivables	(8,466)	(3,450)
Other assets	2,571	(2,949)
Increase (decrease) in		
Accounts payable and accrued expenses	(14,399)	58,824
Other liabilities	(1,071)	-
Income taxes payable	250	250
Deferred franchise fee revenue	(15,700)	28,700
Net cash used in operating activities	(89,285)	(33,134)
CASH FLOW FROM INVESTING ACTIVITIES		
Advances to affiliates	(44,227)	(44,091)
Purchase of property and equipment	-	(95,412)
Acquisition of intangible assets	-	(15,669)
Net cash used in investing activities	(44,227)	(155,172)
CASH FLOWS FROM FINANCING ACTIVITIES		
Advances from affiliates	51,075	96,679
Capital investment	100,000	56,000
Repayment of advances from affiliates	(104,899)	-
Loans from stockholders	87,976	38,217
Net cash provided by financing activities	134,152	190,896
Net increase in cash	640	2,590
Cash - beginning of year	2,590	-
Cash - end of year	$ 3,230	$ 2,590
SUPPLEMENTAL DISCLOSURE OF CASH FLOW INFORMATION		
Cash paid during the year for:		
Income taxes	-	$ 250
Interest	-	$ 125
SUPPLEMENTAL DISCLOSURE OF NON-CASH TRANSACTIONS		
Total capital investment	$138,217	
Conversion of stockholders' loans to equity	(38,217)	
Net cash provided by capital investment	$100,000	

FIGURE 7–7   Bagelz statement of cash flows.

Joe's Departure

At this time, Joe left to pursue other interests.

> Joe was an entrepreneur in the truest sense of the word. We didn't want Joe to go, but his passion was starting companies. His attitude was go, go, go, and he loved to get the company going, but then, when it came to dealing with day-to-day stuff, Joe got completely bored out of his mind. He got us to grow, but he didn't want to deal with the red tape of being a franchisor.

The price for Joe's interest in the company was quickly agreed upon and divided equally among Mike, Wes, and Jamie. Fred and Peter's 50-percent ownership stake remained unaffected. Wes then became president, Mike, vice president, and Jamie, director of training and manager of territory development.

Organizational Structure

The company was growing so rapidly that each team member had to perform multiple functions, making it difficult to define an organizational structure. By 1996, however, the team wanted to develop a more formal management infrastructure. For the present time, Mike, Wes, and Jamie worked as a team, with Jamie ultimately reporting to Mike more than Wes. In addition to the three partners, there were four other full-time corporate employees: a bookkeeper, a controller, a marketing director, and a receptionist.

Mike and his team called Fred for advice but maintained final authority. For example, Fred advised allowing the sale of nonbake units to franchisees who did not already own a bake unit. He reasoned that as a function of demand, bake units would naturally open to support nonbake ones. The team ultimately decided against allowing franchisees to own only nonbake locations. Doing so would put nonbake franchises in a potentially weak negotiating position—they would then be at the mercy of franchisees that operated bake locations to supply their bagels. Supplier-franchisees would have the power to raise wholesale bagel prices, drive nonbake franchisees out of business, and acquire the nonbake facilities. For nonbake franchise locations, franchisees were given the option of purchasing bagels from other franchisees, but all still had the ability to supply a nonbake location internally.

There were seven franchises, and plans were underway to open 53 new franchises by August 1997 and 200 by the year 2000. Mike was aggressively recruiting new franchisees and selling multiple units to existing ones. The team generally required that a potential franchisee have between $60,000 and $70,000 in liquid assets to invest in a store. In this manner, a franchisee could finance a store with a combination of 50 percent equity and 50 percent debt. In addition, the number of stores sold to a particular franchisee also depended upon the number of stores that the franchisee wanted and the number that the team felt the individual could efficiently operate.

Operations

Customers entered a Bagelz store through the front door and walked down an aisle adjacent to the dining area, toward the service counter. (This aisle also served as a queue during peak business hours). The service counter was made of glass showcases spanning the length of the back wall of the store. Between the showcases and the back wall was an employee work area that was five feet wide and as long as the back wall. This area gave employees sufficient room in which to serve customers.

Customers placed their order at the service counter in a cafeteria-style environment. They then moved along the wall, where they could observe their sandwich being assembled behind the glass showcases. Sandwiches were either assembled by the order-taker or, during peak business hours, by a worker specifically assigned to this process. Customers then proceeded to the end of the counter, where they could help themselves to items such as packaged snacks, bottled juice, or prepackaged take-out cream cheese. At the end of the counter, a cashier rang and bagged customers' orders and dispensed cups for self-serve beverages. The self-serve beverage dispensers and condiments were located along a wall in the dining room.

Stores opened at 6:00 A.M. and closed at 5:00 P.M. during the week and at 2:00 P.M. on the weekends. Eighty-five percent of business was done in the morning, with an average customer service throughput time of two minutes. The remaining 15 percent of business was done during lunchtime hours. There was no dinner business, but management's goal was to eventually attract evening customers and remain open until 7:00 P.M. To achieve this, Bagelz first looked to develop the 2:00-to-5:00 afternoon coffee-hour business; it tested several pastries and snack products to complement its cappuccino offerings.

There were major revisions in the operations manual in each of the first four years of the Bagelz franchise. For example, traditionally, bagel making was a boil-and-bake operation. This was a difficult process; it was a hard, hot job, and the baker played an important role in store operations. This role was so critical that the management team had store alarms installed, set to alert the team member on call if the baker was not on site by 3:00 A.M., since it took three hours to prepare the bagels for the 6:00 A.M. opening. Further complicating the situation was that baking required skilled labor. If the scheduled baker did not show up, a skilled replacement had to fill in. But now Bagelz had found a way to make it a bake-only operation without compromising the product's taste. To do this, Bagelz used a newly developed baking technology that provided the same taste as a boil-and-bake bagel without the boiling. This was a faster and cheaper process than the traditional boil-and-bake, but it did not obviate the need for skilled labor.

> In one store, we replaced the regular oven with a new type. After installing it, we noticed that sales continued to climb. To us, this was a clear indication our customers approved.

Management also worked to reduce other costs for the franchisee. Mike formulated a series of bagel-demand charts based on sales patterns. These charts took much of the guesswork out of bagel inventory management for franchisees. Bagels could be made faster; therefore, baking could start later in the morning. There were other benefits as well:

> Before we started installing the new oven, they baked with the oven door open. And it was hot! In one of our stores, we were having a ventilation problem, and it was so hot in the baking area that the light fixtures on the ceiling melted. After installing the new oven, we could bake with the door closed; it was much cooler in the baking area, and there was a utility savings as well: The new oven used only 25 percent as much energy.

Other improvements to production systems further reduced costs. For example, Bagelz sold about 700 dozen bagels per week, and 10 percent of these were poppy seed. Poppy seeds could cost as much as $80 for a 50-pound bag. In the past, bagels had been boiled, placed on seeded boards, seeded on the top, then baked. After baking, the seeds left on the boards had to be discarded, because baking seeds more than once produced a burned-tasting product. Management refined the process by dampening the bagels with a sponge, then dipping them in seed bins that covered each bagel with approximately a quarter of an ounce of seeds. Leftover seeds remained in the bin, effectively eliminating waste and reducing costs by using only half as many seeds as the previous process had.

The Commissary

Mike, Jamie, and Wes owned the central baking facility, called a commissary, which sold bagels, cream cheese, and other products to franchisees. Franchisees were required to purchase cream cheese and bagel dough directly from the commissary, but were permitted to buy other items either from the commissary or from an approved vendor and product list. Because of the commissary's bulk-purchasing power, franchisees were unlikely to obtain a lower price, effectively discouraging them from purchasing products from outside vendors. But the commissary also had to maintain high-quality standards to keep the franchisees from buying elsewhere, because the commissary needed large orders to receive large price discounts. In early 1996 the commissary's cream cheese sales volume reflected America's love of combining cream cheese with bagels, averaging approximately 3,500 pounds per week:

> A lot of people cut cream cheese with water; at the commissary, we don't. That adds to our costs, but it's more than offset by maintaining a high-quality image with our customers. We also make larger bagels—four and a quarter ounces— when others use a four-ounce standard. Because of this, we will never be a cost leader, but the goal is to be seen as a product leader. You see, although you can't tell the difference between a four and four-and-a-quarter ounce bagel, the larger one has a longer shelf life, so we hope the customer will get a fresher bagel.

In the early days of the commissary, there was only one dough-producing machine. Production was started early in the day, so in the event there was a mechanical problem, it could be repaired in time. An additional machine was purchased in 1995, but production still started early in the day so that in the event of an emergency, a store's order could still be met. As the sole source of bagel dough, the commissary had to deliver. Then, in 1996 Mike, Jamie, and Wes developed frozen dough in conjunction with several large manufacturing companies. Bagels were then defrosted. Stores had a double-defrost rack and a single-bake oven, because while defrosting took 30 minutes, baking took only 15. The double defrost-rack kept the production process continually flowing.

Originally, all our stores were doing fresh dough because we weren't able to formulate a frozen dough that tasted the same. But fresh dough only has a shelf life of three days and, therefore, there was minimal distance from the commissary that a store could be located. Because commissaries are a nightmare to set up, this in effect limited company growth potential. Frozen dough has a shelf life of about three months, and cream cheese 30 days, so growth was no longer limited to clusters around commissaries.

Mike, Wes, and Jamie worried about whether to maintain the commissary or to eventually outsource all frozen-dough production. Some franchisees had complained about the commissary's monopoly on dough sales, but once frozen bagel production was outsourced, franchisees could then buy from the lowest-priced producer. They struggled with the decision.

Marketing

Bagelz was continually improving products and store design. Mike and the team felt that Bagelz needed better marketing. For example, to increase coffee revenues, they developed better coffee displays, sold porcelain mugs, and positioned the product with an upscale image:

We even looked into pumping the coffee smell into the store through the air vents. You see, mine was the same exact coffee as other, higher priced coffee competitors, but these sellers displayed the product better, so people saw it as superior and were willing to pay more for it.

Although they wanted to create a deli or gourmet-shop image for Bagelz, the team members also wanted customers to perceive it as having the convenience of fast food. To do this and speed product-assembly times, they switched to presliced meats and premixed cartons of pasteurized eggs that were delivered directly to franchisees from outside vendors. These processes had additional benefits: There was no chance of employee injury from a slicer blade, and sandwich preparation time was reduced. Because the eggs were microwaved, they were always uniform in taste and appearance. Bagelz also added self-serve drink fountains, and its refrigerators were filled with prepackaged cream cheeses.

To better market take-out products, cream cheese containers were custom-printed with the Bagelz logo and put in a display case by the register—in case a customer forgot to get it from the self-serve refrigerator. Previously, a customer had to step out of line to get it, and then step back into line, delaying other customers. Pressure from those waiting to keep the service line moving had resulted in lost sales.

One of the company's greatest advertising successes was travel coffee mugs with the Bagelz name on them. Early on, Bagelz gave them away in exchange for any competitor mug that a customer brought into the store. Other advertising tactics included emphasizing the Z in the Bagelz name, even putting the Z in front of words, as in "Z sandwiches."

Another thing we had been advertising was something called a quarterloaf. There were a lot of people who weren't going to go in to buy a bagel because they simply weren't filling enough. For example, when I'm really hungry, I'm a grinder type of guy: extra sauce, dripping with cheese; it's a beautiful thing. Now, *that's* a sandwich! At first we were thinking of giving extra-thick bread, but others were doing it. The same with submarine sandwiches. Then we came up with the quarterloaf idea, and we knew we had a winner. No one knew what the heck a quarterloaf was, but it sounded good. And most of all, it sounded large.

The quarterloaf was one-fourth the size of a loaf of bread, shaped like a roll, and for an additional 25 cents offered the same sandwich items as a bagel. Because of this, the same sandwich-making area setup could be used for both— giving the impression that Bagelz offered many different menu items without having to coordinate extra preparation processes.

We are constantly looking for items, like the quarterloaf, that you can do a lot with. For example, right now we have a chicken breast, but pretty soon it's going to be a chicken salad. Then it's going to be a chicken Caesar salad. We are using Franchisee Advertising Fund revenues to develop advertising campaigns for all these new products.

Franchisee Advertising Fund

The Franchisee Advertising Fund (FAF) was controlled by franchisees. Two and a half percent of gross sales went to the FAF, and these funds supported media development, media advertising, coupon campaigns, and similar promotions. Discounts from vendors on products such as deli meats and paper goods were negotiated by Mike and approved by FAF's franchisee buying cooperative. It was thought that as the number of store units increased, local FAF chapters would eventually be created. However, Mike planned to continue negotiating vendor-based pricing deals.

We made the deals. We looked to make as large a deal as possible with suppliers. If you could fill their trucks, you would get the lowest possible price—one unit or one truckload costs the same to transport. Because we looked to develop territory clusters of stores, ordering enough to fill a truck became possible. First, we would make a deal with a local supplier, and then with the larger house that distributed to them. We would guarantee the supplier that we would open up a certain number of stores in an area within a given period of time. It has worked fine so far, but if we ever miss projected store openings and usage volumes, it will become a little more difficult.

The team members decided to wait on television advertising. They believed that successful television advertising for food, unlike garage or gas-station advertising, depended directly on how attractive that product looked on the screen. Achieving a high-quality, professional production was expensive and simply wasn't cost-effective for the company at the time. Instead, they saw potential for using the effectiveness of television advertising without spending FAF money by forming strategic alliances with other companies that already advertised on television. Such alliances included developing co-branded units to establish brand recognition in the highly competitive foodservice industry.

Co-Branded Units

Co-branded units offer two different concepts in the same location (e.g., Dunkin' Donuts and Baskin Robbins). Bagelz opened its first co-branded store with Subway. A store adjoining a Subway location had gone out of business, and the site became available. Although Bagelz was able to combine the seating due to Subway's existing setup, Bagelz was not able to combine the back room—something Mike and the team hoped to eventually be able to do. They thought there would be other opportunities to develop co-branded Bagelz and Subway units:

> We were also looking to put together a breakfast program with Fred. Although he was already doing a breakfast program, he was having problems changing Subway's image from strictly a lunch and dinner place. We were looking to use Bagelz as a morning traffic-builder, retrofitting some Subway stores—possibly changing their color scheme to differentiate the co-branded units. If this works, it opens up an enormous number of possibilities, and shared overhead would be a tremendous competitive advantage. But Subway isn't our only option—we see them as one potential brand to do business with, but there are a lot of other franchisors we could co-brand with as well.

One company, a Mobil franchisee, had already opened a Bagelz franchise in his gas station's convenience store. The Mobil owner did not have the room for full-sized baking facilities, nor did he want to lease the space to an existing Bagelz franchisee, so management engineered a scaled-down version of necessary baking equipment. This gave the franchisee potential to open multiple non-bake locations. The Bagelz team considered multiple-unit franchisees key for the company's success:

> If we could be three-to-one or four-to-one nonbake to bake, we would be very happy because you don't make money in the back room—you make money by setting up counters and by getting qualified franchisees to keep them operating.

Future Dilemmas

Mike and the team worried about the appropriate role for the franchisor and the franchisees. They had made so many changes and refinements to the system, they wondered if the business model was clear. It was their hope that those refinements leveraged the competencies of all the players. As a matter of fact, they were betting their futures on it.

Summation of Case Analysis:
Bagelz and Transaction Analysis

The tasks under consideration for a transaction analysis most often fall into these four categories: franchise SDS, outlet operations, advertising and public relations, and product and supply. Following is a categorization of the tasks in the Bagelz case. This is by no means an exhaustive list, but we believe it will help highlight and clarify the process of dissecting a franchise model. We have found this process to help franchisors be explicit about their business models and competitive advantages and to keep franchisees focused on the details. Also, because customer needs evolve, so must your business model. Think about the awesome potential of every franchisee working on the same problems, searching for innovation and better systems and products. The transaction analysis creates the list of priorities whose efficacy as a brand strength should be constantly challenged.

Each item in these lists represents a decision by Bagelz to form its offering in a specific way. It will bake centrally, with excess capacity led by its master baker, Irving Stearns. The total of these tasks is the Bagelz SDS. Its intent is to create a foundation of competitive advantages and the basis of the Bagelz brand.

Franchise SDS (please refer to Table 7–1)

- Centralized baking facility
- Additional dough-making machine at commissary
- Irving Stearns, bagel maker extraordinaire
- Refrigerated cases near cash registers
- Self-serve beverages and cold drink cases
- Pre-sliced meats
- Premixed pasteurized eggs
- Prepackaged cream cheeses
- Fresh vs. frozen dough production
- New style oven in bake locations
- New style of adding toppings to bagels
- Removal of "boiling" aspect from production
- New double defrost rack system
- Use of Subway's legal and architectural departments
- Internal franchisor management infrastructure
- New product development
- New point of distribution: Mobil gas stations
- Territory determinations
- Franchisee recruitment and monitoring

Ongoing Outlet Operations (please refer to Table 7–2)

- Bake and nonbake units
- Field visits by Bagelz managing partners
- Alarm system for 3:00 A.M. baking shift
- Hours of operation
- Operations manual
- Site location search
- Franchisee recruitment
- Bagel sales-demand charts
- Sandwich line-assembly process

Advertising and Public Relations (please refer to Table 7–3)

- Franchising advertising fund
- The use of Z at the end of sandwich names
- Use of Bagelz logo on travel coffee mugs
- Development of quarterloaf bread concept
- Marketing and POS Information
- Co-branding: Bagelz and Subway
- Television advertising in the future

Product Supply (please refer to Table 7–4)

- Franchisee cooperative for raw materials
- Vendor-based product discounts negotiated by Bagelz
- Franchisor-owned commissary

Our next chapter picks up where we have left off here. By evaluating the actual financial consequences of performing a transaction analysis on the profit potential of a business format, we will highlight those areas of a growing system that should be of the highest priority.

8 Financial Analysis

The purpose of this chapter is to show you the links between transactions and their financial ramifications. Every transaction embodies revenue, cost, investment—or all three. How do all of these transactions come together into a system that creates wealth? This chapter answers that question.

The proof of a successful SDS lies first in its ability to generate profit and second in its ability to be precisely duplicated. All too often, success is measured only in terms of revenue without considering profitability or the possibility and effects of growth. Although necessary, revenue is not alone sufficient to measure a franchise's unit economics.

Each transaction in our Chapter 7 discussion of transaction analysis is associated with revenue or a cost and therefore is a line item on the income statement. Therefore, the transaction analysis yields pro forma (projected) financial statements. These not only illustrate the results of the transaction allocation between franchisee and franchisor, but also allow you to prioritize the most important transactions based on their financial impact. Most SDSs have five or six transactions that franchisors should focus on to optimize and maximize cash flow. Let's take a look at the Bagelz pro forma income statement that highlights these line items in Table 8–1.

TABLE 8–1 Bagelz 1999[1] Per-Store Earning (estimated)

		Weekly	Annually	% of Total Revenue Per Store
TOTAL REVENUE PER STORE				
1	Total Revenue	$8,400.00	$436,800.00	100%
COST OF GOODS SOLD				
2	Salaries & Wages	1,848.00	96,096.00	22%
3	Food	1,596.00	82,992.00	19%
	Beverages	756.00	39,312.00	9%
	Paper Supplies	336.00	17,472.00	4%
TOTAL C.O.G.S.		$4,536.00	$235,872.00	54%
GROSS PROFIT ON SALES		$3,864.00	$200,928.00	46%
OPERATING EXPENSES				
4	Royalties	672.00	34,944.00	8%
	Payroll Tax	142.80	7,425.60	1.70%
	Payroll Service	21.00	1,092.00	0.25%
5	Rent	504.00	26,208.00	6.00%
	Electric	210.00	10,920.00	2.50%
	Gas	126.00	6,552.00	1.50%
	Telephone	25.20	1,310.40	0.30%
	Advertising	210.00	10,920.00	2.50%
6 {	Local Advertising	84.00	4,368.00	1.00%
	Promotions	4.20	218.40	0.05%
	Insurance	84.00	4,368.00	1.00%
	Linen & Laundry	16.80	873.60	0.20%
	Repairs & Maintenance	84.00	4,368.00	1.00%
	Rubbish Removal	42.00	2,184.00	0.50%
	Office Supplies	42.00	2,184.00	0.50%
	Uniforms	16.80	873.60	0.20%
	Professional Fees	42.00	2,184.00	0.50%
	Misc.	21.00	1,092.00	0.25%
TOTAL OPERATING EXPENSES		$2,347.80	$122,085.60	27.95%
TOTAL PROFIT FROM STORE OPERATIONS		$1,516.20	$78,842.40	18.05%

Focusing on the Key Transactions

The following list is our take on the Bagelz six key transactions. Bagelz should prioritize its attention and efforts on these items to maximize financial return.

---

1. Bagelz's business plan. All figures are estimated based on industry data and do not necessarily represent the actual financial performance of a Bagelz store operation.

1. **Revenue:** Not surprisingly, the customer is the unit of analysis in the revenue transaction. How much will the average customer spend in a Bagelz restaurant? How many customers can be served in a day or day part? These questions motivate many of the system's activities. *Sell more to each of an increasing number of customers* is the charge of every SDS. Of particular interest is throughput during peak periods, such as lunchtime for Bagelz, morning drive time for Dunkin' Donuts, and Saturday morning for Jiffy Lube.

2. **Labor:** What human assets are required to earn revenue? That question often defines a key competitive advantage of a franchise. A strong brand attracts customers who are willing to pay a premium for a product or service. Labor cost absorbs a percentage of that revenue. The stronger the brand, the *lower* the percentage of labor required to deliver the product or service. Strong brands command premium pricing. By pushing up the unit revenue, you force down the labor *percentage*. McDonald's engaged in a $0.99 price war in 2002 and suffered its first quarterly loss ever in that year. Of course, technology or operating efficiencies push down labor costs. The more streamlined the system's SDS is, the more efficient its labor usage, and therefore the higher the capacity utilization.

3. **Cost of Goods Sold:** After the components of the product are paid for, how much revenue is left to cover other costs? For many franchises, economies of scale in supply are a key competitive advantage. Dunkin' Donuts is one of the largest buyers of coffee in the world. Jiffy Lube is one of the largest buyers of motor oil. Virtually every franchise has the opportunity for regional or national supply contracts. The Bagelz income statement points to food and beverage as key supply needs. Everything that Bagelz buys in those categories, from flour to tomatoes, should be bought under a regional or national contract. Size matters in product purchase, and advantageous national contracts often result in more money for the store operators at the bottom line.

4. **Royalties:** The simple test of a franchise is to look at items 1, 2, and 3 and ask if the advantages in the franchise pay for the royalty. If the advantages of being a franchise are not sufficient to rationalize the ongoing royalty payment, then clearly tension will exist between franchisee and franchisor. The question then arises, What am I paying for as a franchisee if the business model cannot support the royalty, which is essentially the payment for a competitive advantage? A franchisee may begin to wonder if he or she would be better off running the same business as an independent operator. Some franchisors show royalties as a part of cost of goods sold. To develop a comparison with other non-franchised outlets, you should show net revenue as sales minus royalties. Both the franchisee and franchisor should do this. If the comparison doesn't yield positive comparisons for the franchised outlet, why would anyone buy the franchise?

5. **Rent (sometimes referred to as occupancy cost):** This line item directly relates to our SDS discussion. Please refer back to Chapter 4 for a detailed discussion of real estate and the SDS. The most appropriate real estate location for any franchise is the one that produces the lowest *rent as a percentage of revenue* dedicated to occupying that location. It is important not to confuse percentage of rent with the absolute cost of occupying the real estate. When assessing the interconnection between real estate selection and revenue generation, remember that revenue projections arise from customer needs and associated demographics. The best real estate attracts the most revenue at the lowest price, when real estate price is calculated as a percentage of revenue. For example, if your location's rent is $100,00, but the revenue stream is $1 million, then its rent as a percentage of revenue is only 10 percent despite the seemingly high absolute cost. But if another location's rent is $5,500, and the income stream is only $50,000, then the rent as a percentage of revenue is 11 percent, although the absolute amount is lower than at the previous location. Absolute rent cost is one concept to consider, but more important is the ratio of rent to revenue for a given location. Of course, this is important for the franchisee, but it is equally important to the franchisor. Failed locations reflect poorly on the brand and hurt everyone associated with the franchise.

6. **Adverting and Promotion:** Bagelz is typical in the way it allocates advertising costs. The 2.5 percent advertising line item is the system fund used by the franchisor to create materials and sometimes buy media. The local advertising and promotion line items are monies spent by the franchisee in the markets surrounding their store(s). Local advertising or promotion might take the form of the sponsorship of local youth sports teams, whereas the purchase of electronic media would be allocated to the advertising line item.

Prioritizing transactions is a step-by-step process that creates pro forma financial statements. Focusing on the five or six key transactions in the pro forma statements improves net income based on these financial findings and analysis. To complete the analysis—from transactions to financial statements to prioritization of financial statements—we now need to understand the initial investment in the system. This allows us to understand the return on investment (ROI).

It is difficult to properly assess the value of the system until we know the investment necessary to achieve this return. The Uniform Franchise Offering Circular (UFOC) requires franchisors to list the approximate initial investment requirements for a franchisee. Most franchises offer a range of investment. Let's look at Bagelz and the initial investment as found in its disclosure document and laid out in Table 8–2. If you invest $207,600, will you make enough profit from operating your Bagelz franchise to put this money at risk?

TABLE 8–2 Bagelz's UFOC Highlights: Estimated Initial Investment for a Bagelz Franchise Operation

Initial Investment	Lower Cost	Mid-Cost	Higher Cost
Initial franchise fee	$10,000	$10,000	$10,000
Real property	2,500	4,000	8,000
Leasehold improvements	37,000	40,000	46,000
Equipment	55,000	60,000	65,000
Security systems	1,000	1,500	2,000
Freight charges	1,700	2,100	2,500
Outside signage	1,500	2,000	2,500
Opening inventory	5,000	5,000	5,000
Insurance	1,000	1,000	1,000
Supplies	500	750	1,000
Training expenses	600	1,100	2,600
Legal and accounting	1,000	1,000	1,000
Grand opening advertising	2,000	2,000	2,000
Miscellaneous expenses	5,000	5,000	5,000
Working capital (3 months)	23,000	41,000	54,000
Total	$146,800	$176,450	$207,600

Return on Investment

A franchisor cannot be successful unless the franchisees gain a return on their investment. In the next section we analyze ROI and how much is necessary or acceptable for a robust system. Simply stated, ROI is the level of income relative to invested capital. A business's income is derived from two basic sources: cash flow from operations and a capital gain from the harvest or sale of the business. Table 8–3 illustrates Bagelz's ROI under three investment scenarios.

TABLE 8–3 Return by Investment Scenario*

Investment Scenario	Low	Medium	High
Total investment	$146,800	$176,450	$207,600
Total profit from operations	$75,088	$75,088	$75,088
Expected ROI	51%	42.5%	36.2%

*All figures have been estimated based on industry data and do not necessarily represent the actual financial performance of a Bagelz store operation.

ROI is usually calculated on an annual basis. The return scenarios in Table 8–3 appear quite attractive even without the inclusion of capital gain (or loss) on the sale of the franchise. However, return cannot be studied out of the context of risk.

Typically, a franchise is touted as a lower-risk new venture than a standalone operation. Indeed, the International Franchise Association claims a success rate of more than 90 percent among franchises. Although a number of academic studies challenge that number, the size and growth of franchising speaks to increased probabilities of survival compared to a standalone new venture launch. A potential franchise entrepreneur can examine the performance of a number of existing outlets. If the SDS performs consistently, and if the entrepreneur has the commensurate skills, he or she should expect to have an equally profitable performance.

In the Bagelz example, the projected ROI is quite high, but it must be so to attract potential franchisees because it is a relatively new operation. Since performance is achieved over time, the franchisor might be able to charge higher franchisee fees or royalties to new franchisees. That would reduce the return for the franchisee, but if the reduced return is in line with market expectations, and it is better assured because of historical performance, then the franchisor can reap more of the benefit. Increases in the franchise fee clearly increase the investment by the franchisee, just as an increase in the royalty stream effectively reduces the franchisees' net income. Either case results in lowering the ROI for the franchisee.

Conversely, the franchisor can do much to raise the return profile for the franchisee. First, remember some transactions are allocated to the franchisor based upon the belief that economies of scale can be generated. Supply economies (including for equipment) are particularly amenable to reduced cost based on volume. Most non-fee and working capital components of the initial investment in a franchise are subject to purchasing economies. This amounts to $128,000 of the $207,000 initial investment in the Bagelz franchise. A 10 percent reduction in cost because of bulk buying would result in a 6.5 percent increase in operating unit ROI.[1] Of course, more highly leveraged marketing, through national exposure or increased budget due to a higher number of outlets, might increase early revenues. Profitability would increase, and the need to fund operating losses would be reduced or eliminated.

For the franchisor, the ultimate measure of scale and market acceptance of the business model is a success initial public offering and a continued ability to access public capital to augment growth. Our research suggests that public franchisors are competing quite aggressively in the public capital markets. Over the period from 1990 to 2001, excluding 2000's irrational exuberance, public franchisors as a group outperformed the Standard and Poors 500. We discuss this at length in Chapter 12.

Introduction to Case Study: Panera Bread

One of the unique aspects of franchising from the perspective of the franchisee is that the information you need for due diligence is readily available in the marketplace. You can go look at existing operations and make informed judgments. We suggest that how well a franchise allocates transactions will inform you about system competitive advantages only if they result in a financial benefit, the focus of this chapter. By asking each player in a system what each expects from the other, you can infer a realistic understanding of transaction allocation in the firm. Equally important is understanding how execution of the key transactions evolves and improves over time. This process, in essence, defines the financial viability and sustainability of the franchise.

By reading the following case about Panera Bread, you will be able to connect financial analysis and transaction analysis. You will also be able to internalize the process of transaction analysis and see how it can affect your own financial statements. Keep in mind the six significant transaction aspects of the franchise that we highlighted, and then consider their impact on the firm's financial statements by addressing the following questions.

1. **Revenue:** Is Panera Bread's concept of a neighborhood bakery-café robust enough to sustain individual unit economics of its franchisees? Have the most appropriate locations been secured? Panera describes its customer as someone who wants a higher quality meal, quickly, with an inviting atmosphere. Is the customer profile congruent with the franchise's offering?

2. **Labor:** Does Panera's SDS, which incorporates electronic order-taking, self-serve coffee islands, and bakery counters, effectively utilize labor?

3. **Cost of Goods Sold:** Will a profitable balance between the use of frozen dough and fresh dough be achieved to reconcile the organization's commissary network and daily distribution channel? Can forecasting become accurate enough to virtually eliminate daily fresh-baked waste? Will takeaway sales contribute enough to the eat-in sales to make the space and labor allocation more profitable than eat-in only?

4. **Royalties:** Is PR, LLC (the corporate name of the Panera franchisee featured in the case) gaining enough brand awareness, equity, and support to rationalize the royalty payments to the franchisor? Could these two entrepreneurs enjoy the same success if they were not franchisees? Are they getting enough on a weekly, monthly, and yearly basis to continue paying the royalty?

5. **Rent:** Are the revenues from the business sufficient to carry the long-term lease requirements? Panera doesn't own real estate, it only leases. Would purchasing and capitalizing future properties be a better solution than leasing?

6. **Advertising and Promotions:** Panera is still relatively small and not able to buy national media. Is the benefit of the franchisees' contributions to the ongoing advertising funds, both locally and nationally, worth it? How valuable are the franchisees' advertising and promotion expenditures that are executed independently of the franchisor?

Large Motivations Come in Small Packages

On the morning of March 3, 2002, Mitch and Jill Roberts were delighted to welcome to the world their newborn girl, Ruby. Mitch had been "on call" for several weeks, ready to drop everything to race his wife to the hospital. Although Mitch was focused on constructing and launching his next four Panera cafés, his daughter's birth reminded him of how frenetic the pace had been over the past few years.

By the end of 2001, Mitch and his partner David Peterman, who were professionally known as PR Restaurants, LLC,[2] had opened their ninth Panera Bread franchise in Manchester, New Hampshire, with great success. They were obligated to build a total of 20 units to fulfill the ADA[3] they had signed and paid for in 1997. With the widespread accolades given to the Panera Bread concept by the financial press, the growth of PR Restaurants over the next several years would no doubt be exciting. But what was most on their minds was how to best manage the rapid growth of their organization and when to harvest their hard-earned equity.

Pre-Panera: The Saint Louis Bread Company

For most of the 1980s, Ken Rosenthal, a native of St. Louis, Missouri, worked in the sales and design aspects in the women's dress industry. Although successful, he grew tired of this seasonal business that was so dependent on fickle fashion trends. He no longer wanted his entire year's success to depend on whether he correctly guessed the exact length of the newest skirt designs.

In 1987, during this time of personal career struggle, Ken first experienced sourdough bread while on a trip to San Francisco. He enjoyed it so much that he sold his apparel business and moved to San Francisco to study the craft of sourdough breadmaking by apprenticing for a well-known baker. He learned the art of creating a "starter," the core mixture of ingredients that gives sourdough bread its distinctive flavor. When Ken brought the "mother," his original sour mixture, back to St. Louis, he took out a second mortgage on his house and started his first bakery—known as the Saint Louis Bread Company (SLBC). Even though the bakery store was located in a nondescript strip mall, it was an immediate hit. Over time, he added coffee and other beverages to the menu; soups and sandwiches soon followed at the new café.

Through internal funding and the acquisition of new partners, the café grew organically to 19 company-owned stores in the greater St. Louis area; one unit had been franchised, for a total of 20 units by 1993. Company-owned store sales had grown to approximately $20 million, and although Ken knew he had a winning concept, he also knew that the demand for high-quality food served fast and at an affordable price far outstripped supply. Unfortunately, Ken lacked the necessary capital to fuel the growth of his unique café concept.

A Potential Partner: Au Bon Pain

Ken Rosenthal met Ron Shaich, the CEO of Au Bon Pain (ABP), at an industry conference in 1993. The two began to discuss their common interest—bakery cafés.

Au Bon Pain ("Good Bread") was modeled after the street cafés in France that featured flavorful food and drinks. Based in Massachusetts, Au Bon Pain specialized in Parisian-style baked goods and coffee beverages situated in trendy boutique locations in major metropolitan cities such as Boston, New York, and Chicago.

During their conversations, there was something that captured Ron's imagination about the Saint Louis Bread Company—the vision of a "neighborhood bakery-café." He envisioned thousands of these cafés that would not be constrained, as Au Bon Pain was, by high-rise buildings and downtown locations. Furthermore, although Au Bon Pain had become an established brand, the Saint Louis Bread Company was still in its infancy. Ron began to think about the opportunities for a joint venture or partnership. He saw far greater potential in terms of sheer number of units for the Saint Louis Bread Company because of its suburban concept as well as its higher top-line sales revenue, lower cost structures, and subsequently attractive bottom-line figures. Ron also understood that one of his directives as CEO of a public company was to return value to the shareholders—and he believed the only way to continue to do so was through an aggressive growth strategy.

Shortly after their meeting, Ron fell in love with the Saint Louis Bread Company concept and wanted to acquire the 20 units from Ken. Au Bon Pain proceeded to purchase the Saint Louis Bread Company in 1993 for approximately $24 million. By 1995, systemwide sales for the Saint Louis Bread Company division were $44 million, and it grew from 20 to 45 units. Ron knew he had something special in the neighborhood bakery-café concept. Little did he know, however, that he would be recognized as a pioneer in a rapidly evolving segment of the restaurant industry.

Fast-Casual Dining

Fast-casual is an emerging segment in the $380 billion[4] restaurant industry. Although no single definition can clearly describe this segment, a survey of fast-casual consumers reported (1) good quality food, (2) convenience to home, and (3) good value for money as the key elements of success.

Fast-casual accounts for $19 billion or 5 percent of restaurant industry sales. However, the demand for fast-casual is rapidly increasing. People who live and work in the suburbs are often faced with lunch options that mainly consist of fast food and greasy spoons. Panera Bread is moving into that suburban void and catering to the crowd of aging baby boomers and young mothers who eat out more often and are tired of the high-fat fare of fast-food chains. As a result, Panera grew at a rate of 56 percent from 1999 to 2000. Furthermore, the market share of fast-casual in terms of sales accounted for 18.1 percent in 2000 compared to 14.9 percent in 1999. All other types of food services, such as sandwiches (D'Angelos), pizza (Pizza Hut), family (Denny's), and chicken (Kentucky Fried Chicken), lost market share over the past three years .

Although there does not seem to be any direct head-to-head competition, eateries like Einstein's Bagels, Boston Market, and Schlotzky's Deli fall into the fast-casual segment. According to Panera, anyone who sells breakfast for $5 within 5 minutes or lunch for $10 within 10 minutes is a potential competitor. Some noted fast-casual competitors might be New York's Cosi, Inc., Baja Mexican Grill, Peet's, and Boston Market. Although a quick-service restaurant (QSR)[5] giant such as McDonald's could decide to enter the market segment, if it does so, it will encounter Panera's nearly 525 franchised units (in operation at the end of 2002).

Panera Bread Is Born

With the dramatic growth of the Saint Louis Bread Company, Ron turned his attention away from Au Bon Pain to further develop his vision of the neighborhood bakery-café concept. With little brand identity outside of St. Louis, Ron needed a new name for the Saint Louis Bread Company that would convey a positive image throughout the country. "Panera" was chosen for its play on "pain," which is "bread" in French as well as "basket of bread" in Spanish. The 45 units in St. Louis retained their original name because of their strong brand identity in the local market.

The Panera neighborhood bakery-café concept consists of providing fresh baked goods, beverages (hot and cold), and various sandwiches, soups, and salads. All these items are presented in a fast, convenient, and friendly atmosphere. One example of convenience is the self-serve hot beverage stations and free refill allowance. Additionally, the environs of a café have some measure of ambience, including warm yellow/orange painted walls, hardwood tables and chairs, a working fireplace in select locations, light music, trendy lights, couches, and colorful wall art. This combination creates an inviting respite for main mealtimes as well as what the company terms "chill-out" times—those occasions when we just need a refreshing break from our daily routine surroundings.

In 1998 system-wide sales from Panera and the Saint Louis Bread Company bakery-cafés reached $114 million from 115 units. However, sales from the preexisting Au Bon Pain units were declining. In May 1999 Ron Shaich decided to sell the Au Bon Pain division to Bruckmann, Rosser, Sherrill & Co., LP.[6] Now consisting solely of Panera stores and as the operator of the Saint Louis Bread Company in Missouri, Panera ended 1999 with system-wide sales of $171 million from 181 units. Thirty-four area development agreements (ADAs) had been signed with franchisees for a total commitment of 643 bakery-cafés. The year 2000 ended with system-wide sales of Panera (without the ABP division) of $151 million from 262 units. In 2001 Panera's net income rose 92 percent to $13 million, while revenues increased 33 percent to $201 million from 369 units in 30 states.

The Panera Franchise Concept

The Panera franchise program of selling ADAs instead of individual units was designed to avoid the mom-and-pop environment of inexperienced entrepreneurs that is typical of many other franchise systems. Panera Bread, the franchisor, made a strategic decision to promote more sophisticated and experienced entrepreneurs as multiunit franchisees. In the end the system would have fewer franchisees, but potentially a larger collective knowledge base. Some of the Panera franchisees are not only multiunit operators, but are also franchisees of other restaurant chains. For example, the largest Panera franchisee with 39[7] units was previously one of McDonald's largest franchisees with 40 units. In the Boston-metro territory the Panera units are owned by a Springfield, Missouri, operator who also owns 21 Wendy's units. Presently, there are 39 territories under agreement, accounting for an estimated 733 committed units; 525 units (including corporate growth) were open by the end of 2002.

According to the ADA, the Panera franchisee must pay a development fee of $5,000 for each Panera Bread bakery-café that may be opened under the agreement. The number of units that may be developed under a particular ADA is determined by a variety of factors, including population statistics, local competition, real estate availability, and the number of units estimated to thrive within the development area. The initial franchise fee for each Panera Bread bakery-café under an ADA is $35,000, including the $5,000 development fee. The ADA fee must be paid up front for all units to be developed, although the franchise fee is due prior to opening a new location. A royalty of 5 percent of gross sales must be paid annually. Furthermore, up to 2.6 percent of gross sales must be paid for the national advertising fund (when called for by corporate), 2 percent for local advertising, and 0.4 percent for marketing administration fees.[8] See figures 8–1, 8–2, and 8–3 for unit pro forma financial statements.

Service Delivery System

Panera's success depends on its ability to deliver fresh breads daily to its customers through its company-owned and franchised locations. Because the company's nationwide expansion was based on selling ADAs, the franchisor had to develop an equally scaleable system to support the foundation of its brand—dough. Each Panera Bread location bakes all its breads and other products fresh daily. To achieve this goal, each location uses two kinds of dough.

For all the sourdough-based products, fresh dough produced at one of Panera's company-owned dough facilities is delivered daily to each unit. As of February 2002, Panera Bread operated 11 fresh dough commissaries to serve its 39 ADAs. Additionally, frozen dough used in the remaining non-sourdough products is produced in a commissary in Missouri and delivered twice per week through an independent food distributor.

Annual Income Statement			% of Sales
Revenues	$	1,700,000	
5% Royalty Fee	$	85,000	5.0%
Cost of Goods Sold (31.5%)	$	535,500	31.5%
Gross Profit	$	1,079,500	63.5%
Labor	$	480,000	28.2%
Operating Expenses	$	120,000	7.1%
Advertising Expenses (1.5%)	$	25,500	1.5%
Fixed Expenses	$	70,000	4.1%
Occupancy Expenses	$	110,000	6.5%
Interest Expense (10%)	$	21,000	1.2%
Income before Tax	$	253,000	14.9%
Tax (35%)	$	88,550	5.2%
Net Income (in rent case)	$	**164,450**	**9.7%**
Depreciation	$	65,000	3.8%
EBITDA	$	**339,000**	**19.9%**

Operating Expenses include cost of utilities, repairs and maintenance, office supplies, etc.
Fixed Expenses include taxes, depreciation, cost of insurance, lease payments for equipment.
Occupany Expenses include base rent, real estate taxes, common area maintenance.

FIGURE 8–1 Single-unit Panera Bread Franchise pro forma income statement.

The estimated cost for building and equipping a sourdough commissary is approximately $1 million. Panera's strategy is to expand its ADAs around an existing commissary to maximize capacity and distribution. But because of the importance of the daily fresh dough, Panera has built commissaries in undeveloped areas, even when only a single Panera café would be utilizing dough capacity. The ideal number of distribution points for each commissary is between 20 and 30 units. Panera is also responsible for the daily transportation of the dough to the outlying units. Across the system, dough prices are set uniformly at 30 percent of retail prices regardless of transportation distance.

Panera is currently experimenting with "commissary-less" cafés that would have their own dough production as well as existing baking functions on site. This format would require a larger facility and additional labor, adding approximately $125,000 to annual unit operating expenses. Presently under consideration is whether to add an additional oven, at a cost of $40,000, to the existing store format to allow for new product introductions.

Balance Sheet
(typical non-freestanding unit at end of Year 1)

ASSETS

Cash	200,000
A/R	-
Inventory	16,900
Prepaid Expenses	35,000
Total Current Assets	251,900
Property and Equipment	175,000
Land	-
Furniture, fixtures and equipment	97,000
Leasehold Improvements	300,000
Property under capital leases	-
Total assets	823,900

LIABILITIES & SHAREHOLDER'S EQUITY

A/P	20,500
Notes payable	-
Current portion - LTD	14,000
Current portion of capital lease	-
Total Current Liabilities	34,500
Long-Term Debt	196,000
Capital Lease Obligations	-
Other long-term liabilities	-
Total Long-Term Liabilities	196,000
Shareholders' Equity	
Paid-In Capital	593,400
Retained Earnings	164,450
Total liabilities and equity	823,900

FIGURE 8–2 Single-unit Panera Bread Franchise pro forma balance sheet.

PR Restaurants, LLC

PR Restaurants, LLC, was founded in 1997 by David Peterman (the P) and Mitchell Roberts (the R) as a franchisee of Panera Bread, LLC. Between 2000 and 2003, Mitch and David opened nine bakery-cafés; their ADA covers the area outside Route 128 in Massachusetts and all of New Hampshire, Vermont, and Maine. PR Restaurants was one of Panera Bread's first five franchisees. In just a short time, PR Restaurants became Panera's leading franchisee in same-store sales. Same-store sales are a key metric in most retail operations for measuring the revenue growth of stores that were in existence a year earlier. Another measure, system sales, includes new stores and tends to mask the condition of the individual store.

By age 37, Mitch had accomplished much. Between college and business school, he spent 5 years in real estate development learning the ropes. After graduating from MIT's Sloan School, Mitch worked for 8 years at Au Bon Pain, leaving as head of corporate real estate development. When Mitch became a franchisee, he was able to leverage his 13 years of experience in real estate and 8 years in the Au Bon Pain business.

Cash Flows from Operations

Net Income		164,450
Depreciation and Amortization		65,000
A/R		-
Inventory		(10,140)
Prepaid Expenses		(35,000)
A/P		12,300
Income Taxes payable		-
Other long-term liabilities		-
	Cash flow from operation	196,610

Cash Flows from Investing

Purchases of property and equipment		(65,000)
Proceeds from sale of property and equipment		-
Acquisition of license agreements		-
Change in other assets		-
	Cash flow from Investing	(65,000)

Cash Flows from Financing

Proceeds from long-term borrowings and revolving line of credit		-
Principal payments on long-term borrowings		(14,000)
Principal payments on capital lease obligations		-
Proceeds from sale of Common Stock and capital contributions		-
	Cash flow from Financing	(14,000)

Cash at the beginning of the year	200,000
Cash inflow (outflow) throughout the year	117,610
Cash at the end of the year	317,610

FIGURE 8–3 Single-unit Panera Bread Franchise pro forma cash flow statement.

At 49 years old, David had spent the previous 29 years of his life building a remarkable career in the food and restaurant industry. After attending UCLA, David got his first taste of the industry as a manager of a local International House of Pancakes (IHOP). His longest stint was approximately 15 years in the Taco Bell franchise system as both a district manager and then regional vice president of Taco Bell in Los Angeles. Prior to becoming a Panera franchisee, David served as Au Bon Pain's senior vice president of operations, overseeing the company's 186 cafés and 4,000 store employees.

With the dream of owning his own business, Mitch approached David while they were both working at Au Bon Pain about his interest in a Panera franchisee partnership. With Mitch's experience in real estate and David's experience in operations, they complemented each other quite well. While Mitch was inspecting a site for the next Au Bon Pain unit, he negotiated a deal with Panera's CEO, Ron Shaich, to allow Mitch and David to open their first Panera unit there. According to Mitch, their relationship with Ron was critical to their ability to leave Au Bon Pain and launch their first Panera franchise. The store broke even in 5 weeks, business boomed, and as they say, the rest is (for the most part) history.

Getting Started

To get started, Mitch and David raised $1.3 million from friends, family, and angel investors. Their first step was to prepay their ADA, which obligated them to build 20 units. This created an ownership distribution in which Mitch and David each owned 40 percent of the company, and the rest of the investors owned 20 percent. This seed capital was used as follows:[9]

- $100,000 in franchise fees for the entire 20-unit ADA

- $50,000 startup costs, including attorneys

- $60,000 for David's salary for 6 months

- $600,000 for the first store's leasehold improvements

- $500,000 for franchisee fees and working capital

PR Restaurant Operations

Mitch and David understood Panera's expansion strategy of clustering new Panera locations around existing commissaries. Prior to opening a new restaurant, careful thought, extensive research, and a bit of luck contribute to finding a real estate location that is "most right" given the parameters of the Panera format. To date, Panera locations are between 3,500 and 4,500 square feet in size, as shown in Figure 8–5. Typical locations are malls, strip centers, and freestanding locations that are usually leased for 10 years with two 5-year options. There are currently approximately 25 freestanding units in the Panera system; as yet, none of PR Restaurants' units are freestanding.

CATEGORY	ACTUAL OR ESTIMATED AMOUNT	METHOD OF PAYMENT	WHEN DUE	TO WHOM PAID
Franchise Fee (See Note 1)	$35,000	Lump sum	Upon execution of franchise agreement	Panera
Real Property (See Note 2)	(See Note 2)	(See Note 2)	(See Note 2)	(See Note 2)
Leasehold Improvements (See Note 2)		Lump sum	As incurred	General contractor
Equipment (See Note 2)		Lump sum	Upon delivery before opening	Equipment vendors

CATEGORY	ACTUAL OR ESTIMATED AMOUNT	METHOD OF PAYMENT	WHEN DUE	TO WHOM PAID
Fixtures		Lump sum	Upon delivery before opening	Vendors
Furniture		Lump sum	Upon delivery before opening	Vendors
Consultant Fees (See Note 4)		Lump sum		Architect, engineer, expeditor, etc.
Supplies & Inventory (See Note 5)		Lump sum	Upon delivery before opening	Panera, and other suppliers
Smallwares		Lump sum	Upon delivery before opening	Suppliers
Signage		Lump sum	Upon delivery before opening	Suppliers
Additional Funds (3 Months; see Note 6)	$175,000 to $245,000	Lump sum	As incurred before opening	Vendors, suppliers, employees, utilities, landlord, etc.
TOTAL	$842,561 to $1,5111,746 (excluding real estate and related costs as well as landlord allowances)			

Note 1: We will apply $5,000 of the development fee paid under an ADA toward the initial franchise fee. (See Item 5 for details.)

Note 2: The total estimated initial investment does not include real estate. Panera Bread Bakery-Cafés are typically located in malls, strip centers, and freestanding locations. The cost of purchasing or leasing and developing a site will vary considerably depending on such factors such as location, size, and local real estate market. You must purchase or lease a building of approximately 4,200 to 4,500 square feet and pay the cost of site work and/or leasehold improvements. During 2001, all sites developed by Panera were leased with lease costs (as averaged throughout the initial term of the lease) ranging from $6,000 to $17,500 per month base rent, triple net, and with an allowance for tenant improvements ranging from $0 to $600,000. Leases may also require percentage rent.

Note 3: We estimate the cost of purchasing equipment to range from $150,000 to $200,000, including a computerized cash register system, computer hardware, and proprietary software, but not including any costs for POS and computer training. You purchase your computer system from Micros, Inc. (see Item 11), who will require you to attend training at a cost of $6,595 for the first store.

Note 4: The consultant fees include, at the high end of the range, an estimated impact fee of $35,000, which may be imposed by the municipality.

Note 5: Proprietary ingredients must be purchased from us, our affiliates, or our designated suppliers (see Item 8). Licensed ingredients may be purchased from our approved suppliers or other suppliers that we approve (see Item 8). other items must meet our quality standards or be purchased from an approved supplier (see Item 8). The cost of purchasing POP materials, training materials, and forms is estimated to range from $4,000 to $5,000. We estimate the cost of the opening food, paper, chemicals, and uniforms order to range from $16,675 to $21,000.

Note 6: This estimate includes working capital for the first 3 months and general operating expenses, such as lease payments, inventory, payroll expenses, facility expenses, insurance, pest control, security, repairs and maintenance, and complimentary sales and other costs. This estimate also includes your preopening expenses during the 6 months prior to opening and includes such items as professional fees, organizational expenses, utility deposits, and salaries and expenses during training of your operating partner (described in Item 15) and your other personnel whose training is required by the franchise agreement and/or the ADA. Because you and/or your operating partner and your other personnel for your bakery-café, as well as personnel in management positions and personnel that will work in more than one bakery-café (see Item 11), these expenses are included for your first bakery-café. Consequently, the additional funds necessary for your first bakery-café tend to be on the high end of the estimated range, while additional funds required for subsequent bakery-cafés that you open will tend to fall on the lower end of the estimated range. These figures are estimates based upon our experience in opening and operating company-owned bakery-cafés, and we cannot assure you that you will have additional expenses in starting your Panera Bread Bakery-Cafés.

Except as otherwise noted, none of these payments are refundable. These payments are only estimates, and your costs may be higher, depending on your particular circumstances. Panera relied on its experiences in opening both company-owned Panera Bread Bakery-Cafés and franchisee-owned Bread Bakery-Cafés to compile these estimates. You should review these figures carefully with a business advisor, accountant, or attorney before making any decision to purchase a franchise. We do not offer any financing for your initial investment or other items. The availability and terms of financing with third-party lenders will depend on factors such as the availability of financing generally, your credit worthiness, and policies of lending institutions concerning the type of business to be operated.

If you purchase an existing company-owned Panera Bread Bakery-Café, you may have to make a greater or smaller investment, depending on the circumstances, than the estimated initial investments shown above. The price and terms of payment for such Panera Bread Bakery-Cafés will be established by mutual agreement. We do not have sufficient experience with non-traditional locations to be able to estimate the initial investment for those locations.

Upon signing an ADA application, you must pay us a $15,000 deposit, which is described in Item 5. If you sign an ADA, you will be required to pay us a development fee (see Item 5) and also will need funds for working capital, in an estimated amount of $10,000 to $50,000, to pursue your development obligations. There is no other initial investment required upon execution of an ADA. However, an initial investment will be required for each Panera Bread Bakery-Café at each location you open. Our current estimate of this investment is described above.

FIGURE 8–4 Initial investment for Panera Bread franchise (Panera Bread Company UFOC, April 2002).

The average working capital required by PR Restaurants to open the doors of a new location is approximately $765,000; this includes real estate development, leasehold improvements, preopening salaries, startup marketing costs, and losses to breakeven. Profitability often begins within 2 to 3 weeks of opening.

As early adopters of the Panera franchise concept, Mitch and David pay a royalty fee of 4.5 percent instead of the current standard 5 percent rate. The other fees required from them as franchisees are 1.6 percent of sales for advertising[10] and the franchise/ADA fee of $35,000 per unit (including $5,000 paid towards the ADA). Clearly, the franchisor lowered the royalty to increase the projected ROI. With upwards of $2.0 million in sales, the half percent royalty reduction means an additional $10,000 of net income each year.

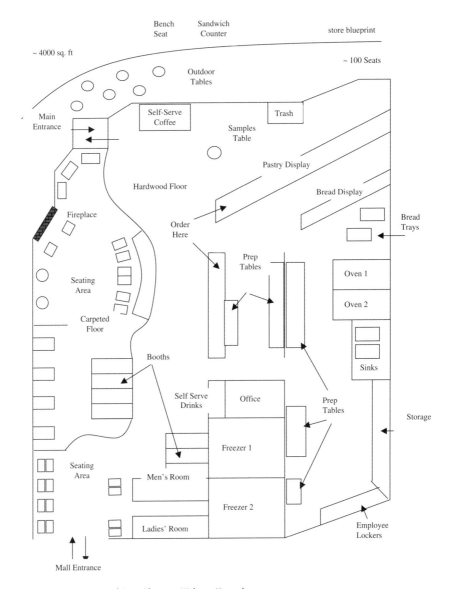

FIGURE 8–5 Panera Bread Store Blueprint, Woburn, Massachusetts.

Average Panera Bread franchisee unit sales are $1.7 million per unit, but over the past 18 months, there has been a 6.6 percent increase in new units' sales to $1.9 million.[11] In comparison, PR Restaurants' units average $2.1 million in store sales with a 12 percent to 18 percent store-level profit. In comparison to other industry players, the average Chili's restaurant's average sales per square foot are $240 compared to Panera's average sales per square foot of $475.[12] PR

Restaurants' average breakfast sale is approximately $3. The average lunch sale is approximately $8; however, this figure may be slightly misleading because the average party size tends to be larger at lunch. The average ticket sale is captured by transaction total, which does not necessarily account for customer count. Similarly, the average dinner check also tends to be larger parties. The "chill-out" time is more of a menu issue when more sweets and coffee are sold; there does not seem to be a distinct average for this period, but it may be most similar to breakfast.

The most significant unit cost is food and labor, followed by real estate, with lease costs ranging from $5,000 to $17,500 per month. The most important factors for a restaurant's success generally fall into three buckets—location, food, and customer service. In the fast-casual as well as the larger QSR industry this is not any different. According to Mitch, Panera has been fortunate to be the hottest new concept in some time and therefore has been able to attract some of the best talent in the restaurant management industry. Among the entire Panera system, PR Restaurants has some of the highest average management salaries; during 2001, the average general manager salary with bonuses was $68,000, with assistant manager's earning between $35,000 to $50,000. The highest management salary was approximately $80,000. Each store has a general manager and three assistant managers. The organization currently has two district managers, but will have to hire another as the expansion continues. A controller is also on the horizon as the next internal personnel to hire. As for turnover rates, Panera has performed better than the industry averages. As of the end of 2001, its general manager turnover was zero, assistant managers approximately 30 percent, and hourly staff turnover of only 60 percent to 70 percent as opposed to industry averages of 100 percent or more.

As in every privately held, small-scale entrepreneurial business, especially those that are highly capital intensive, questions of value and harvest are always ongoing concerns. The short-term questions of lifestyle and disbursements to the primary shareholders (owners) are balanced against long-term questions of value and eventual harvest. Although the partners of PR Restaurants earn market-rate salaries for their operational positions in the organization, the value of taking intermittent disbursements becomes increasingly questionable considering the state of the economy and specifically the return available through financial markets. According to Mitch, PR Restaurants will continue to reinvest its "profits" back into the business; he is confident that it is the best investment vehicle currently available.

From Here to 20?

With store number nine up and running smoothly, Mitch and David turned their attention to the next opening. Although the process had become more standardized with each new location, both knew that they would need additional personnel to help them manage their future rapid growth. They were confident that they would create an appropriate corporate infrastructure that would at once keep their hands in the daily operations and alleviate some of the frenetic pace of the last years.

As the second quarter of 2002 began to unfold, the question for Mitch and David began to change from, How will we get to 20 units? to What do we do now that we know we will get to 20? In fact, Mitch said one day, "We can't grow fast enough [to meet the market demand for Panera]." If their expansion plans proceeded as scheduled, PR Restaurants would complete its 20th unit by the end of 2004—less than three years away. Although the franchisor stated its goal of 1,500 units to be opened over the next several years, in Mitch's opinion that would be just the tip of the iceberg. His personal projection fell in the range of 4,000 based on the population statistics and restaurant density (unit per capita) of local markets such as New Hampshire and the 14-year old St. Louis market.[13]

With their respective family's welfares and four new stores slated for construction on their minds, both Mitch and David wondered when would be the right time to harvest their equity. Should they sell at the end of the year with 13 units operating so that the new owner could develop the remaining seven? Should they sell once their 20-unit obligation was complete? Should they renegotiate for a larger territory and an additional ADA agreement? Or should they simply run the 20 units as a lifestyle business that would continue to throw off a healthy positive cash flow for years to come?

The financial return would suggest that Panera, and Mitch and David in particular, have a service and product that is delivered effectively and efficiently. These partners will have to continue to stay current with customer needs and make the changes to the system, efficiently allocating transactions, to stay competitive. We'll explore Mitch and David's harvest options later in the book.

The chart in Figure 8–4 provides an estimate of the initial investment for a Panera Bread bakery-café (single unit with a "bake-off"[14] facility).

Endnotes

1. An initial investment of $207,000 less the 10 percent savings on the $128,000 of investment with national contract implications reduces the total maximum investment by $12,800. The reduced investment should still yield store net income of $75,088 (from Table 8–1), an increase in ROI of 6.4 percent.

2. This case was written in 2002, and all financial information and statistics were based on 2001 data. All information in this case (and the figures) was derived from Panera's UFOC, *www.panerabread.com*, and discussions with management.

3. An ADA is a contract between franchisee and franchisor that obligates and enables the franchisee to build a predetermined number of outlets in an exclusive territory.

4. "Restaurant Industry Operations Report," National Restaurant Association, Deloitte & Touche, 2001.

5. QSR refers to "Quick Service Restaurants," commonly known as fast-food restaurants.

6. Bruckmann, Rosser, Sherrill & Co., LP (BRS), is a New York-based private equity investment firm with approximately $1.2 billion in funds under management. BRS specializes in management buyouts and recapitalizations of high-quality, middle-market companies with strong market positions and/or growth potential.

7. As of January 2002.

8. Panera Bread Company UFOC, March 2002.

9. See Figure 8–4 for estimated initial investment costs for a general franchisee.

10. A 1.2 percent contribution goes to the local marketing budget; 0.4 percent is contributed to advertising production.

11. For quarter ending December 29, 2001, Panera experienced a 6.3 percent increase in same-store sales. "Panera Bread Co.'s Comp. Sales Jump 6.3%." *Yankee Food Service*, April 2002, p. 14.

12. Based on Chili's sales of $2.4 million and average store footprint of 10,000 square feet and Panera's sales of $1.9 million and average store footprint of 4,000 square feet.

13. St. Louis' population is approximately 2 million, with 43 Saint Louis Bread Company locations. Manchester, New Hampshire's population is approximately 60,000, with two Panera Bread locations.

14. "Bake-off" refers to the process of baking the preordered dough into daily product selection.

9 The Dynamics of the Franchisee– Franchisor Relationship

What separates the great franchises from the mediocre? What makes some franchises hum like a finely tuned engine and others sound like a broken record? Our belief is that beyond all the systems, spreadsheets, and technologies, the fundamental success factor for franchises is an understanding that the franchisor–franchisee alliance is an intimate business relationship. This leads to our discussion of the dynamic relationship between franchisor and franchisees and the important role it plays above and beyond all the quantitative material and data that comprises the "potentially successful" franchise. Relational dynamics is the way in which the franchisee and franchisor interact to exploit opportunities, handle conflict, communicate about current operations, and plan for the future.

The subject of conflict in franchising is well documented in the press. Almost 50 percent of all franchisors are in a lawsuit at any given time. Thirty percent of franchisees are unhappy enough with the relationship to consider severing it. Conflict is not totally unhealthy for any business. Questioning, probing, arguing, and even fighting can sometimes produce very healthy results. Pizza Hut had dramatically contentious relations with its franchisees in the late 1970s that led to a revised license agreement and a successful new launch of its pizza-delivery program. However, when conflict reaches the courts, it drains time, talent, and money from a franchise system, and conflict at that level seldom results in a healthy relationship going forward.

Like several of our other topics, relational dynamics is a concept that can be separated into four individual parts but that can be fully appreciated only by the integration of all the parts working together in a dynamic fashion.

We briefly break down "relational dynamics" into its individual parts, and then present a case study that reflects the relative importance that each component below brings to a franchise system. The individual components of relational dynamics in franchising are:

1. **Wealth Creation:** A view by each player about how the franchise system will help them become wealthy or at least will provide a market ROI. For some people, this is simply an income stream or the accumulation of assets. For others, it includes wanting to be in the industry they are involved with, the product or service they provide, the people they serve, their role in the business, and the degree of control in decision making.

2. **Communications:** Franchising is a long-term contractual relationship facing many challenges because both people and markets change. Communication, both formal and informal, is at the core of a relationship flexible enough to last over time.

3. **The Brand:** How do the franchisor and franchisee value the brand and their collective role in maintaining and building it? When there is perceived fairness in brand building, role definition, and execution, then the relationship remains healthy.

4. **Exit Costs:** What happens when a franchisee becomes unhappy with the franchisor? He or she likely looks at the long-term value of the relationship versus the cost of exiting the relationship. That calculation is more measurable than you might expect.

Let's look at each of these components more closely.

Wealth Creation

As we've stated numerous times throughout this book, one of the main reasons for becoming involved in franchising is wealth creation. With most license agreements averaging 15 years in length, we doubt anyone would become either a franchisor or a franchisee without the absolute expectation of creating long-term, sustainable wealth. In fact, of the more than 600 franchisees we surveyed, *all* of them expected the venture to create some personal wealth beyond their management salary. The trick, as if you could make it that simple, is to turn this great franchising idea into real wealth. Believe it or not, your success may rest not only on the quality of your product or service, but also on the quality of your partnerships with those you depend upon and those who depend on you.

The franchisee must make a series of investments in the franchise. The initial investment is disclosed in the United States through the Uniform Franchise Offering Circular (UFOC) and can range from a few thousand dollars to several million dollars. The operating results of the franchise are expected to provide a return on that investment. Often, over the life of a franchise agreement, reinvestment in property, plant, and equipment is required. Again, operating results need to support that additional investment.

When the operating results fall short, the franchisee tends to look to the franchisor for an explanation. Most systems have some under-performing stores. But when a significant minority of stores under-perform, the franchisees often lash out at the franchisor. There is a two-pronged focus of franchisee wrath. First, are the royalty payments too high and thus strangling profitability? Second, are the services provided by the franchisor appropriate and sufficient? Look at a franchisor's balance sheet for royalties payable to get an indication of the health of the franchisee–franchisor relationship. If accounts receivables are rising and days receivable are increasing, there may be franchisee conflict brewing. When franchisees become pressed financially, the first bill extended is the royalty payment. Ultimately, the franchisor cannot survive without an overwhelming majority of franchisees that are making a market or better ROI. When financial return does not meet franchisee expectation, conflict ensues and changes to the relationship occur. A small number of outlets in trouble results in closure or franchisor acquisition. A large number of under-performing outlets affect royalties or services. Those changes can happen through renegotiation of the license agreement or in litigation. The market simply will not allow status quo with under-performing operating stores.

Communication

Franchisees as a group and each franchisee individually must find a way to manage their relationship with the franchisor, and vice versa. Not enough attention is paid to how partners, who commit to as many as 20 years of working together, will remain focused enough to protect the brand and be flexible enough to react to constantly changing market forces. It is this very ability to manage the franchise relationship in a dynamic way that keeps a system viable for the long run. Additionally, when the franchise relationship builds in mechanisms to adjust to market changes, the formal legal boundaries of the license agreement should not constrain competitive advantage. In other words, no contract can be written that anticipates every change that may occur over the course of a 20-year period. But when both the franchisor and franchisee are committed to communicate openly and believe there is equity in the relationship, then the appropriate adjustments can and will be made in manners that benefit both parties.

This is the essence of relational dynamics—making adjustments to the relationship in response to market demand that benefit both parties and enable them to reach their mutually dependent goals of wealth creation. The role and interpersonal skills of the franchisor's field personnel is the key to the informal communications system in the franchise relationship. When franchisees believe their field support contact with the franchisor is clearly and accurately communicating, the level of conflict remains healthy. This is true even when the message is not one the franchisee wants to hear! Frequent and direct contact with the franchisee by trusted franchisor personnel is essential to a positive relational dynamic.

Informal communication is wrapped around a more formal system of contact that often includes

- Written store reviews with clearly delineated expectations and performance feedback.
- Advertising and promotional materials and strategy that is planned in advance and delivered to operating units.
- Regional and national meetings to provide education and a venue for strategic planning with franchisee input.
- Formalized business planning at the franchisee level with custom tools (such as customized electronic spreadsheet programs, store growth capital planning tools, human resource management support).
- Training aids such as curriculum, videos, and certification.

Also important to franchisees is their assessment of the distribution of the revenue generated by the franchise. Franchising is a classic "relational exchange." That is, the franchisee and franchisor both see their current income and future wealth as tied to the performance of their franchise partner. They equate preservation of the relationship with the *fair* distribution of the benefits generated by the relationship. Clearly, fair does not necessarily mean equal. Fairness, however, is subjectively assessed by a franchisee. If fairness is perceived to be absent in the distribution, then the franchisee will assess alternatives to the current relationship or start behaving badly.

Value of Trademark or Brand

The question of a franchise's value rears its head in the discussion of relational dynamics in a different sense than it does when you are a prospective franchisor or franchisee first considering a franchise opportunity. From the relational dynamics perspective, the question of a franchise's value is, Now that I am a party to this franchise relationship, what is the value of continuing to be so?— not, Should I do this at all?

That assessment to continue as a franchisee ultimately values the trademark or brand value that produces profits. How much it costs to exit the franchise relationship tells us a lot about how valuable the relationship is. There are always costs to exiting a business relationship. So, a franchisee says, "Am I unhappy enough to bear the expense of severing the relationship?" When franchisees see the trademark as able to grow and sustain value, they try to work through problems. However, if they see little value in the trademark at present or over time, then it's fairly reasonable to contemplate leaving the system. There is evidence that if franchisees aren't rewarded by the brand in the first 7 years of the relationship, then contemplation changes to action. It's an interesting twist we call the "franchise seven-year itch." As we soon discuss, one way to calculate the present and future value of your stake in the franchise is to determine your exit costs.

The franchise relationship is based upon the belief that the alliance will generate efficiencies resulting in greater returns to the participants than if they pursued similar opportunities independently. The franchisor and franchisee share a common trademark or brand, which is the embodiment of the value of the franchise relationship. The two must manage the part of their relationship that centers on this shared asset. If they understand the issues likely to cause conflict that erodes brand value, the partners can design and implement policies to control disagreement and to support the long-term relationship. The connection between forethought and real-time policy implementation enables more effective adjusts and supports the constant effort to prevent disruptions to the wealth stream whenever and however possible.

Exit Costs

Either party may make the decision to exit the franchise relationship. This choice carries with it both direct and indirect costs. In this discussion we assume that the franchisee's exit is followed by the decision to continue to operate as an independent. You could, of course, try to sell the franchise instead. This can be difficult if poor performance is the underlying cause of your dissatisfaction. The sale price would be significantly depressed. In either case—sale or exit to become an independent operation—understanding exit costs is essential to making a sound decision.

You should assess your exit costs while your relationships are strong, before conflict arises. As an integral part of a relational dynamics management process, assessing these costs will confirm your understanding of the value of the franchise. Based on this confirmation, you will see the value in managing and planning for conflict before it happens. Only in the worst situations will you have to put your knowledge of exit costs into action to terminate the relationship. In contrast, when returns meet expectations and you are ready to sell the franchise, exit cost knowledge will help you assess the value of your firm and establish a sale price.

Previous research has shown that dissatisfaction may arise in a conflict situation when the cost of remaining in the relationship exceeds the perceived cost of exit. These costs vary wildly by franchise, but the greater importance is not magnitude—it is the comparison of cost of exit and benefit of staying in the relationship. Conflict in the relationship usually comes from one or more of the categories we describe in Table 9–1 when they do not yield the benefits that the franchisee expects. Conflict generally arises for franchisees when they perceive diminished value from the very franchise concepts that were purported to make the system unique. Think of it this way: The value you receive from the franchisor would cost you something to replace if you weren't a franchisee. The less value received from the franchisor, the less expensive it would be to leave the system. Therefore, perceived exit costs correlate with trademark value. Higher exit costs mean you think it will be expensive to replace the value received from the franchisor. If there is conflict with the franchisor and the exit costs are high, you'll work harder to solve the conflict. This brand capital would be lost to the franchisee upon exit from the franchise relationship. In the simplest terms, the amount of loss that would be incurred is equal to the value of the brand capital.

To help determine the value of exit costs, we assessed the investments that franchisees often make and placed them into four categories: business format, expense, asset, and psychic. Table 9–1 categorizes several exit costs and describes the perceived effect of each cost.

The variables in the first category, business format, deal with the SDS, operating system, or training program. The business format variables dominate the exit cost calculation because these comprise the foundation of the franchise. The second category, expense, reflects what appears to be the direct expense associated with exit, such as legal fees. The third category is psychic costs—clearly, great personal psychological expenses are incurred by an entrepreneur as investments are made in the franchise relationship with other parties. The fourth category, the asset, deals with the costs of converting physical assets to avoid legal infringements on the rights of the franchise you have exited. Some of these exit costs are easier to quantify than others.

TABLE 9–1 Exit Cost Analysis

Perceived Exit Costs	Relationship Category	Cost Analysis
Exiting will increase training cost.	Business Format	How many days of training do you currently receive from the franchisor?
Exiting will require operating changes.	Business Format	Will you have to replace special/proprietary tools, equipment, or software?
Company investment is unique to the relationship.	Business Format	Some of the services you receive from the franchisor are difficult or impossible to replace. How much will that increase the cost of delivering your product?

TABLE 9.1 Exit Cost Analysis (Continued)

Exiting will be costly in lost customer goodwill.	Business Format	The brand of the franchise generates sales. If you change the name of the business from the franchise name to an independent name, how much revenue will be lost?
Exiting will be costly in finding alternative suppliers.	Expense	How will you buy your supplies as an independent versus a franchisee? You'll no longer have access to national or regional supply contracts.
Exiting will increase marketing budget.	Expense	You'll have to advertise your new name and logo. Also, you'll probably not have the marketing economies of the franchise system. How much will that increase your marketing budget?
Exiting will be costly in legal expense.	Expense	A franchise license agreement is a contract that is not easily severed and almost always requires legal counsel.
Company has invested time and energy into the relationship.	Psychic	Most franchisees report they have built informal relationships in the franchise system that provide benefits. What if these relationships were severed? What costs or lost opportunities might result?
Exiting will be costly in store conversion.	Asset	Both external and internal signage has to be changed if you exit; this is the single biggest store conversion cost.

Using this exit cost assessment as a framework for determining not only the actual costs of exit, but also of the value of the trademark presently and subsequently, will make the transition into a relational dynamics management process that is much simpler and standardized.

The relational dynamics management process of creating wealth, communicating goals and execution requirements, clearly defining roles in building brands, and assessing exit costs is another tool for solidifying the value of your franchise. Relationships are the vehicle that enable, empower, and support every other physical or financial effort. Once franchisee and franchisor understand that wealth creation is the common goal, everything else falls into place.

Introduction to Case Study: Quick Lube Franchisee Company (QLFC)

When reading about the Quick Lube Franchisee Company, you'll see the manifestation of conflict in franchising on all four of the dimensions discussed in this chapter. While you are reading the case, we recommend keeping the following four concepts in mind. As a guide, we have provided the general definition of each category in italics and then a hint as to how you will see each in the case. Although the names of people and companies are fictitious, the events are a true depiction of the vastly complicated human and organizational interactions between a growing and profitable franchisee and a franchisor.

1. **Wealth Creation:** *A view by each player about how the franchise system will help them become wealthy, or at least provide a market return on investment.* The change in control of the franchisor almost always causes concern among franchisees. In this case study we see a franchisee who now wonders how the multiple roles of "Big Oil" will cause an unfocused approach to wealth creation for the franchisees.

2. **Communications:** *Franchising, as a long-term contractual relationship, faces many challenges because both people and markets change. A relationship based on both formal and informal methods of communications is at the core of a relationship flexible enough to last over time.* When there is trauma in the franchisor, the field support personnel have to go into high gear with communications. We see little of this from the new franchise owner. The franchisee, QLFC, panics and quickly seeks refuge in the courts.

3. **Brand:** *How do the franchisor and franchisee value the brand and their collective role in maintaining and building it? When there is perceived fairness in brand-building role definition and execution, then the relationship remains healthy.* The franchisor is suddenly the franchisee's biggest supplier. This is a huge red flag for the franchisee: What brand is going to get promoted, Quick Lube or Big Oil? When there is brand confusion, the franchisees invariably feel stress. Unless there is absolute clarity from the franchisor, this stress is likely to elevate to negative conflict.

4. **Exit Costs:** *What happens when a franchisee becomes unhappy with the franchisor? She likely looks at the long-term value of the relationship versus the cost of exiting the relationship. That calculation is more measurable than you might expect.* A consequence of brand confusion is a lowering of exit costs. If the franchisee believes that the franchisor is diluting the brand (in this case with a supplier brand), then losing that brand and operating under another name is not a big hurdle. This case is a particularly good example of how brand concerns for a franchisee lead to dramatic action. A company with $30 million of revenue suing a multibillion-oil company is a David versus Goliath battle and not a completely rational action!

Quick Lube Franchise Corporation

It had been a year since Huston, a major oil company, had bought 80 percent of Super Lube, Inc., the number one franchisor of quick lubrication and oil-change service centers in the United States, with 1,000 outlets. As a result of that take-over, Super Lube's largest franchisee, QLFC, found itself in the position where its principal supplier, lead financing vehicle, and franchisor were the same entity. Was this an opportunity or a disaster? In April 1998 Frank Herget, founder, chairman, and CEO of QLFC, was faced with one of the most important decisions of his life.

Historical Background.   Super Lube was the innovator of the quick-lube concept, serving the lube, motor oil, and filter needs of motorists in a specialized building with highly refined procedures. It was founded in March 1986 by Jeff Martin. Frank Herget was one of the four founding members of Martin's management team. After a few years, Herget became frustrated with life at the franchisor's headquarters in Dallas, Texas. He believed that the future of the Super Lube was in operating service centers. That put him at odds with founder, chairman, and CEO Jeff Martin, who was passionately committed to franchising service centers as fast as possible. Martin and Herget had known each other for a long time, so they sought a mutually acceptable way to resolve their differences. Their discussions quickly resulted in the decision that Herget would buy a company-owned service center in northern California by swapping his Super Lube founder's stock valued at $64,000, which he had purchased originally for $13,000. Quick Lube Franchise Corporation was founded.

Early Success and Growth.   Success in his first service center inspired growth. Eventually, QLFC controlled service-center development and operating rights to a geographic area covering parts of California and Washington with the potential for over 90 service centers. Herget's long-term goal was to build QLFC into a big chain of Super Lube service centers that would have a public stock offering or merge with a larger company. See Table 9–2 for QLFC's 10-year growth trend.

TABLE 9–2 QLFC's 10-Year Growth

	'89	'90	'91	'92	'93	'94	'95	'96	'97	'98
Service Centers	2	3	4	7	16	25	34	44	46	47
Sales ($ Mill.)	.5	1.6	2.1	3.8	8.5	15.5	19	27	28	30

QUICK LUBE FRANCHISE CORP.

FY 1998[1] Budget Worksheet

	APR	MAY	JUN	JUL	AUG	SEP	OCT	NOV	DEC	JAN	FEB	MAR	TOTAL
SALES	2,424,718	2,444,629	2,756,829	2,816,765	2,872,074	2,358,273	2,619,415	2,435,022	2,494,696	2,733,469	2,464,172	2,795,804	**31,215,866**
COST OF SALES	544,689	549,348	613,728	626,809	639,126	529,542	588,628	547,137	573,063	627,574	565,836	642,144	**7,047,624**
VARIABLE EXPENSES (2)	805,251	826,956	894,782	914,080	943,260	790,276	893,236	819,709	844,626	911,313	826,811	949,576	**10,419,876**
FIXED EXPENSES	358,640	349,858	351,828	363,917	371,498	366,260	371,988	391,686	378,485	388,381	399,375	393,974	**4,485,890**
REAL ESTATE COST	320,377	337,372	340,652	341,353	352,053	352,053	372,030	372,030	392,337	392,452	392,452	410,552	**4,375,713**
STORE OPERATING INCOME	395,761	381,095	555,839	570,606	566,137	320,142	393,533	304,460	306,185	413,749	279,698	399,558	**4,886,763**
OVERHEAD	255,515	261,573	245,083	241,089	263,458	278,333	258,655	274,724	277,974	269,551	279,819	275,440	**3,181,214**
OPERATING INCOME	140,246	119,522	310,756	329,517	302,679	41,809	134,878	29,736	28,211	144,198	(121)	124,118	**1,705,549**
OTHER INCOME	7,392	7,392	7,392	7,392	7,392	7,392	7,392	7,392	7,392	7,392	7,392	7,392	**88,704**
DROPPED SITE EXPENSE	(8,333)	(8,333)	(8,333)	(8,333)	(8,333)	(8,333)	(8,333)	(8,333)	(8,333)	(8,333)	(8,333)	(8,333)	**(99,996)**
MINORITY INTEREST	686	613	(2,610)	(3,254)	(3,145)	2,065	511	4,529	4,346	1,290	6,564	2,459	**14,054**
INTEREST EXPENSE	(5,495)	(5,495)	(5,495)	(5,495)	(5,495)	(5,495)	(5,495)	(5,495)	(5,495)	(5,495)	(5,495)	(5,495)	**(65,940)**
TAXABLE INCOME	134,496	113,699	301,710	319,827	293,098	37,438	128,953	27,829	26,121	139,052	7	120,141	**1,642,371**
INCOME TAX EXPENSE	54921	47253	119971	126613	115680	17885	53211	17790	16727	58652	6880	51779	**687,362**
NET INCOME	79,575	66,446	181,739	193,214	177,418	19,553	75,742	10,039	9,394	80,400	(6,873)	68,362	**955,009**

(1) Budget Revised March 21, 1997

(2) Royalties to the franchisor equal 7% of gross sales

FIGURE 9–1 QLFC's budget worksheet.

QUICK LUBE FRANCHISE CORP.
Consolidated Balance Sheets

	Year Ended March 31	
	1998	**1997**
ASSETS		
CURRENT ASSETS		
Cash	$740,551	$665,106
Accounts receivable, net		
doubtful accounts of $61,000		
in 1998 and $44,000 in 1997	518,116	309,427
Construction advances receivable	508,168	137,412
Due from government agency		407,678
Inventory	1,093,241	1,074,513
Prepaid expenses other	407,578	401,562
TOTAL CURRENT ASSETS	3,267,654	2,995,698
PROPERTY AND EQUIPMENT		
Land	351,772	351,772
Buildings	3,171,950	2,519,845
Furniture, fixtures and equipment	2,988,073	2,644,801
Leasehold improvements	242,434	183,635
Property under capital leases	703,778	703,778
Construction in progress	68,138	531,594
	7,526,145	6,935,425
Less accumulated depreciation and amortization	(1,290,565)	(854,473)
	6,235,580	6,080,952
OTHER ASSETS		
Area development and license agreements, net of accumulated amortization	923,970	988,314
Other intangibles, net accumulated amortization	273,737	316,960
Other	151,604	208,898
	$10,852,545	$10,590,822

FIGURE 9–2 QLFC's consolidated balance sheets.

Herget financed QLFC's growth with both equity and debt (figures 9–2, 9–3a and 9–3b). Most of the additional equity came from former Super Lube employees who left the franchisor to join QLFC in senior management positions. They purchased stock in QLFC with cash realized by selling their stock in Super Lube. A key member of Herget's team was Mark Roberts, who had been Super Lube's CFO until 1993. He brought much needed financial sophistication to QLFC.

QUICK LUBE FRANCHISE CORP.
Consolidated Balance Sheets

	Year Ended March 31	
	1997	1996
LIABILITIES AND SHAREHOLDERS' EQUITY		
CURRENT LIABILITIES		
Accounts payable & accrued expenses	$3,085,318	$3,198,694
Income taxes payable	37,224	256,293
Note payable		250,000
Current portion - LTD	203,629	174,134
Current portion of capital lease	19,655	17,178
TOTAL CURRENT LIABILITIES	3,345,826	3,896,299
LONG-TERM DEBT, less current	2,848,573	3,052,597
CAPITAL LEASE OBLIGATIONS, less current	628,199	648,552
OTHER LONG-TERM LIABILITIES	731,783	483,534
MINORITY INTEREST	2,602	13,821
TOTAL LONG-TERM LIABILITIES	4,211,157	4,198,504
SHAREHOLDERS' EQUITY		
Common stock, par value $.01/share authorized		
10,000,000 shares; issued 1,080,000 shares	10,800	10,800
Additional paid-in capital	1,041,170	774,267
Retained earnings	2,243,592	1,710,952
	3,295,562	2,496,019
	$10,852,545	$10,590,822

FIGURE 9–3a QLFC's consolidated balance sheets.

The primary debt requirement was for financing new service centers. In 1998 the average cost of land acquisition and construction had risen to $750,000 per service center from about $350,000 ten years earlier.

QUICK LUBE FRANCHISE CORP.

Consolidated Cash Flow

	Year Ended March 31		
OPERATING ACTIVITIES	**1998**	**1997**	**1996**
Net Income	$532,640	$764,794	$524,211
Adjustments to reconcile net income to net cash provided by operating activities:			
Depreciation and amortization	612,063	526,750	414,971
Provision for losses on accounts receivable	16,615	30,510	5,559
Provision for deferred income taxes	(15,045)	12,519	50,388
Minority interest in losses of subsidiaries	(11,217)	(129,589)	(83,726)
Loss (gain) on disposition of property and equipment	33,301	(420)	N/A
Changes in operating assets and liabilities:			
Accounts receivable	(225,304)	(58,700)	(135,585)
Inventory	(18,728)	(273,559)	(286,037)
Prepaid expenses and other	(6,016)	(102,117)	(34,334)
Accounts payable and accrued expenses	(113,376)	559,456	1,409,042
Income taxes payable	(219,069)	404,068	(620,434)
Due from shareholders and affiliates	N/A	N/A	(43,742)
Other long-term liabilities	263,294	167,501	84,697
NET CASH PROVIDED BY OPERATING ACTIVITIES	849,158	1,901,213	1,285,010
INVESTING ACTIVITIES			
Purchases of property and equipment	(599,327)	(1,922,892)	(1,922,852)
Proceeds from sale of property and equipment	374,592	8,523	782,519
Acquisition of license agreements	(44,000)	(127,000)	(117,000)
Acquisition of other intangibles	(2,615)	(327,549)	(2,500)
Change in construction advance receivable	(370,756)	593,017	(601,525)
Change in other assets	43,894	(138,816)	11,908
NET CASH USED IN INVESTING ACTIVITIES	(598,212)	(1,914,717)	(1,849,450)
FINANCING ACTIVITIES			
Proceeds from long-term borrowings and revolving line of credit	4,940,000	4,026,441	2,448,071
Proceeds from borrowings from related parties	N/A	N/A	19,600
Principal payments on long-term borrowings	(5,364,529)	(3,463,693)	(2,658,534)
Principal payments on borrowings from related parties		(19,600)	(7,216)
Principal payments on capital lease obligations	(17,876)	(38,048)	N/A
Proceeds from sale of Common Stock and capital contributions	266,903	97,201	19,600
NET CASH PROVIDED BY (USED IN) FINANCING ACTIVITIES	(175,502)	602,301	(178,479)
INCREASE (DECREASE) IN CASH	75,444	588,797	(742,919)
Cash at beginning of year	665,106	76,309	819,228

FIGURE 9–3b QLFC's consolidated cash flow report.

Growth was originally achieved through off-balance-sheet real estate part-nerships. An Oregon bank lent about $4 million, and a Texas bank lent almost $3 million. However, rapid growth wasn't possible until QLFC struck a deal with Huston Oil for $6.5 million of subordinated debt. The Huston debt was 8 percent interest-only for five years and then amortized on a straight-line basis in years six through ten. The real estate developed with the Huston financing was kept in the company. QLFC was contractually committed to purchasing Huston products. See figures 9–3a and 9–3b for QLFC's financial statements.

Super Lube's Relationship with Its Franchisees.   Despite bridge financing of $10 million at the end of 1992, followed by a successful IPO, Super Lube's growth continued to outpace its ability to finance it. By the mid-1990s, Super Lube was in technical default to its debt holders. Huston struck a deal to acquire 80 percent of the company in a debt-restructuring scheme. However, during the time of Super Lube's mounting financial problems and the subsequent Huston deal, franchisees grew increasingly discontented.

A franchise relationship is governed by a contract called a license agreement. As a business format franchise, a franchisor offers a franchisee the rights to engage in a business system by using the franchisor's trade name, trademark, ser-vice marks, know-how, and method of doing business. The franchisee is contrac-tually bound to a system of operation and to pay the franchisor a royalty in the form of a percentage of top-line sales.

The Super Lube license agreement called for the franchisor to perform prod-uct development and quality-assurance tasks. Super Lube had made a strategic decision early in its existence to sell franchises on the basis of area development agreements. These franchisees had grown to become a group of sophisticated, fully integrated companies. As the franchisees grew with multiple outlets and became increasingly self-reliant, the royalty became difficult to justify. When the franchisor failed to perform its contractually obligated tasks as its financial prob-lems grew more burdensome by the mid-1990s, a franchisee revolt began to sur-face.

The Huston Era Begins.   The new owner, Huston Oil, quickly moved to replace virtually the entire management team at Super Lube. The new CEO was previously a long-term employee of a K-Mart subsidiary. He took a hard-line position on how the franchise system would operate and insisted that Huston motor oil would be an important part of it. The first national convention after the Huston takeover was a disaster. The franchisees, already frustrated, were dis-mayed by the focus of the franchisor on motor oil sales instead of service center-level profitability.

Herget decided to make a thorough analysis of the historical relationship between QLFC and Super Lube. Three months of research and documentation led to QLFC calling for a meeting with Huston to review the findings and address concerns. The meeting was held at the franchisor's offices with Herget and the franchisor's CEO and executive vice president. Herget described the meeting:

The session amounted to a three-hour monologue by me, followed by Super Lube's rejection of the past as relevant to the relationship. I was politely asked to trust that the future performance of the franchisor would be better and to treat the past as sunk cost. In response to my concern that Huston might have a conflict of interest in selling me product as well as being the franchisor and having an obligation to promote service center profitability, they answered that Huston bailed Super Lube out of a mess and the franchisees should be grateful, not combative.

Litigation.   The QLFC board of directors received Herget's report and told him to select a law firm and to pursue litigation against Huston. QLFC's 3 months of research was supplied to the law firm. A suit against Huston was filed three months after the failed QLFC/Huston "summit."

Huston denied the charges and filed a counter suit. Document search, depositions, and general legal maneuvering had been going on for about 3 months when QLFC's attorneys received a call from Huston requesting a meeting. Herget immediately called a board meeting and prepared to make a recommendation for QLFC's strategic plan.

10 Understanding the Basics of U.S. Franchise Laws

Because the legalities associated with franchising play such a critical role in its existence and continued success, we have enlisted the help of a well know franchise lawyer, Andrew Sherman, to explain the sometimes complex nature of franchise law. This chapter lays out the very basic framework every franchise entrepreneur needs to understand. However, the legal landscape of franchising is complex and difficult to understand. No one should expect to navigate legalities without the support of a lawyer who specializes in franchising.

Recent Key Trends in U.S. Franchising

An Overview of Federal and State Franchise Regulation of U.S. Franchises

Current and prospective franchisors need to have a full understanding of the complex regulatory framework that governs the definition, offer, and sale of franchises and business opportunities in the United States. The offer and sale of a franchise in the United States is regulated at both the federal and state levels. At the federal level, the Federal Trade Commission (FTC) in 1979 adopted its trade regulation rule 436 (the "FTC Rule") that specifies the minimum amount of disclosure that must be made to a prospective franchisee in the United States. In addition to the FTC Rule, over a dozen states have adopted their own rules and regulations for the offer and sale of franchises within their borders. Known as the registration states, they include most of the nation's largest commercial marketplaces, such as California, New York, and Illinois. These states generally follow a more detailed disclosure format, known as the Uniform Franchise Offering Circular (the UFOC).

The UFOC was originally developed by the Midwest Securities Commissioners Association in 1975. The monitoring of and revisions to the UFOC are now under the authority of the North American Securities Administrators Association (NASAA). Each of the registration states has developed and adopted its own statutory version of the UFOC. Both current and prospective franchisors and their counsel should check the differences among the states carefully.

A new version of the UFOC was adopted by NASAA in April 1993 and approved by the FTC in December 1993. As of January 1, 1995, the registration states had approved the new UFOC and mandated its use for filings in their states. The new UFOC Guidelines ("Guidelines") require that the offering circular be written in "plain English." Such plain English disclosures must be made "clearly, concisely and in a narrative form that is understandable by a person unfamiliar with the franchise business and should not contain technical language, repetitive phrases or 'legal antiques.'"

A Brief Review of the Evolution of Franchise Regulation

The laws governing the offer and sale of franchises in the United States began in 1970, when the state of California adopted its Franchise Investment Law. Shortly thereafter, the FTC commenced its hearings to begin the development of the federal law governing franchising. After seven years of public comment and debate, the FTC adopted its trade regulation rule that is formally titled "Disclosure Requirements and Prohibitions Concerning Franchising and Business Opportunity Venture" on December 21, 1978, to be effective October 21, 1979. Many states followed the lead of California, and there are now 15 states that regulate franchise offers and sales.

The states that require full registration of a franchise offering prior to the "offering" or selling of a franchise are *California, Illinois, Indiana, Maryland, Minnesota, New York, North Dakota, Rhode Island, South Dakota, Virginia,* and *Washington.*

Other states that regulate franchise offers include *Hawaii,* which requires filing of an offering circular with the state authorities and delivery of an offering circular to prospective franchisees; *Michigan and Wisconsin,* which require filing of a Notice of Intent to Offer and Sell Franchises; *Oregon,* which requires only that pre-sale disclosure be delivered to prospective investors; and *Texas,* which requires the filing of a notice of exemption with the appropriate state authorities under the Texas Business Opportunity Act.

Among other principles, the FTC Rule requires that every franchisor offering franchises in the United States deliver an offering circular (containing certain specified disclosure items) to all prospective franchisees (within certain specified time requirements). The FTC has adopted and enforced its rule pursuant to its power and authority to regulate unfair and deceptive trade practices. The FTC Rule sets forth the minimum level of protection that shall be afforded to prospective franchisees. To the extent that a registration state offers its citizens a greater level of protection, the FTC Rule will not preempt state law. There is no private right of action under the FTC Rule; however, the FTC itself may bring an enforcement action against a franchisor that does not meet its requirements. Penalties for noncompliance have included asset impoundments, cease and desist orders, injunctions, consent orders, mandated rescission or restitution for injured franchisees, and civil fines of up to $10,000 per violation.

The FTC Rule regulates two types of offerings: (1) *package and product franchises* and (2) *business opportunity ventures*. The first type involves three characteristics: (i) the franchisee sells goods or services that meet the franchisor's quality standards (in cases where the franchisee operates under the franchisor's trademark, service mark, trade name, advertising, or other commercial symbol designating the franchisor "Mark") that are identified by the franchisor's Mark, (ii) the franchisor exercises significant assistance in the franchisee's method of operation, and (iii) the franchisee is required to make payment of $500 or more to the franchisor or a person affiliated with the franchisor at any time before, to within six months after, the business opens.

Business Opportunity Ventures also involve three characteristics: (i) the franchisee sells goods or services that are supplied by the franchisor or a person affiliated with the franchisor; (ii) the franchisor assists the franchisee in any way with respect to securing accounts for the franchisee, or securing locations or sites for vending machines or rack displays, or providing the services of a person able to do either; and (iii) the franchisee is required to make payment of $500 or more to the franchisor or a person affiliated with the franchisor at any time before, to within six months after, the business opens.

Relationships covered by the FTC Rule include those within the definition of a "franchise" and those represented as being within the definition when the relationship is entered into, regardless of whether, in fact, they are within the definition. The FTC Rule exempts (1) fractional franchises, (2) leased department arrangements, and (3) purely verbal agreements. The FTC Rule excludes (1) relationships between employer/employees and among general business partners, (2) membership in retailer-owned cooperatives, (3) certification and testing services, and (4) single trademark licenses.

The disclosure document required by the FTC Rule must include information on the following 20 subjects:

1. Identifying information about the franchisor.
2. Business experience of the franchisor's directors and key executives.
3. The franchisor's business experience.

4. Litigation history of the franchisor and its directors and key executives.

5. Bankruptcy history of the franchisor and its directors and key executives.

6. Description of the franchise.

7. Money required to be paid by the franchisee to obtain or commence the franchise operation.

8. Continuing expenses to the franchisee in operating the franchise business that are payable in whole or in part to the franchisor.

9. A list of persons, including the franchisor and any of its affiliates, with whom the franchisee is required or advised to do business.

10. Realty, personalty, services, and so on that the franchisee is required to purchase, lease, or rent and a list of any person with whom such transactions must be made.

11. Description of consideration paid (such as royalties, commissions, etc.) by third parties to the franchisor or any of its affiliates as a result of franchisee purchases from such third parties.

12. Description of any franchisor assistance in financing the purchase of a franchise.

13. Restrictions placed on a franchisee's conduct of its business.

14. Required personal participation by the franchisee.

15. Termination, cancellation, and renewal of the franchise.

16. Statistical information about the number of franchises and their rate of termination.

17. Franchisor's right to select or approve a site for the franchise.

18. Training programs for the franchisee.

19. Celebrity involvement with the franchise.

20. Financial information about the franchisor.

The information must be current as of the completion of the franchisor's most recent fiscal year. In addition, a revision to the document must be promptly prepared whenever there has been a material change in the information contained in the document. The FTC Rule requires that the disclosure document must be given to a prospective franchisee at the earlier of either (1) the prospective franchisee's *first personal meeting* with the franchisor; or (2) *ten business days* prior to the execution of a contract; or (3) *ten business days* before the payment of money relating to the franchise relationship. In addition to the disclosure document, the franchisee must receive a copy of all agreements that it will be asked to sign at least *five business days* prior to the execution of the agreements. A business day is any day other than Saturday, Sunday, or the following national holidays: New Year's Day, Washington's Birthday, Memorial Day, Independence Day, Labor Day, Columbus Day, Veteran's Day, Thanksgiving, and Christmas Day.

The timing requirements described above apply nationwide and preempt any lesser timing requirements contained in state laws. The 10-day and 5-day disclosure periods may run concurrently, and sales contacts with the prospective franchisee may continue during those periods.

It is an unfair or deceptive act or practice within the meaning of Section 5 of the FTC Act for any franchisor or franchise broker to

1. Fail to furnish prospective franchisees, within the timeframe established by the Rule, with a disclosure document containing information on 20 different subjects relating to the franchisor, the franchise business, and the terms of the franchise agreement

2. Make any representations about the actual or potential sales, income, or profits of existing or prospective franchisees except in the manner set forth in the rule

3. Fail to furnish prospective franchisees, within the timeframe established by the rule, with copies of the franchisor's standard form of franchise agreement and copies of the final agreements to be signed by the parties

4. Fail to return to prospective franchisees any funds or deposits (such as down payments) identified as refundable in the disclosure document

State Franchise Laws

The goal of the FTC Rule is to create a minimum U.S. federal standard of disclosure applicable to all franchisor offerings and to permit states to provide additional protection as they see fit. Thus, while the FTC Rule has the force and effect of federal law and, like other federal substantive regulations, preempts state and local laws to the extent that these laws conflict, the FTC has determined that the rule will not preempt state or local laws and regulations that either are consistent with the rule or, even if inconsistent, would provide protection to prospective franchisees equal to or greater than that imposed by the rule.

Examples of state laws or regulations that would not be preempted by the Rule include state provisions requiring the registration of franchisors and franchise salespersons, state requirements for escrow or bonding arrangements, and state-required disclosure obligations set forth in the Rule. Moreover, the Rule does not affect state laws or regulations that regulate the franchisor–franchisee relationship, such as termination practices, contract provisions, and financing arrangements.

Definitions Under State Law.   Each state franchise disclosure statute has its own definition of a franchise, which is similar to, but not the same as, the definition set forth in the FTC Rule. If the proposed relationship meets this definition, then the franchisor must comply with the applicable registration and disclosure laws.

There are four major types of state definitions of a franchise or business opportunity:

  A. Majority State Definition. In the states of California, Illinois, Indiana, Maryland, Michigan, North Dakota, Oregon, Rhode Island, and Wisconsin a franchise is defined as having three essential elements:

  1. A franchisee is granted the right to engage in the business of offering, selling, or distributing goods or services under a marketing plan or system prescribed in substantial part by a franchisor.

  2. The operation of the franchisee's business that is substantially associated with the franchisor's trademark or other commercial symbol designating the franchisor or its affiliate.

  3. The franchisee is required to pay a fee.

  B. Minority State Definition. The states of Hawaii, Minnesota, South Dakota, and Washington have adopted a somewhat broader definition of *franchise*. In these states, a franchise is defined as having the following three essential elements:

  1. A franchisee is granted the right to engage in the business of offering or distributing goods or services using the franchisor's trade name or other commercial symbol or related characteristics.

  2. The franchisor and franchisee have a common interest in the marketing of goods or services.

  3. The franchisee pays a fee.

  C. New York Definition. The state of New York has a unique definition. Under its law a franchisee is defined by these guidelines:

  1. The franchisor is paid a fee by the franchisee.

  2. Either essentially associated with the franchisor's trademark *or* the franchisee operates under a marketing plan or system prescribed in substantial part by the franchisor.

  D. Virginia Definition. The Commonwealth of Virginia also has its own definition of a franchise, which stipulates that

  1. A franchisee is granted the right to engage in the business of offering or distributing goods or services at retail under a marketing plan or system prescribed in substantial part by a franchisor.

  2. The franchisee's business is substantially associated with the franchisor's trademark.

Virginia and New York have definitions that are broad in certain respects. Virginia does not have a "fee" element to its definition. New York requires a fee, but specifies *either* association with franchisor's trademark *or* a marketing plan prescribed by the franchisor. Therefore, in New York, no trademark license is required for a franchise relationship to exist. However, the regulations in New

York exclude from the definition of a franchise any relationship in which a franchisor does not provide significant assistance to, or exert significant controls over, a franchisee.

Guidelines for Determining What Is a Franchise

There are many reasons why a company may not want to structure a relationship that falls under the definition of a franchise under federal or state law. Some of these reasons are appropriate legal or strategic reasons, while others are not. Some of the most common reasons are

a. An overseas franchisor that is uncomfortable with concepts of disclosure that may not be required in their country of origin.
b. A mid-sized or large company who feels that its industry is not ready for, or will react adversely to, the kinds of controls that a franchise relationship typically implies.
c. A company or individual officer who would prefer not to disclose an aspect of its (or his or her) past (this raises other legal problems).
d. A small company concerned with the perceived costs of preparing and maintaining the legal documents.
e. The belief that by becoming a franchisor, the company somehow increases its chances of being sued (a myth).
f. Some other specific circumstances or myth or fear that the company's management team has towards franchising.

Before dealing with the parameters developed by the courts and regulatory authorities, which provide some insight into which relationships will be considered a franchise and which will not, we usually try to solve a company's problem with creative thinking and structural alternatives. For example, under (a) above, an overseas franchisor may want to set up a new subsidiary in lieu of disclosing the parent company's (usually privately held) financial statements. If the subsidiary is properly capitalized and certain other specific conditions met, the confidentiality of the parent company's data may be preserved. Under (b), we have often created the "non-franchise franchisor," which is a company that has essentially agreed to prepare and provide a UFOC even though the details of its relationships are in a regulatory gray area. In this way the franchisor appeases the regulators but also placates the industry participants who may be more comfortable with a "strategic partner" or "licensee" designation than a franchisor–franchise relationship.

If the company still insists on avoiding compliance with these laws, then we go through an exercise of determining from a cost-benefit analysis which leg of the "three-legged stool" it will agree to sacrifice. In today's brand-driven environment, the willingness to license the system without the brand to avoid the trademark license leg has not been very popular. Similarly, in an economy where "cash flow is king," most of these clients have not been willing to waive the initial franchise fee or wait over 6 months for their financial rewards. The regulators long ago figured out the age-old trick of "hiding" the franchise fee in a training program or initial inventory package. So, it is often the third leg of the stool, the one that is most difficult to interpret, where the creative structuring must take place. The courts and the federal and state regulators have not provided much clear guidance as to the *degrees* of support or the *degrees* of assistance that will meet the definition and those which will not. The mandatory use of an operating system or marketing plan will meet the third element of the test, but what if the use of the system is optional? What if the plan or system is not detailed and provides room for discretion by the franchisee without penalty for adopting the plan or system to meet local market conditions? If you choose this path, does allowing this degree of discretion and flexibility sacrifice your ability to maintain quality control?

In addition, in a competitive environment where most growing companies are trying to provide *more* support and assistance (as well as exercise more control) to their partners in the distribution channel, would providing less than the norm just to avoid the definition of a franchise really make sense? Franchisors should not make these legal and strategic decisions hastily without properly analyzing the long-term implications.

FTC Analysis.   The term *franchise* is defined in Section 436.2(d) of the FTC Rule. There are three key components to this definition: (1) the franchisee's goods and/or services are to be offered and sold under the franchisor's trademarks; (2) the franchisee is required to make a minimum $500 payment to the franchisor; and (3) the franchisor exercises significant control of, or provides significant assistance to, the franchisee's method of operation. Each of these components is outlined below.

> *Trademark.* This element is satisfied when the franchisee is given the right to distribute goods or services under the franchisor's trademark or service mark.
>
> *Required Payment.* This element is met if a franchisee is required to pay the franchisor at least $500 as a condition of obtaining the franchise or of commencing operations. Payments made at any time prior to, or within 6 months after commencing operations will be aggregated to determine if the $500 threshold is met. The payments may be required by the franchise agreement, an ancillary agreement between the parties, or by practical necessity (such as required supplies that are only available from the franchisor).
>
> *Significant Control and Assistance.* The key to this element is that the control or assistance must be "significant." According to the "Final Guides to the Franchising and Business Opportunities Ventures Trade Regulation Rule" (the "Final Guides"), published by the FTC, the term *significant* "relates to the degree to which the franchisee is dependent

upon the franchisor's superior business expertise." The Final Guides state that the dependence on the business expertise of the franchisor may be conveyed by the franchisor's controls over the franchisee's methods of operation or by the franchisor furnishing assistance to the franchisee in areas related to methods of operations. The presence of *any one* of the following types of control or assistance may suggest the existence of "significant control or assistance" sufficient to satisfy this prong of the definition of a franchise:

Types of Control or Assistance

- Site approval
- Formal sales, repair, or business training
- Site design/appearance requirements
- Establishing accounting systems
- Dictating hours of operation
- Furnishing management, marketing, or production techniques
- Personnel advice
- Accounting practices
- Site selection assistance
- Personnel policies/practices
- Furnishing detailed operations manual
- Required participation in, or financial contribution to, promotional campaigns
- Restrictions on customers
- Restrictions on sales area or location

There is a wide variety of strategic questions and structural issues to consider when conducting this analysis, including

- Do we anticipate the relationship to be short-term or long-term? In other words, are we just dating or really serious about getting married?
- Are we ready to sacrifice the ability to build brand awareness and increase the value of other intangible assets on our balance sheet in a brand-driven competitive environment?
- Are we prepared to deliver the level and the quality of training and support that is typically implied and expected in the franchisor–franchisee relationship?
- Will we be converting or keeping in place existing distributors, sales representatives, or other components of the current distribution channel? How will the franchising program *truly* differ?

- While considering the operational dynamics of the proposed relationship, how interdependent do we really need or want to be? Are we truly inextricably intertwined with synergistic and shared goals, or would a more casual commitment suffice? Would a joint venture or strategic partnering relationship adequately suffice?

- To what extent will training, support, marketing, and other key functions truly be uniform and centralized? Or will a more flexible system suffice?

- Could we "unbundle" the license of the intellectual property being offered, making items an optional menu of support and services rather than making them mandatory and integrated?

- If we choose to operate in the gray area and without a UFOC, how comfortable are we and our management team with living the possibility of a regulatory investigation and or a system wide rescission offer if the relationship is subsequently deemed to be a franchise? How comfortable with this strategy are we if our company is publicly traded?

- To what extent will market conditions dictate that we maintain control over the product mix, warranty policies, discounting policies, and so on or the need to conduct quality-control audits or make pricing suggestions?

Again, you don't want to emasculate key strategic aspects of the program merely to avoid compliance with federal and state franchise laws. Remember that the courts and the regulators are likely to examine the "totality of the relationship," with an emphasis on reality and practice rather than the written word of the contract or offering materials. For example, if you take the position that the support services are optional, but in practice 99 percent of your franchisees have elected to use and pay for them, then the reality of the situation will probably prevail. If the marketing plan or operating system is prescribed in substantial part by you in practice, and there will be adverse consequences to the other party if these procedures and standards are not followed, whether or not your agreement says so, then you will have difficulty supporting your position that you are not a franchise. Although a "community of interest" is not generally a term that provides much insight, here are some factors directly considered by the court in arriving at this determination:

- The franchisor's advertising claims to prospective franchisees that a successful marketing plan is available.

- The contemplation of nationwide or area-wide distribution on an exclusive or semi-exclusive basis, possibly with multiple levels of jurisdiction (such as regional and location distributorships and arrangements) designed to establish uniformity of prices and marketing terms.

- Reservation of control by the franchisor over matters such as customer terms and payments, credit practices, and warranties and representations made to customers.

- The franchisor's rendering of collateral services to the franchisee.

- Any prohibition or limitation on the franchisee's sale of competitive or noncompetitive products.

- A requirement that the franchisee observe the franchisor's direction or obtain the franchisor's approval for site selection, trade names, advertising, signs, appearance of the franchisee's business premises, fixtures and equipment used in the business, employee uniforms, hours of operation, housekeeping procedures, and so on.

- The franchisor's implementation of its requirements regarding the conduct of the business by inspection and reporting procedures.

- The franchisor's right to take corrective measures that may be at the franchisee's expense.

- Comprehensive advertising or other promotional programs, especially if the programs identify the location of the franchisee and if the franchisee's advertising or promotional activities require the franchisor's approval.

- Grant of an exclusive territory and the sale of products or services at bona fide wholesale prices.

- Percentage discounts (although insubstantial) and mutual advertising and soliciting by the franchisor and the franchisee.

- Volume discounts attained by a system of distributors and subdistributors, and mutual advertising.

- Use of the franchisor's confidential operating manuals or forms by the franchisee and mutual opportunity for profit.

- Grant of an exclusive patent and an exclusive territory, and a training program for which the franchisor receives payment from the franchisee.

- Required purchases from the franchisor, an exclusive territory, franchisor-supplied advertising, the provision of leads to the franchisee, and prohibitions on selling competitive products.

- The franchisor's selection of locations and required purchases through the franchisor.

- Performance of services devised by the franchisor, franchisor-approved forms, mutual service of customers, franchisor approval of the franchisee's presentations, and mutual financial benefit.

- The franchisee's production of products under the franchisor's patent, technical assistance, training, the franchisee's ability to subfranchise, and required record keeping.

- The franchisor's selection of locations, the franchisee's purchase of product from the franchisor for regularly serviced accounts, and required record keeping.

Preparing the Disclosure Document: Choosing the Appropriate Format

In many ways, the choice of the appropriate format for the franchisor's franchise offering circular is difficult and complex, because the requirements of the FTC Rule, the UFOC guidelines, and the particular state laws must all be coordinated. The format selection process is a decision regarding the *form* in which the disclosure is made but is not a choice of which law shall govern. Even if the UFOC format is selected, the federal laws governing the timing of the delivery of the disclosure document, the restrictions on the use of earnings claims, and the penalties available to the FTC for noncompliance still apply.

Depending on the targeted markets selected by the company, most franchisors have elected to adopt the UFOC format in the preparation of their disclosure documents. Because many registration states do not accept the FTC Rule format (even though the FTC has endorsed the UFOC format), it is simply more cost-effective to have only one primary document for use in connection with franchise offers and sales. If the franchisor will be limiting its marketing activities to states that do *not* have registration statutes, then the FTC Rule format may offer certain advantages. For example, the FTC Rule format generally requires less information than the UFOC format does in the areas of training and personnel of the franchisor, the litigation history of the franchisor (FTC Rule requires a 7-year history, while the UFOC format requires a 10-year history), history of termination and nonrenewable (FTC, 1 year; UFOC, 3 years), bankruptcy history (FTC, 7 years; UFOC, 10 years), and sanctions under Canadian law (required by UFOC but not FTC), and it requires less stringent disclosure regarding the refundability of payments made by the franchisee.

The FTC Rule format may also be easier for the early-stage franchisor to satisfy, because it allows for a three-year phase-in period for the use of audited financials. Under the UFOC format, audited financials are required from the onset, and if the financial condition of the franchisor is weak, then many state administrators will impose costly escrow and bonding procedures or require personal (or parent company, for a subsidiary) guaranties of performance. In some registration states, a financially weak franchisor will be denied registration until its condition improves. Early-stage franchisors that are grossly undercapitalized, have a negative net worth, or may have suffered significant recent operating losses should be prepared for an uphill battle with the state franchise examiners before approval will be granted.

Preparing the Disclosure Document Under UFOC Guidelines. The UFOC format of franchise disclosure consists of 23 categories of information (Table 10–1) that must be provided by the franchisor to the prospective franchisee at least 10 business days prior to the execution of the franchise agreement. Because this format has been adopted by many states as a matter of law, franchisors may not change the order in which information is presented, nor may any of the disclosure items be omitted in the document. In addition, many sections of the UFOC must be a mirror image of the actual franchise agreement (and related documents) that the franchisee will be expected to sign. There should be no factual or legal inconsistencies between the UFOC and the franchise agreement.

TABLE 10–1 UFOC Format of Franchise Disclosure

Cover Page:	NASAA has sought to create a generic cover page by moving state-specific information to Item 23 (Receipt) or to exhibits to the offering circular. Information moved off of the cover page includes state-mandated language regarding offering circular delivery requirements and related disclaimers, addresses of administrators, and the list of registered agents, subfranchisors, and franchise brokers. The Guidelines mandate disclosure of certain risk factors. A franchisor must use prescribed language to disclose as a risk that its franchise agreement includes an out-of-state form and/or choice of law provision. State regulators may require additional risk factor disclosures.
Item 1:	THE FRANCHISOR, ITS PREDECESSORS AND AFFILIATES. Franchisors must identify themselves by using "we," initials, or two words of reference. "Franchisor" and "Franchisee" are not to be used. The entities for which disclosure must be made are expanded to include franchisor's affiliates. The number of years of the franchisor's predecessors is reduced from 15 to 10. Agents for service of process may be disclosed in Item 1, Item 23 (Receipt), or an exhibit to the offering circular. In addition, franchisors must disclose, in general terms, "any regulations specific to the industry in which the franchise business operates." Regulations that are applicable to businesses generally need not be disclosed.
Item 2:	BUSINESS EXPERIENCE. This section requires disclosure of the identity of each director, trustee, general partner (where applicable) and officer or manager of the franchisor who will have significant responsibility in connection with the operation of the franchisor's business or in the support services to be provided to franchisees. The principal occupation of each person listed in Item 2 for the past five years must be disclosed, including dates of employment, nature of the position, and the identity of the employer. The identity and background of each franchise broker (if any) authorized to represent the franchisor must also be disclosed in this Item.

TABLE 10–1 UFOC Format of Franchise Disclosure (Continued)

Item 3:	LITIGATION. A full and frank discussion of any litigation, arbitration, or administrative hearings affecting the franchisor, its officers, directors, or sales representatives over the past 10 years should be included in this section. The formal case name, location of the dispute, nature of the claim, and the current status of each action must be disclosed. Item 3 does not require disclosure of all types of litigation but rather focuses on specific allegations and proceedings that would be of particular concern to the prospective franchisee. "Ordinary routine litigation incidental to the business" is not to be considered material. Litigation is deemed "ordinary routine" if it "ordinarily results from the business and does not depart from the normal kind of actions in the business."
Item 4:	BANKRUPTCY. This section requires the franchisor to disclose whether the company or any of its predecessors, officers, or general partners have, during the past 10 years, been adjudged bankrupt or reorganized due to insolvency. The court in which the bankruptcy or reorganization proceeding occurred, the formal case title, and any material facts and circumstances surrounding the proceeding must be disclosed.
Item 5:	INITIAL FRANCHISE FEE. The initial franchise fee and related payments to the franchisor prior to opening the franchise must be disclosed in this section. The manner in which the payments are made, the use of the proceeds by the franchisor, and whether or not the fee is refundable in whole or in part must be disclosed. If the initial franchise fee is not uniform, the franchisor must disclose the formula or range of initial fees received by it in the most recent fiscal year prior to the application date.
Item 6:	OTHER FEES. A tabular form of any other initial or recurring fee payable by the franchisee to the franchisor or any affiliate must be disclosed and the nature of each fee fully discussed, including but not limited to royalty payments, training fees, audit fees, public offering review fees, advertising contributions, mandatory insurance requirements, transfer fees, renewal fees, lease negotiation fees, and any consulting fees charged by the franchisor or an affiliate for special services. The amount, time of the payment, and refundability of each type of payment should be disclosed. A "remarks" column or footnotes may be used to elaborate on the information about the fees disclosed in the table. In addition, if fees are paid to a franchisee cooperative, the franchisor must disclose the voting power of its outlets in the cooperative. Further, the range of any fees imposed by that cooperative must be disclosed if the franchisor's outlets have controlling voting power.

TABLE 10–1 UFOC Format of Franchise Disclosure (Continued)

Item 7:	INITIAL INVESTMENT. Each component of the franchisee's initial investment that the franchisee is required to expend in order to open the franchised business must be estimated in this section, in a prescribed tabular form, regardless of whether such payments are made directly to the franchisor. Real estate, equipment, fixtures, security deposits, inventory, construction costs, working capital, accounting and legal fees, license and permit fees, and any other costs and expenditures should be disclosed. The disclosure should include to whom such payments are made, under what general terms and conditions, and what portion, if any, is refundable. A payment must be disclosed if it is required to be paid during the "initial phase" of the business. The Guidelines instruct that "[a] reasonable time for the initial phase of the business is at least three months or a reasonable period for the industry." The Guidelines also require disclosure of additional funds required during the initial phase and the factors, basis, and experience upon which the franchisor bases its calculation.
Item 8:	RESTRICTIONS ON SERVICES OF PRODUCTS AND SERVICES. Any obligation of the franchisee to purchase goods, services, supplies, fixtures, equipment, or inventory that relates to the establishment or operation of the franchised business from a source designated by the franchisor should be disclosed. The terms of the purchase or lease as well as any minimum-volume purchasing requirements must be disclosed. If the franchisor will or may derive direct or indirect income based on these purchases from required sources, then the nature and amount of such income must be fully disclosed. Remember that such obligations must be able to withstand the scrutiny of U.S. antitrust laws. In addition to disclosing whether the franchisor or its affiliates will or may derive revenue or material consideration as a result of franchisees' required purchases or leases, the franchisor must also disclose the estimated proportion of these required purchases and leases to all purchases and leases by the franchisee of goods and services necessary to establish and operate the franchise. The franchisor must disclose whether there are any purchasing or distribution cooperatives serving its system. The franchisor must disclose, based on immediately preceding years' financial statements, its (1) total revenues; (2) revenues derived from required purchases and leases of products and services; and (3) the percentage of its total revenues from such required purchases and leases. If the franchisor's affiliates also sell or lease products or services to franchisees, the franchisor must also disclose the percentage of the affiliates revenues derived from these sales or leases. Any fees required for approval of a new supplier must also be disclosed. In addition, the franchisor must disclose whether it offers franchisees inducements, such as renewal or additional franchises, for purchasing goods or products from designated or approved sources.

TABLE 10–1 UFOC Format of Franchise Disclosure (Continued)

Item 9:	FRANCHISEES' OBLIGATIONS. Franchisors must set forth the franchisees' obligations in a prescribed tabular form with regard to 24 specific categories. The table must cite the relevant sections of both the franchise agreement and offering circular.
Item 10:	FINANCING. In this section the franchisor must disclose the terms and conditions of any financing arrangements offered to franchisees either by the franchisor or any of its affiliates. The exact terms of any direct or indirect debt financing, equipment or real estate leasing programs, operating lines of credit, or inventory financing must be disclosed. If any of these financing programs is offered by an affiliate, then the exact relationship between the franchisor and the affiliate must be disclosed. Terms that may be detrimental to the franchisee upon default, such as a confession of judgment, waiver of defenses, or acceleration clauses, must be disclosed in this Item of the UFOC. The terms and conditions of "indirect offers of financing" made to franchisees must be disclosed. An "indirect offer of financing" includes (1) a written arrangement between the franchisor, or its affiliate, and a lender to offer financing to franchisees; (2) an arrangement in which the franchisor or its affiliate receives benefits from a lender for franchisee financing; and (3) the franchisor's guarantee of a note, lease, or obligation of the franchisee. Franchisors are permitted, but not required, to make disclosure in tabular form. Franchisors must disclose the annual percentage rate of interest (APR) charged for financing, computed in accordance with Sections 106–107 of the Consumer Protection Credit Act, 15 U.S.C. (sections) 106–107. If the APR varies depending on when the financing is issued, franchisor must disclose the APR as of a disclosed recent date. Franchisor must disclose to the franchisee the consequences of any default of its obligations, including operation of any cross-default provisions, acceleration of amounts due, and payment of court costs and attorneys' fees. In addition, franchisors must include in the offering circular specimen copies of any financing documents.
Item 11:	FRANCHISOR'S OBLIGATIONS. This section is one of the most important to the prospective franchisee because it discusses the initial and ongoing support and services provided by the franchisor. Franchisors must disclose only those preopening obligations that they are contractually required to provide to franchisees. Preopening assistance that the franchisor intends to provide, but to which it is not contractually bound to provide, may not be included. Accordingly, this disclosure must begin with the following sentence: "[e]xcept as listed below,

TABLE 10–1 UFOC Format of Franchise Disclosure (Continued)

Item 11: *(continued)*	(franchisor) need not provide any assistance to you." Franchisors must make comprehensive disclosures regarding advertising, including (1) the type of media in which the advertising may be distributed; (2) whether the media coverage is local, regional or national in scope; (3) the source of the advertising (e.g., inhouse or advertising agency); (4) the conditions under which franchisees are permitted to use their own advertising; and (5) if applicable, the manner in which the franchisee advertising council operates and advises the franchisor. Franchisors must make specific disclosures regarding local or regional advertising cooperatives, including (1) how the area and/or membership of the cooperative is defined; (2) how franchisees' contributions to the cooperative are calculated; (3) who is responsible for administration of the cooperative; (4) whether cooperatives must operate from written governing documents and whether the documents are available for review by franchisees; (5) whether cooperatives must prepare annual or periodic financial statements and whether such statements are available for review by franchisees; and (6) whether the franchisor has the power to form, change, dissolve or merge cooperatives. Franchisors must disclose information about advertising funds they administer, including (1) the basis upon which franchisor-owned outlets contribute to the fund; (2) whether franchisees contribute at a uniform rate; and (3) the percentages of the fund spent on production, media placement, administrative, and other expenses. Franchisors must also disclose whether they are obligated to advertise in the area in which the franchise is to be located and the percentage of funds used for advertising that is principally a solicitation for the sale of franchises. Franchisors are required to disclose whether franchisees must buy or use electronic cash registers or computer systems. If there is such a requirement, the franchisor must describe in nontechnical language (1) the hardware components; (2) the software program; and (3) whether such hardware and software are proprietary property of the franchisor, an affiliate, or a third party. If the hardware or software is not proprietary, the franchisor must disclose (1) whether the franchisee has any contractual obligation to upgrade or update the equipment, and if so, any limitations on the frequency and cost of such obligation; (2) how it will be used in the franchise; and (3) whether the franchisor has any independent access to information or data in the system. The new Guidelines expand disclosure regarding site selection procedures to include the factors considered by the franchisor in site selection or approval. In addition, a copy of the table of contents of the franchise Operating Manual must be included in the offering circular unless the prospective franchisee will view the manual before purchasing the franchise.

TABLE 10–1 UFOC Format of Franchise Disclosure (Continued)

Item 12:	TERRITORY. The exact territory or exclusive area, if any, to be granted by the franchisor to the franchisee should be disclosed, as well as the right to adjust the size of this territory in the event that certain contractual conditions are not met, such as the failure to achieve certain performance quotas. The right of the franchisor to establish company-owned units or to grant franchises to others within the territory must be disclosed. A detailed description and/or map of the franchisee's territory should be included as an exhibit to the franchise agreement. In addition to disclosing whether it has established or may establish additional franchised or company-owned outlets that may compete with franchisees' outlets, the franchisor must disclose whether it has established or may establish "other channels of distribution" under its mark. The franchisor must disclose the conditions under which it will approve the relocation of a franchise or the establishment of additional franchises. In addition, a franchisor must disclose whether it or an affiliate operates or has plans to operate another chain or channel of distribution under a different trademark to sell goods or services that are similar to those offered by the franchise. If the franchisor operates competing systems, it must also disclose the methods it will use to resolve conflicts between them regarding territory, customers, and franchisor support. If the principal business address of the competing system is the same as franchisor's, it must also disclose whether it maintains separate offices and training facilities.
Item 13:	TRADEMARKS. Franchisors need only disclose the principal trademarks, rather than all trademarks, to be licensed to the franchisee. If a principal trademark is not federally registered, franchisors must include a statement that "[b]y not having a Principal Register federal registration for (trademark), franchisor does not have certain presumptive legal rights granted by a registration."
Item 14:	PATENTS, COPYRIGHTS AND PROPRIETARY INFORMATION. If the franchisor claims proprietary rights in confidential information or trade secrets, it must disclose the general subject matter of its proprietary rights and the terms and conditions under which they may be used by the franchisee.
Item 15:	OBLIGATION TO PARTICIPATE IN THE ACTUAL OPERATION OF THE FRANCHISED BUSINESS. Franchisors are required to disclose obligations arising from its practices, personal guarantees, and confidentiality or noncompetition agreements.
Item 16:	RESTRICTIONS ON WHAT THE FRANCHISEE MAY SELL. In this section the franchisor must disclose any special contractual provisions or other circumstances that limit either the types of products and services the franchisee may offer or the types or location of the customers to whom the products and services may be offered.

TABLE 10–1 UFOC Format of Franchise Disclosure (Continued)

Item 17:	RENEWAL, TERMINATION, TRANSFER, AND DISPUTE RESOLUTION. The disclosures must be presented in a prescribed tabular form. The table must contain abbreviated summaries regarding 23 specific categories with references to relevant sections of the franchise agreement. Preceding the table, the offering circular must state: "[t]his table lists important provisions of the franchise and related agreements. You should read these provisions in the agreements attached to this offering circular."
Item 18:	PUBLIC FIGURES. Any compensation or benefit given to a public figure in return for an endorsement of the franchise and/or products and services offered by the franchisee must be disclosed. The extent to which the public figure owns or is involved in the management of the franchisor must also be disclosed. The disclosure is only required if a public figure endorses or recommends an investment in the franchise to prospective franchisees. Consequently, franchisors need not disclose franchisees' rights to use the names of public figures that are featured in consumer advertising or other promotional efforts.
Item 19:	EARNINGS CLAIMS. If the franchisor is willing to provide the prospective franchisee with sample earnings claims or projections, they must be discussed in Item 19.
Item 20:	LIST OF FRANCHISE OUTLETS. A full summary of the number of franchises sold, number of operational units, and number of company-owned units, including an estimate of franchise sales for the upcoming fiscal year broken down by state. The names, addresses, and telephone numbers of franchisees should be included in this Item. With the exception of the list of franchise names, addresses, and telephone numbers, franchisors must disclose all information required by this Item in tabular form. The franchisor must disclose the number of franchised and company-owned outlets sold, opened, and closed in its system as of the close of each of its last three fiscal years. Operational outlets must be listed separately from those not opened, and disclosure must be provided on a state-by-state basis. The franchisor may limit its disclosure of the franchisees' names, addresses, and telephone numbers to those franchised outlets in the state in which the franchise offering is made if there are 100 outlets in such state. If there are fewer than 100 in the state, the franchisor must disclose the names, addresses, and telephone numbers of franchised outlets from contiguous states and, if necessary, the next closest states until at least 100 are listed. For the three-year period immediately before the close of its most recent fiscal year, the franchisor must disclose the number of franchised outlets which have (1) had a change in "controlling ownership interest"; (2) been canceled or terminated; (3) not been renewed;

TABLE 10–1 UFOC Format of Franchise Disclosure (Continued)

Item 20: *(continued)*	(4) been reacquired by the franchisor; or (5) otherwise ceased to do business in the system. The franchisor must disclose the last known home address of every franchisee who has had an outlet terminated, canceled, not renewed, or who otherwise voluntarily or involuntarily ceased to do business under the franchise agreement during the most recently completed fiscal year end or who has not communicated with the franchisor within 10 weeks of the application date. In addition, the franchisor must disclose information about company-owned outlets that are substantially similar to its franchised outlets. The same table may be used for both franchised and company-owned outlets so long as the data regarding each is set out in a distinct manner.
Item 21:	FINANCIAL STATEMENTS. The franchisor must include its balance sheet for the last two fiscal years. Disclosures of statements of operations, stockholder's equity, and cash flow are required for the franchisor's last three fiscal years. If the most recent balance sheet and statement of operations are as of a date more than 90 days before the application date, the franchisor must also include an unaudited balance sheet and statement of operations for a period falling within 90 days of the application. If the franchisor does not have audited financial statements for its last three fiscal years, it may provide either (1) an audited financial statement for its last fiscal year and, if the audit is not within 90 days of the application date, an unaudited balance sheet and income statement for a period falling within 90 days of application; or (2) an unaudited balance sheet as of the date within 90 days of the application and an audited income statement from the start of its fiscal year through the date of the audited balance sheet.
Item 22:	CONTRACTS. A copy of the franchise agreement as well as any other related documents to be signed by the franchisee in connection with the ownership and operation of the franchised business must be attached as exhibits to the UFOC.
Item 23:	RECEIPT. Franchisor are required to provide two copies of the Receipt in the offering circular, one to be kept by the prospective franchisee and the other to be returned to the franchisor. The franchisor must disclose the name, principal business address, and telephone number of any subfranchisor or franchise broker offering the franchise in the state. The Receipt must contain an itemized listing of all exhibits to the offering circular. If not previously disclosed in Item 1, the franchisor must disclose the name(s) and address(es) of its agent(s) authorized to receive service of process.

The Mechanics of the Registration Process

Each of the registration states has slightly different procedures and requirements for the approval of a franchisor prior to offers and sales being authorized. In all cases, however, the package of disclosure documents is assembled, consisting of an offering circular, franchise agreement, supplemental agreements, financial statements, franchise roster, mandated cover pages, acknowledgment of receipt, and the special forms that are required by each state, such as corporation verification statements, salesperson disclosure forms, and consent to service of process documents. The franchisor and its counsel should check the specific requirements of each state carefully. Initial filing fees range from $250 to $750, with renewal filings usually ranging between $100 to $250.

The first step is for counsel to "custom tailor" the UFOC format to meet the special requirements or additional disclosures required under the particular state regulations. Once the documents are ready and all signatures have been obtained, the package is filed with the state franchise administrator and a specific franchise examiner (usually an attorney) is assigned to the franchisor. The level of scrutiny applied by the examiner in reviewing the offering materials will vary from state to state and from franchisor to franchisor. The sales history, financial strength, litigation record, reputation of legal counsel, time pressures and workload of the examiner, geographic desirability of the state, and the general reputation of the franchisor will have an impact on the level of review and the timetable for approval. Franchisors should expect to see at least one "comment letter" from the examiner requesting certain changes or additional information as a condition of approval and registration. The procedure can go as quickly as 6 weeks or as slowly as 6 months, depending on the concerns of the examiner and the skills and experience of legal counsel.

The initial and ongoing reporting and disclosure requirements vary from state to state. For example, the filing of an amendment to the offering circular is required in the event of a material change; however, each state has different regulations as to the definition of a material change. Similarly, although all registration states require the annual filing of a renewal application or annual report, only Maryland requires that quarterly reports be filed. When advertising materials are developed for use in attracting franchisees, they must be approved in advance by all registration states, except Virginia and Hawaii. All franchise registration states except Virginia require the filing of salesperson disclosure forms. California, New York, Illinois, and Washington require their own special forms. It is critical that the franchisor's legal compliance officer stay abreast of all of these special filing requirements.

About the Chapter Author

Andrew J. Sherman is a Capital Partner in the Washington, D.C., office of McDermott, Will & Emery, an international law firm with nearly 1,000 attorneys worldwide. Mr. Sherman is a recognized international authority on the legal and strategic issues affecting small and growing companies and serves as Chairman of the firm's International Franchising, Licensing and Distribution Group. Mr. Sherman is an Adjunct Professor in the Masters of Business Administration (MBA) program at the University of Maryland and Georgetown University, where he teaches courses on business growth, franchising, capital formation, and entrepreneurship. Mr. Sherman is the author of 11 books on the legal and strategic aspects of business growth and franchising. His most recently published books include *The Complete Guide to Running and Growing Your Business,* published by Random House in December 1997, and *Franchising and Licensing: Two Ways to Building Your Business* (2nd edition) published by AMACOM. His newest book, *Fast Track Business Growth,* was published by Kiplinger's in January 2002. Mr. Sherman can be reached at (202) 756-8610 or by email: *ajsherman@mwe.com.*

11 International Franchising

Franchising in a Foreign Country from a U.S. Base

The Southland Ice Company opened its first convenience store in 1927 and called it a Tote'm. In 1946 the company changed its store name to 7-Eleven to reflect its operating hours. The company entered franchising in 1964, signed its first United States area licensing agreement in 1968, and signed the first international licensing agreement with Mexico in 1971. In 1991 Southland Corporation, the quintessential American company was purchased by its Japanese franchisee. In 2003 almost 80% of 7-Eleven's 24,400 stores are located outside of the United States.

Because franchising is a vehicle for growth, many franchisors ask, "Why stop at U.S. national borders?" Here in Chapter Eleven we outline several aspects of franchising that you, as franchisor, should consider before entering a particular country. At the end of the chapter we offer some additional resources for further information.

International franchising has taken on new meaning in the last ten years. Before 1990, U.S. franchise presence abroad meant a McDonald's in Tokyo or one next to the Spanish Steps in Rome. However even as early as the 1970s, several European based franchises existed, such as Dynorod and Prontaprint. By

2003, thousands of U.S. franchises in food, retail, and services had moved into emerging markets around the globe. Why?

The U.S. franchise market, set to reach 1 trillion dollars in 2003, may be nearing saturation for existing franchises like MacDonald's that have very high historical growth rates. *Saturation* means the market will no longer support the company's historical growth, whether new outlet growth or same store sales growth. The opening of trade and international commerce "globalization" that occurred throughout the 1990s is another factor. Still another reason is that franchising simply works. Because it is a proven business model that has generated wealth in the United States, the next logical step is clearly to export the system abroad. The risks are certainly greater, but if the reward resembles even a fraction of what it has been in the U.S., many businesspeople are prepared to accept them.

Rather than focusing on the myriad opportunities available to franchisors willing to expand abroad, this chapter will outline the risks involved in doing so. A 1995 report by Arthur Andersen showed that two-thirds of all U.S. franchisors who decided to expand abroad did so based on first contact from a prospective foreign franchisee.[1] As international franchising becomes even more commonplace, we believe that making decisions about it can become a more structured, calculated process, with the benefit of greater experience and information.

The proliferation of the Internet and international trade in general, mean that the resources now exist to allow you to make shrewd decisions in the international arena. This chapter guides you through the decision making with a checklist of criteria to consider when looking for a foreign country in which to locate new franchises. As a franchisee you will know how the franchisor should be making the decision to expand internationally. Each criterion is accompanied by an explanation and a list of resources for determining whether or not the criterion is prohibitive, restrictive, or conducive to franchising. Once the preliminary country decision has been made by the franchisor, the next step, meeting potential partners and finding local professional service, will be identified.

Using The International Franchising Checklist

The checklist below will help you assess the risks and opportunities inherent in franchising abroad. Each country criterion in the checklist is structured according to whether or not it is prohibitive (significantly reduces the chance of opening stores profitably versus the U.S. operation), restrictive (extends the time it takes to open profitable outlets) or conducive to franchising (will add in the speed of opening new stores and or profitability). Unfortunately, determining whether or not a country poses an opportunity is not as simple as adding up the results of particular questions and taking the average. Some criteria, such as language and

---

1.   Woolweaver, Charles L. "International Franchising Checklist: Short- and Long-term Considerations." FranchiseConsulting.net. *http://www.franchiseconsulting.net/ ?source=overture.* 2002.

culture, can be restrictive, and not all criteria are equally important. If the laws of the country prohibit franchising, proceed no further! But if the laws are merely restrictive and the criteria in other areas such as purchasing power and economic stability are conducive, then an opportunity could still exist. We recommend using the checklist to get a sense of the issues that will pose the biggest challenges to a system, rather than as a tool for eliminating opportunities. The countries that pose the best opportunities nonetheless will have their share of restrictive characteristics—success in realizing those opportunities will depend on your ability to overcome those.

The checklist is also intended to convey how much conviction, resources, and creativity are necessary for success. Although many franchisors see it as a low-cost bet, setting up a franchise operation in a foreign country invariably requires significantly more time, capital, and other resources than setting up another domestic one. With an established income stream in the United States, some franchisors see fees from international markets as "icing on the cake." They reason that brand damage in another country will not bleed over into the U.S. and that they will not have to apply franchisor resources to the international market. "If it works, fine. If it doesn't, then no harm has been done." This line of reasoning could not be more misguided.

Contractual requirements will certainly require the franchisor to expend some resources to assist international partners. Further, implied good faith (sometimes legally) requires the franchisor to make a reasonable effort to support an international franchisee. Of course, distance almost always creates the need for enhanced communications and further use of resources. If the expansion fails the brand will be harmed regardless of geography. Not only do you need creativity to get over the hurdles outlined in the checklist, but you may also have to change the franchise to suit the country in question. Vegan burgers in India are essential in all of the traditional hamburger franchises. Papa John's Pizza franchise varies its take out and dine-in business models based on local customs and zoning laws. The successful international franchisor will be armed not only with good information and contacts, but also with plenty of flexibility and conviction.

The checklist is shown in its entirety in Table 11–1; we then go through the list question by question and give you more detail about how to find and evaluate the answers. Although the international business environment is always in a state of change, we believe this list can become an important part of any international franchise system's annual strategic review and plan.

TABLE 11–1 Checklist for International Franchising

1. Is the country's legal and regulatory environment for franchising: • Prohibitive • Restrictive • Conducive	6. Is the economic and political stability of the country: • Prohibitive • Restrictive • Conducive
2. Are import rules and customs procedures: • Prohibitive • Restrictive • Conducive	7. The franchises currently operating in the country suggest that overall it is: • Prohibitive • Restrictive • Conducive
3. For franchising, are tax rates: • Prohibitive • Restrictive • Conducive	8. The effect of differences in language for the franchise: • Prohibitive • Restrictive • Conducive
4. Are the cost and availability of labor: • Prohibitive • Restrictive • Conducive	9. The effect of cultural differences on the franchise: • Prohibitive • Restrictive • Conducive
5. Is the purchasing power of the population: • Prohibitive • Restrictive • Conducive	

Using the Checklist.

    1. Is the country's legal and regulatory environment for franchising:

- Prohibitive?
- Restrictive?
- Conducive?

Outside the United States, most countries do not have laws that specifically address franchising. The franchise-specific laws that do exist in several countries usually pertain to disclosure agreements, but some go as far as to regulate the amount and duration of the royalties due from the franchisee.

The general application laws[2] to which you should pay especially close attention are those that pertain to monetary exchange, employment and intellectual property. For example in Europe, such issues as minimum wage, long statutory maternity leave, or paternity leave may affect your decisions. If the government regulates the import and export of currencies, it may complicate, or even prohibit, the export of the payments due you. And employment laws that restrict the firing of employees could also add significant costs down the road. In terms of intellectual property, it is crucial for you to know whether or not the law protects the system's patents, trademarks, and copyrights. If intellectual property laws exist, you must determine whether or not these laws are being purposefully and effectively enforced. Loosely enforced intellectual property laws put your logo and brand at risk and expansion in those countries carries extreme risk.

Obviously a country that forbids franchising altogether (such as Mexico before 1991)[3], or that severely restricts currency exchange, would be considered prohibitive. If a country allows franchising but has non-existent or unenforced intellectual property laws, you should consider it restrictive. One that allows franchising by law, and that enforces intellectual property laws according to international standards, is conducive to franchising. Please refer to up to date information regarding intellectual property, patents, and trademarks at the following sites. In the UK: *www.patent.gov.uk*, and in the U.S.: *www.uspto.gov.*[4]

Assessing the country's legal and regulatory environment for franchising: One useful document that summarizes the existing franchise-specific laws in various countries is available for free download from a company called Franchise Consulting. Visit *http://www.franchiseconsulting.net* and click on "International Franchising" from the main page to find the download called "Compliance with Foreign Country Disclosure."

Because most countries do not have very specific laws, the first order of business in determining the level of intellectual property protection in a country is to determine whether or not the country is a member or observer of the World Trade Organization (WTO). All members of the WTO must sign on the Agreement on Trade Related Aspects of Intellectual Property Rights, or the TRIPS agreement. For a list of WTO member and observer countries, visit the WTO online at: *http://www.wto.org* and click on "The WTO." It is also helpful to use the site's search option to find and read an explanation of the TRIPS agreement and the intellectual property law enforcement rules that it contains.

Although a country's membership in the WTO is highly significant, it is important to keep in mind that this alone does not guarantee that its intellectual

---

2. A general application law refers to contract or case law that exist in a country and is applied to the general business environment, not specifically or only to franchising.
3. Herrmann-Ferkl, Claudia. "Viva Mexico: Open for Expansion." *International Franchising Magazine.* Spring 2002, Vol. 1, No. 1. Pp. 17–22.
4. Additional intellectual property rights web links are listed at the end of this chapter.

property laws are well enforced. For example, China and Mexico are two WTO members that have had major grievances filed against them in the area of intellectual property piracy. To find out what the actual climate for intellectual property protection is in the country, we recommend referring to the U.S. Department of State's Country Commercial Guides. These useful tools may be found online at *http://www.export.gov.* From the main page, click on "Country and Industry Market Research."

    2. Are import rules and customs procedures:

- Prohibitive?
- Restrictive?
- Conducive?

The franchisor may have to import raw materials and supplies to its franchises in the given country. These inputs will range from intellectual property and training personnel to raw material, For that reason, it is important to determine the state of the country's supply infra-structure and import and customs procedures. If the franchise is a restaurant and heavy import duties are imposed upon certain foodstuffs, those added costs might make the country a restrictive or prohibitive place to do business. Likewise, if customs procedures are overly complex or inconsistently applied and enforced, the effect may be deleterious to a new franchise venture. For example, McDonald's in Russia built food-processing plants to supply their restaurants and to ensure quality. Low import duties and efficient customs procedures consistent with international standards will of course be conducive to a franchising operation.

Assessing the country's import and customs procedures: The U.S. Department of Commerce has an excellent system in place for determining what the import tariffs and duties will be for specific products going to specific countries. This information can be found online by going to the DOC's International Trade Administration website at *http://www.export.gov* and clicking on "Tariffs and Taxes." Simply enter the information about the products to be exported and select the country of interest, or call 1-800 USA TRADE for assistance. The aforementioned Department of State Country Commercial Guides provide relevant information about the country's customs procedures, and will usually make a note if they have received complaints from U.S. companies about customs procedures.

    3. Are corporate tax rates:

- Prohibitive?
- Restrictive?
- Conducive?

No one wants to do business in a country that takes too much in the way of taxes. The nature of franchising is such that the franchisor will likely only have to pay taxes on the income earned from foreign royalties to the United States' IRS. However, the franchisee will certainly will have to pay taxes to the foreign government at its tax rate. The franchisee is already paying royalties and advertising fees to the franchisor based on revenue, not profits. Therefore, a high foreign tax rate on top of that could mean the difference between a franchise that is profitable, and one that is not. Before setting up an operation abroad, you must have a complete understanding of the tax structures in place for that country. A foreign tax rate that is above 35% could be restrictive or prohibitive whereas one that is below would be conducive to franchising.

Assessing the country's corporate tax rates: A number of print and online resources exist for investigating foreign tax structures (although the best resource is a good foreign tax advisor). Consult "The Worldwide Corporate Tax Guide," published by Ernst & Young. The most recent edition is always available online for free downloading. Visit *http://www.ey.com* and do a search based on the title of the document. Tax rates and related information can be found by country. Another resource is the International Monetary Fund's (IMF) Country Information page. Visit *http://www.imf.org* and click on "Country Information." These comprehensive country reports give extensive coverage in the area of tax policy.

4. Are the cost and availability of labor:

- Prohibitive?
- Restrictive?
- Conducive?

When it comes to franchising, labor affordability and availability are often key ingredients for success. In the current world environment, we often see two extremes. The first is the high cost of labor in developed countries such as Japan and Germany, in which the labor pool is limited, people are relatively well educated, and the cost of living is high. The other extreme is found in developing countries in which labor is cheap and abundant, but in which workers may be less well educated and training is difficult and/or expensive. Depending on the type of franchise, either of these extremes can be prohibitive or restrictive to franchise development. However there are many nations, such as China or the countries of Latin America that have sufficiently sophisticated labor at a lower cost than in the United States. Labor environments like these would be conducive to franchising.

Assessing the country's cost and availability of labor: The IMF is a good place to start looking for information on the labor markets of specific countries. The country reports at *http://www.imf.org* also contain facts on labor cost and availability. The United Nations Statistics Division is also an excellent source for broader socio-economic demographic information. This site gives literacy rates and education levels, broken down by age and sex for over 100 countries. It also segments population according to age, geographical location and more. Find these and other statistics at: *http://www.un.org/Depts/unsd/*.

5. Is the purchasing power of the population:

- Prohibitive?
- Restrictive?
- Conducive?

The purchasing power of any given population is generally related to the issue of cost, availability and literacy of labor. We have found that education levels can be a good indicator of real purchasing power of a target segment. If 50% of the population is illiterate and only a third of the population has more than 7 years of schooling, chances are that labor costs and purchasing power will be low. Conversely, a highly educated and literate population usually indicates a high cost of labor and good purchasing power. When it comes to franchising, low purchasing power need not be an indicator of a prohibitive, or even restrictive, environment for franchising. For example, fast food franchises have done well in developing countries because they offer a relatively high-quality though inexpensive product. However if purchasing power is too low, the environment will be prohibitive, because no one will be able to afford the good or service being offered by the franchise. Thus, an environment conducive to franchising is one in which the purchasing power of the population *is appropriate to purchase* the good or service you plan to offer.

Assessing the purchasing power of the population: In theory, finding the purchasing power of the population in a given country should be a matter of converting the foreign GNP per capita into U.S. dollars at the prevailing exchange rates. But the major problem with this method is that it assumes a dollar in one country buys the same amount of good or service as it does in another. As anyone who has purchased a Pepsi in Mexico knows, prices are relative; some things are more or less expensive depending upon the country where you buy them. As a result, purchasing power is better measured using the principal of Purchasing Power Parity (PPP), which takes into account differences between countries in measures such as inflation, price and wage controls, and import tariffs. The World Bank has calculated Year 2000 Gross National Income using the PPP method for over 200 countries. This data is available by visiting *http://www.worldbank.org/data/*. Click on "International Comparison Program" and follow the links for "PPP" data.

6. Is the economic and political stability of the country:

- Prohibitive?
- Restrictive?
- Conducive?

Perhaps the greatest risks in franchising abroad are those that involve political and economic disruptions. Wars, coups d'etat, nationalizations, runaway inflation, governments in default—these create an international businessperson's nightmare. And as we have seen over the last ten years, these events can disrupt countries that the conventional wisdom has said were safe bets. Take, for example, the truncated moves to an open economy in Venezuela or the economic morass in Japan. We gauge economic and political stability by how long a country has managed to ward off these kinds of disruptions and keep its economy and political system in relative equilibrium. A country that has experienced stability for fifty years or more is one that is conducive to international franchising. Countries in this category include those of North America and much of Western Europe, as well as Australia, and New Zealand.

Countries that have experienced disruptive turmoil in the past twenty years are restrictive, and one that is in turmoil is prohibitive to franchising. Eastern Europe is a clear example of the turmoil, risk and opportunity in the last twenty years. As always in business, with greater risk comes greater potential reward. Because almost every developing economy has experienced disruption in the past twenty years, it is up to you to do the necessary research and decide whether the return is worth the risk. As the next section will illustrate, many have determined that it is.

Assessing the economic and political stability of the country: The level of economic and political stability of a country is often referred to as country risk. The most authoritative evaluator of country risk is the *International Country Risk Guide* published by the Political Risk Services group (PRS) (*http://www.prs-group.com; http://www.prsonline.com/.*) This expensive resource is used by finance professionals and researchers the world over. The survey covers 140 nations and is compiled using a complex methodology that analyzes economic, financial and political factors for risk. Other less exhaustive (and free) resources includes the Central Intelligence Agency's World Factbook. These country profiles are available online at: *http://www.odci.gov/*; click on The World Factbook under Library and Reference on the main page. The Department of State's Country Reports contain information about the economic and political environment of countries. These can be found at: *http://www.export.gov* by clicking on Country and Industry Market Research. Finally, the Economist Intelligence Unit is an excellent source of up-to-date country information at: *http://www.eiu.com/.*

7. The franchises currently operating in the country suggest that overall it is:

- Prohibitive
- Restrictive
- Conducive

One of the surest ways to determine the viability of a particular country for franchising is to see which franchises are already doing business there. Chances are, if someone has achieved success, so can others. If there were no franchises at all in a given country, that location could be a prohibitive one to move into unless you are willing to commit significant resources. If there are but a few there, or if the number of franchises is declining, the country is probably restrictive of franchising. But if there are a number of franchises operating in the country, and if they have grown steadily in number, then that country is probably conducive to franchising.

Assessing the number of franchises in a country: In its Country Reports, the Department of State usually mentions the number of U.S. franchises operating in the given country. It will also specifically note franchising as a good opportunity for U.S. franchisors if it sees significant growth in the industry. The International Franchise Association has compiled this existing franchise data for 52 countries into concise reports which can be found online at: *http://www.franchise.org/international.asp.* Click on Franchisor Services for the reports.

Another approach is to look at the World Franchising website where the Top 50 international franchisors in food, service and retail are listed: *http://www.franchiseintl.com/.* From there, you can investigate individual companies to see in exactly which countries franchises have opened. There is some correlation between travel patterns of U.S. tourists abroad and the viability of U.S. franchises. Of course, the specific context of the country is crucial. We doubt that Jiffy Lube would work in India (too many small workshops by the roadside), or a lawn care franchise in Singapore (too few houses with lawns).

8. The effect of differences in language for the franchise:

- Prohibitive
- Restrictive
- Conducive

Although language is one of the biggest hurdles in realizing international business opportunities, it is a surmountable one. You will have to have all documents drawn up in duplicate, one in English, the other in the foreign language. It greatly helps if you speak the foreign language in question, but even if you plan a large-scale overseas initiative, it may be unrealistic to expect to be fluent in ten languages. Finding bilingual franchisees whenever possible and hiring a consultant, a tax professional and an attorney from the local area who can assist you with communication and paperwork will greatly reduce the language barrier risk. Many franchisors have found that partnering with a Master Franchisee from the country in question makes the most sense. For example, Cartridge World is an Australian franchisor that sells large regional franchise rights to franchisees who can then re-sell those rights or operate the large territory. The company's business strategy combines refilling printer cartridges for inkjet and laser printers, photocopy and fax machines with fast customer service at convenient retail locations. The combination of retail and office business makes it more difficult to define territories. Larger territories make it easier for a Master Franchisee, who knows the territory better than the franchisor to build the right number of outlets. Using this method, you can manage franchisee operations for the whole country (or region, if it's a large country) and minimize the points of contact. Of course you need to find the right individual, but that is a necessary task in any relationship-based business arrangement.

9. The effects of cultural differences on the franchise are:

- Prohibitive

- Restrictive

- Conducive

Unfortunately, there is no guidebook available for determining which foreign countries would be most receptive to franchising, but culture can be a make or break factor in setting up internationally. You can start by looking first at the nature of your offering or menu and then on the physical service delivery system. For instance, in India beef is not widely eaten for cultural reasons, therefore a fast-food franchise such as McDonald's must take this fact into account when developing their menu there or suffer the consequences. In other countries, décor and signage might have to be adjusted to suit local tastes, or the actual products and services offered might have to be altered. High Street locations in Great Britain often have severe signage restrictions.

The best way to get a sense of the cultural differences in a country is to go there and to see first-hand how comparable local businesses are set up. Cultural differences present a complex set of variables. For example, companies that do business with the U.S. Government must adhere to the Foreign Corrupt Practices Act wherever they trade. While we agree with this anti-corruption law, it can severely limit opportunities in cultures where bribery is a normal way of doing business, can be charged to the P&L and provide the local competition with a financial competitive advantage. Additionally, we recommend looking at what the existing franchises have done regarding cultural differences to make themselves fit in locally and to be successful.

Getting Serious: After You Have Selected a Country. Once you have selected the country to enter, it is time to begin forging business relationships in that country. At this stage, the best resource available to U.S. franchisors wishing to set up shop abroad is the U.S. Government. The government has a vested interest in seeing U.S. business expand overseas, and it has an excellent system for facilitating this through the Department of State and the International Trade Administration. The U.S. Commercial Service has offices at U.S. embassies in over 100 countries with the express intent of assisting U.S. companies that wish to enter those markets. For a relatively small fee, this service will conduct primary market research, locate potential partners (Master Franchisees and franchisees), find proven local consultants and tax and legal professionals, conduct background checks, and even host networking events at the embassy. To find out more about the Commercial Service visit *http://www.export.gov* and click on Country & Industry Market Research.

International Market Entry Strategies.   A U.S. franchisor can be lured into entering a foreign country by an enthusiastic and wealthy prospective franchisee. This generally happens when a foreign entrepreneur comes to the United States, sees or uses a U.S. franchise, and then gets excited about launching the concept in his or her home country. A large franchise fee, and the perception that if the opportunity goes poorly abroad it won't hurt the company's U.S. image, can lead the franchisor into a hastily conceived relationship. These relationships seldom result in financial success.

There are no shortcuts. Entry into a foreign country from a U.S. base is a "back to basics" task that should always begin with an examination of the opportunity using the Franchise Relationship Model. Then, you can make use of this chapter as a guide to further international due diligence. Finally, you should develop and execute your entry strategy for the international launch.

Franchise Launching into a Foreign Country.   There is a wide spectrum of strategies to enter an international market, described in Table 11–2. From left to right, the spectrum identifies the extent of franchisor involvement in the unit operations.

TABLE 11–2 Spectrum of Market Entrance Strategies

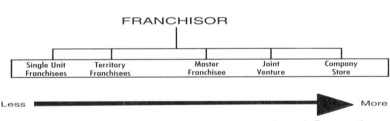

The sale of a single franchised unit is the most problematic approach to entering a foreign market. There is typically little or no brand awareness in the foreign country. One unit is at best a "beta site," as described in earlier chapters, but with the franchisee as the risk bearer. This can seem appealing because it brings in fees with what seems to be little brand or capital risk. However, your ability to gain real market intelligence and market share, and hence your probability of success, are limited. To support the site you would have to commit major resources for training, field operations, and marketing. Putting that overhead in place for one franchised unit might not make financial sense.

You may want faster growth and larger up front franchise fees and decide instead to sell territory franchise rights to a select well-capitalized franchisee. They will likely be a national of the foreign country and committed to an extensive development and operation of outlets. Marketing the sale of large franchise territories is often directed to bankers, lawyers and accountants in the targeted nation. These professionals often provide a communications conduit to wealthy business-minded nationals. Territory franchise sales usually include a large up front franchise fee and incremental payments along the way that help underwrite franchisor support. Thus you will have incentives to ramp up support for the franchisee as development increases. Multiple territory franchisees can be sold in a given country in an attempt to build critical mass. However, this "carpet bombing" approach can also magnify new country entry, operations, and marketing glitches.

The next level of involvement is to establish a relationship with a master franchisee, by selling him or her rights to share in your benefits and responsibilities in a country or section of a country. In a Master Franchisee arrangement you assign rights and responsibilities in the license agreement. The master franchisee is then responsible for opening outlets under his or her ownership or selling outlets to other franchisees that they will support in the fashion of a franchisor. That usually includes site selection, training, marketing and field operations support. The master franchisee receives a percentage of the royalty fees that you would normally receive.

An explicit partnership is the joint venture. In this case, the franchisor becomes a partner with the franchisee, bearing a percentage of both the new outlet capitalization requirements and the management functions. This is a way for the franchisor to enter a market with a partner "on the ground," but also to have significant control of the operation. However, because capital requirements are expressly shared, this scenario is also a much more capital-intensive strategy for entering a foreign country.

Lastly, the franchisor can take a "grass roots" approach similar to the strategy we recommend in the opening chapter of this book. The franchisor opens company owned stores in a methodical manner to test the service delivery system in the context of the foreign market. After initial success, you can build upon the initial markets, and upon further success, you can begin selling franchises or even offer the company owned outlets for sale to franchisees.

It is also worth mentioning the issue of physical proximity of a new base of operations from a franchisor's U.S. headquarters. Many franchisors tend to base their first international headquarters in Great Britain for several reasons: the relative close proximity to the Eastern U.S., the similarity of language and culture, and the relative closeness to other parts of Europe, Asia, and the Middle East.

Conclusion

The lure of international markets for U.S. franchisors is understandable. Huge market potential driven by populations far exceeding U.S. totals, more open borders than ever and more ubiquitous communication of brands can mean vastly increased growth. However, there is no risk-free approach to entering a foreign country from a U.S. base. The lure of up-front fees and support-free royalties is an illusion. A failed franchise effort in a foreign country may very well have far-reaching negative brand implications, truncate future international expansion, and result in litigation. A Franchise relationship Model Approach will ensure a disciplined due diligence and a more accurate assessment of the risk-return scenarios.

Further Reading

Mendelsohn, Martin and Brennan, Michael. *The International Encyclopedia of Franchising.* London: Kluwer Law International, 1999.

> The International Encyclopedia of Franchising has an introduction summarizing the considerations that should be taken when franchising internationally. It is then broken down into 15 sections, each one country or region (the EU) specific, and written by a law professional or researcher from that country. Each section gives a history of franchising and details the country's legal and tax system as it pertains to international franchising.

Eds. Asbill, Richard M. and Goldman, Steven M. *Fundamentals of International Franchising.* Chicago: International Bar Association, 2001.

> Fundamentals of International Franchising was prepared for the American Bar Association's Forum on Franchising. It gives detailed information on what considerations need to be made in the areas of tax and law by franchisors when they go international. It is not country specific, but is very useful as a general guide and in describing the interaction of U.S. tax and legal policies with foreign ones.

International Institute for the Unification of Private Law. *Guide to International Master Franchise Arrangements.* Rome: UNIDROIT, 1998.

> The Guide to International Master Franchise Arrangements is devoted exclusively to the type of deal most often used by international franchisors. The work is not country specific, but goes through the considerations and procedures that a franchisor should take into account in drawing up a contract with any international master franchisee.

Web Sites

www.franchise.org

> IFA - The International Franchise Association, founded in 1960, is a member-ship organization of franchisors, franchisees and suppliers.

www.bison1.com

> This is an interesting site that has an alphabetical list of franchises with links to their home page. Companies are also listed by industry category. Initial investment, current press releases, a list of books on franchising and franchise financing resources are listed

Official websites of intellectual property authorities

Argentina	Brasil
INPI—Instituto Nacional de la Propriedad Industrial (in Spanish only)	*INPI*—Instituto Nacional de Propriedade Intelectual (in Portuguese, English, French and Spanish)
Canada	**México**
CIPO/OPIC— Canadian Intellectual Property Office / L'Office de la propriété intellectuelle du Canada (in English and French)	*IMPI*—Instituto Mexicano de la Propriedad Industrial (in Spanish and English)
Perú	**United States**
INDECOPI—Instituto Nacional de Defensa de la Competencia y de la Protección de la Propriedad Intelectual (in Spanish only)	*U.S. PTO*—U.S. Patent and Trademark Office *U.S. Copyright Office* *Plant Variety Protection Office*
Uruguay	
DNPI—Dirección Nacional de la Propriedad Industrial	

12 Harvest

The holy grail of entrepreneurship is "cashing out." Some people sell their business and others transfer ownership and or management responsibility. Entrepreneurs call this the "harvest" of the business. It is sometimes referred to as an exit strategy. Clearly, every entrepreneur eventually exits the business, be it by sale, bankruptcy, or death. We prefer the word *harvest* because it connotes a natural and positive conclusion to a well-planned series of events.

Everything we've talked about in this book can be optimized only if harvest is well thought out from the beginning of planning, prior to execution. Seldom is wealth achieved in a haphazard manner. A harvest strategy is not a luxury, it is a requirement. You must evaluate the ways that value can be maximized and the avenues most appropriate for realizing the wealth created in your company. If you perform a detailed examination of opportunity, then construct an SDS designed to meet demand in a competitive manner, the dynamic operation and growth of the system will create wealth, but wealth is ephemeral if not used. A harvest strategy secures that wealth for the shareholders.

Both entrepreneurs and the general business public sometimes misunderstand the harvest as being simply an unplanned exit from a deal. This is seldom the case. Although luck, chance, or coincidence often plays a role, it is not the compelling reason for a successful harvest—harvest should be a planned ingredient of any business opportunity.

Harvest is a way for both entrepreneurs and investors to extract value from their firm. Note that you cannot plan a harvest strategy without examining the needs of multiple stakeholders. Who has a vested interest in the success of the franchise system? Anyone included in your answer is likely to be a stakeholder. That list is likely to include investors, banks, founding management, key employees, and even some suppliers. William Petty[1] describes harvest as "the owners' and investors' strategy for achieving after-tax cash flows on their investment." This implies, and we agree, that multiple stakeholders can be satisfied in a harvest event. Harvest is intimately important for most outside investors. Except for investors in publicly held companies (only 5 percent of franchisors) who look for share appreciation and dividends, they cannot reap any reward for their risk without a harvest of the investment.

Many entrepreneurs ignore the harvest issue until many years after the launch of the business, but it should be planned at the beginning of the venture. Business owners get so excited about the new firm and the need for survival that harvest seems a distant event that will take care of itself once they are successful. Without a plan, however, the entrepreneur can become trapped in the business. A franchisee operates her business with the expectation of making a profit each year. Harvest is selling that expectation to someone else, reaping a payout of expected earnings earlier rather than later.

There is a category of investment called "the living dead," an investment that never achieves a harvest *and* never fails. The investor can't write off the investment as a loss for tax purposes, but doesn't get the investment back or a return on the investment. Living dead companies typically break even or make a small profit over the life of the business. The operator receives a salary but creates no wealth. It's very difficult to ever extract money from the business for investors because there is no excess cash flow and usually no buyer of the company. When management tires of the struggle, the firm simply winds down and assets (if any) are sold.

Fortunately for you, franchising provides a unique, if sometimes complicated, environment for harvest. The contractual relationship between the franchisor and franchisees and the bias in franchising toward growth creates "value inflection points" that provide harvest opportunities for both the franchisor and the franchisees. For each inflection point, there is an appropriate harvest strategy. We address harvest from the perspectives of both the franchiser and the franchisee and their likely investors and at the same time address which strategy is most likely to maximize return for each party. TIP 12–1 illustrates a unique harvest opportunity in the 7-Eleven franchise system.

---

1.   Petty, William. (1995). "Harvesting." In William Bygrave (Ed.), *Portable MBA in Entrepreneurship*. John Wiley and Sons.

TIP 12–1 Theory into Practice

Franchising: A Unique Harvest Opportunity—7-Eleven

The opinion of franchisees affects the harvest strategy of the franchisor. An unhappy group of franchisees would certainly depress franchisor value. Alternately, franchisees can become shareholders in a public franchisor. Clearly, a large group of wealthy franchisees will play a role in the future of the franchisor. A franchisee or group of franchisees can even get big enough to buy the franchisor. The biggest such event in franchise history occurred in 1991. The Ito-Yokado Company, known as the IY Group, signed the original licensing agreement with Southland to form 7-Eleven Japan and become the franchise in that country in November of 1973. The IY Group later founded 7-Eleven Hawaii in 1989. In a dramatic turn of events IY Group bought the franchisor, 7-Eleven, in 1991. The success of the IY Group as a franchisee gave it both operating credibility and the financial strength to buy the franchisor.

The IY Group now owns more than 21,000 7-Eleven stores throughout the world. There are more than 5,700 stores in the United States and Canada and 9,100 stores in Japan. Besides convenience stores, the IY Group also owns superstores, restaurants (Denny's Japan), specialty stores, food manufacturing and processing companies, and finance/insurance companies. Its stock is listed on the NASDAQ as IYCOY. The IY Group owns about 73 percent of 7-Eleven Inc. and 51 percent of 7-Eleven Japan.

The IY Group's revenues for its fiscal year ending February 2002 were $22.3 billion with a total net income of $390 million. 7-Eleven Japan's revenues for its fiscal year ending February 2002 were $2.9 billion with total net income of $612 million. 7-Eleven's revenues for its fiscal year ending December 2001 were $9.8 billion with total net income of $103 million.

In its latest venture, 7-Eleven Japan along with Uni-President Group, a Taiwanese company that operates 7-Eleven stores in Taiwan, will be opening 500 stores in China over the next five years.

Harvest Options

Although there are a number of variations on the harvest theme, they boil down to five basic options:

1. An initial public offering
2. A trade sale to or merger with another company
3. Increasing (and extracting) free cash flow
4. A management buyout (MBO)
5. An employee stock ownership plan

All these options are viable for a given situation. However, the franchise environment provides a roadmap for harvest that is dependent on your role as a franchisor or franchisee and on the specific nature of the relationship, that is, whether you are a single unit owner, a multiple-unit owner, or a multiple-unit and multiple-system owner.

The Initial Public Offering

An Ideal Harvest Strategy for the Franchisor

An IPO harvest strategy is the perfect transaction to leverage franchisor growth. The IPO provides cash to the franchisor firm and liquidity to the non-management investors. These investors, certainly venture capitalists, will almost always have a bias toward an IPO. If a company qualifies for an IPO, it typically yields the highest percentage return to shareholders. Qualification for an IPO centers on the scale of the firm, the quality of the management team, and the prospects for sustainable and profitable growth. Taking a company public invariably means the entrepreneur will not exit the deal as either an investor or manager, but may realize some of his investment through the sale of a percentage of his equity.

Few new investors in an IPO like to see the founders realizing all their shares. Such actions signal a lack of confidence in the future of the company. Because an IPO raises money for growth and the new investors provide the lead entrepreneur and management with growth capital, they would not be as likely to provide those funds to a company whose leader was leaving. An IPO is, to a great extent, the public's belief in the vision and capabilities of the executive team. Further, executive "lock-up" (the amount of time an executive cannot sell stock after the IPO) can be as little as 6 months or up to 2 years or even longer.

Although an IPO is often the preferred harvest strategy for the investors in the franchisor, a trade sale is cheaper to execute and allows investors to exit completely, which is often what venture capitalists want. With an IPO, the franchisor and the investor goals are in complete alignment. As we've said, the investor is seeking the maximum ROI. The franchisor is seeking to simultaneously meet the harvest requirements of the investors and gain additional growth capital. The IPO investor is specifically interested in companies that have a steep growth trajectory, making the franchisor a likely candidate in the public capital marketplace.

Let's review the ramp up to an IPO. The prospective franchisor recognizes an opportunity based on a perceived demand and builds an SDS to meet that demand. To test the SDS, a single beta site is constructed. Success with the beta leads to the build out of enough outlets to create economies of scale in a definable market, maybe 4 to 10 stores. Again successful, the firm then begins an aggressive franchise sales program to penetrate a targeted geographic region, maybe 100 outlets. If the franchise can prove unit profitability with 100 stores, it has a great IPO story to tell! The original investors can cash out at the IPO, and the franchisor can raise a round of capital to grow the system to national presence. Owners of shares of a publicly trade company can easily turn their shares into cash. They can watch the growth and profitability progress of the franchisor and make the hold-or-fold investment decision. Once a company has accessed public capital, it can return a number of times for additional funds through new offerings.

IPO: A Rare Experience for the Franchisee

In contrast to franchisors, few franchisees go public. Even the largest in a given system has a specified and (almost always) limited development plan. Franchisees are usually constrained by a defined geography and even a limited right to the trademark under the term of the license agreement. The growth potential is simply not exciting enough for the public capital markets.

A Word of Caution

Although IPOs are attractive in many ways, the fact remains that many privately held firms will never go public. But that's okay because some firms *should not* go public. An IPO certainly will not create immediate liquidity for the entrepreneur, because it may be several years before founding management are legally permitted to sell sizeable amounts of shares. Clearly, without either of these needs, pursuing an IPO simply does not make sense for your company.

The attractiveness or appropriateness of an IPO is also directly affected by the status and appetite of the capital markets. When stocks are booming and financial capital is abundant, then companies are encouraged to execute an IPO. However, markets can turn quickly. In 2000 there were 354 IPOs. In the following year there were 60 percent fewer IPOs that raised 85 percent less money. In other words, the capital markets needs may not coincide with your harvest strategy. The franchisor considering going public needs to communicate that strategy with investors and with franchisees from the inception of the strategy, but especially during the ramp-up period prior to the IPO. There should be a clear understanding among the players, franchisor, franchisees, and investors about the market parameters that will influence the "go" or "no-go" decision.

A Trade Sale or Merger with Another Company: A Franchisor's View

Why would someone give you a lot of money for your company? Because she believes she can make more money than you did. The sale of one company to another or merger of two companies occurs because the players believe the combined entity will better create wealth for the owners. Franchisors can uniquely position themselves for a trade sale in at least two ways:

A supplier might buy the franchisor to secure the channel of distribution. Because franchising is a highly efficient channel of distribution, the suppliers to a franchise have a vested interest in maintaining their distribution network. Those suppliers become logical candidates to purchase the franchisor. Why did Pennzoil purchase Jiffy Lube? Pennzoil needed to secure sales of millions of gallons of motor oil annually. The strategy in a supplier-related trade sale is to mirror your development of outlets in geographic locations with the distribution needs of a major supplier. Developing a relationship with key suppliers leverages your company. Volume discounts, extended trade payable terms, and even investment capital can come from suppliers. Relationship building is both art and science. Clearly, the supplier has a vested interest in a customers' success.

A company might buy a franchisor to acquire the franchising growth skills of the company. A second strategy is related to franchising as a competency. The knowledge of and ability to create a franchise system is a transferable skill. Another company might have a division or even a concept that requires a concept growth expert. Alternately, a conglomerate might purchase a sophisticated franchisor, then follow-up with the purchase of what they might see as less well-managed franchises. By purchasing a franchise company, the acquirer gains the franchising knowledge that can be transferred to other concepts. That appears to have been the strategy of Allied Domecq, a major international spirits company. They acquired Dunkin' Donuts and almost immediately put the management team to work buying other franchisors. The result was Allied's acquisition of Baskin Robbins and Togo's Restaurant. TIP 12–2 discusses some of these very brands.

A trade sale or merger with another company: The franchisee view of a trade sale as harvest for the franchisee is a rare but growing phenomenon. The license agreement of virtually every franchise system precludes the sale of a franchise without the approval of the franchisor. Additionally, the franchisor almost always has a right of first refusal. A right of first refusal chills buying activity. If you negotiate a favorable purchase of a franchise, then the franchisor is likely to step in and take the deal. The prospective purchaser is left with nothing for his effort but a lot of opportunity cost. However, some firms become "professional franchisees" and look for back-office expertise in the management of franchise systems. These companies are almost always privately held, and obtaining specific information about them is very difficult. However, the anecdotal information is that execution expertise and franchising experience is a powerful way to combine the ownership of a number of different franchises under one corporate entity.

The more likely trade sale for a franchisee is the sale of the franchise to an already existing franchisee in your own franchised system. Aside from increasing free cash flow, this may be the predominant harvest strategy for franchisees. Again, timing is an important component of maximizing harvest value. If you own a single franchise, then sale at a point of increasing revenues is likely to most benefit you. It's important to understand the nature of the trade area you occupy and its relationship to contiguous trade areas. Because franchise licenses are granted for long terms, it is likely that the markets will evolve and might grow in terms of the number of outlets it can hold versus that prescribed in the older agreements. Sale of your store may contractually "unlock" this market for development. Therefore, your store may be worth more than the revenue might suggest.

For multiple unit franchisees, timing is even more important. At what point does investment in new stores provide diminished harvest returns? Let's develop a hypothetical example. A franchisee owns a territory with an estimated capacity of 100 stores. He or she chooses a trade sale harvest strategy. Should the franchisee build all 100 stores or sell while there is still growth potential in the territory? That decision is a part of our valuation discussion later in this chapter. TIP 12–2 illustrates a growing harvest trend in the franchised food service industry.

Merger of the Franchise Company with a Known Brand Manager

Successful franchise companies are great brand managers. The value of the brand might be extended to another branded product to add value to both. Pepsi bought Pizza Hut, Kentucky Fried Chicken (now KFC), and Taco Bell. The three franchises eventually were spun out in 1997 as a separate company called Tricon, which is presently called YUM! In just under 2 years the stock price more than doubled, followed by a precipitous decline in the next 16 months. Over the next 24 months, the stock rose consistently. With the inclusion of two other brands, Long John Silver's and A&W All American, the organization—however volatile its share value has been—appears to understand brand management in a franchise environment. Franchisors have been experimenting with franchise system combinations for a number of years (Dunkin'-Baskin-Togos and Pizza Hut-KFC-Taco are the most prominent).

Harvesting Trends in Food Service

During the last quarter of the 20th century, it became clear that the rate at which food consumed away from home (fast food, take-away, sit-down) would be growing much faster than packaged goods sales through supermarkets and the like. As a result, many package goods and spirits companies purchased franchised food service companies; for example, Pillsbury acquired Burger King; PepsiCo purchased Pizza Hut, Taco Bell, and Kentucky Fried Chicken; and Allied Domecq acquired Baskin Robbins in 1976 and then Dunkin' Donuts in 1990. Also entering this fray were several nonfranchised businesses, among them the General Mills purchase of Darden Restaurants (Red Lobster) in 1976.

By the turn of the millennium, as restaurant sales growth slowed to the rate of packaged goods sales, these acquisitions, save Dunkin' Donuts and Baskin Robbins, were floated to the public or sold to private equity investors. During the same period, many franchisee networks had grown to substantial size and harvested their growth by either public ownership—for example, Apple South (an Applebee's franchisee), Quality Dining and Caroll Corporation (Burger King franchisees), Marcus Group (a diversified food service franchisee in the Midwest), and PJ America (a Papa John's franchisee)—or by sale back to their respective franchisors. That these franchisor buybacks often resulted in tens of millions of dollars for the franchisee gives a solid indication of just how much wealth could be created through franchise ownership. Interestingly, many of these successful, publicly owned, territorial operators jettisoned their original franchise business and high stock prices to create new concepts of their own. This strategy ultimately failed for most (Quality Dining and Apple South are now Avado Brands) and destroyed the value they had created as successful regional franchisees.

Increasing the Free Cash Flow

Free cash flow is the amount of cash left after running a stable and efficient business in a defined period—for example, one year. Generally, free cash flow is used to invest in new assets, reduce debt, or return money to investors. For a franchisee, that means when growth of new outlets you own is slowed or stopped, you will begin to take cash out of the business over and above your management salary. That is the essence of a free cash-flow harvest strategy. Let's review the calculation for free cash flow.

A. Free Cash Flow

= Operating Income

– Taxes on operating income

+ Depreciation and other noncash expenses

– Increases in net working capital during the year

– Capital expenditures for the year (for replacement and support of growth)

The Franchisor Perspective.   Because franchising is predominantly a growth option, reinvestment of cash flow into new assets for expansion is almost always assumed. Increases in cash will increase the rate of growth and preclude distribution of cash flow as a primary harvest strategy. The only time increasing free cash flow is a viable harvest option for a franchisor is when system growth is stalled because of market saturation. In this circumstance, cash builds from the franchisee royalty payments. The natural inclination and indeed the core competency of the franchisor is growth, and therefore when market saturation occurs, the franchisor looks to acquire franchised stores or to begin another concept.

The Franchisee Perspective.   Conversely, the franchisee usually has a limited regional growth capability (by license agreement). When growth is slowed, the reinvestment of cash flows into new assets becomes problematic, if not impossible. Therefore, increasing free cash flow for the franchisee investor is a logical harvest strategy. This strategy is one of retaining within the firm only the amount of cash necessary to maintain the current markets and not trying to grow the present markets or expand into new markets. Timing is crucial to the free cash flow strategy for any firm, but it is much more important in franchising. The license agreement grants trademark rights to the franchisee for a limited time in a limited geographic region. The timing of increasing cash flows must be aligned with the optimal development of the territory the franchisee owns. That territory can be as small as one trade area for one store, or it can be much larger, even into hundreds of outlets. The amount of time to grow to an optimal size (defined as serving the needs of the target customers in your geographic area) must be subtracted from the total term of the license agreement. The amount of time left on the license agreement after optimal growth is achieved multiplied by the annual free cash flow the franchisee can expect to get from operating at a status quo growth rate equals the total harvest payment.

Of course, no one can really "expect" cash flow. We discount the projected cash flow by some percentage to reflect the risk that the cash flows will not manifest. Also, remember that many franchises have a renewal term. The contractual rights, term, and cost of renewal vary widely in franchising. You should *increase* the discount rate for any renewal term when planning a cash flow harvest strategy.

Franchisees face both advantages and disadvantages with the increasing cash flows strategy. The advantages are twofold: First, the franchisee retains ownership of the company, which gives him strategic flexibility to reverse course and redirect cash flows into growth if an opportunity presents itself or to sell outright if an attractive offer is made. Second, this strategy does not require the franchisee or an advisor to find a motivated and financially capable buyer. Finding and negotiating the sale of a company is a time- and energy-consuming experience. A failed deal not only ends without a harvest—it typically takes a toll on the operating excellence of the firm.

There are also several disadvantages to the strategy of increasing cash flows. The franchise that doesn't expand tends to lose touch with the dynamic changes that are occurring in the marketplace. The infrastructure support systems atrophy, and it may be difficult to regain momentum. We use the term *expansion complacency* to describe this phenomenon. McDonald's founder Ray Kroc once said, "Green and growing or ripe and rotting." There is dramatically less excitement in maintaining a company than in growing a firm. Keeping yourself and key employees motivated to pursue excellence can be a challenge in a stagnant environment. Exacerbating the motivation problem is that the career path for management is clearly limited in this scenario. Additionally, there is a risk that expansion complacency will forfeit competitive advantage to the competition. If good locations emerge in a market and you pass, your competitor might move in.

Franchisors are reticent to grant lengthy exclusive territory contracts to franchisees because of the problem they define as *franchisee underinvesting*. Underinvesting is another way of saying the franchisee has decided to stop building new stores and instead distribute the increased free cash flow to the investors (especially themselves!). This reaction is intuitively sound. If you have one store that is making a lot of money, then you might want a second or third or fourth store, especially when the franchisor offers or encourages this expansion. But when the territory is limited, and the franchisor asks you to put in another store between two of your good performers, you may hesitate, thinking, Won't this new store cannibalize the sales of the other two because of its proximity? In this case your rationale will simply be to underinvest and consequently not build the third store.

Management Buyout

MBOs are typically classified as financial engineering strategies. In an MBO a small group of senior managers within the firm attempt to purchase the company from the existing shareholders. These transactions often include some form of leveraged financing, but only in the larger cases. For the smaller ones (especially franchisees operations), the team may be able to raise the necessary funds from their own resources. On the franchisor side, management seldom has the resources to complete the transaction. So, like the takeover artists of the 1980s, Carl Icahn and T. Boone Pickens, management will seek some equity and usually heavy debt financing to consummate these deals. A heavily leveraged deal puts pressure on the company to increase free cash flow for debt service.

A leveraged buy out or management buy out (LBO/MBO) strategy can make sense when the acquirer of the franchisor uses the base royalty stream to secure debt and infuses significant equity capital into the company. As we discussed, that is a very difficult task for a franchisor because of the franchisor's ongoing need to funnel free cash flow into growth plans. Another tactic of the LBO/MBO is to sell off assets of the company to reduce debt. This usually occurs where there are parts of the business that are not relevant for the new owner. That is unlikely to be the case for a franchise. Unfortunately for the franchisor, an LBO/MBO signals a dramatic retreat from growth. In this case, selling franchises and gaining the support of the franchisees becomes exceedingly difficult.

Interestingly, small-scale MBOs might not be a bad strategy for a franchisee, especially one with multiple outlets. Training support from the franchisor, including corporate "universities," operating manuals, and continuing education programs, tends to develop highly competent unit operators. Without corporate overhead or growth requirements, these managers can effectively increase free cash flow to pay off the purchase price of an outlet out of future earnings. Because bank financing is difficult in these small-scale transactions, the selling franchisee will probably have to carry the debt on the transaction, clearly a high-risk proposition. Although failure to meet debt payments would result in a return of the outlet, the seller will likely get a store in poor condition. Also, will the seller be prepared to reenter an operating role? If a franchisee owns multiple units, then a portfolio approach can be taken with the sale of individual outlets to individual buyers, therefore spreading the risk.

Employee Stock Ownership Plan (ESOP)

A leveraged ESOP borrows money from the company or another financial institution to buy the company's stock, whether all at once or in parts. The entrepreneur may or may not exit the company, but in either case he or she gets a large amount of money—in essence, the annualized stream of free cash flow in one or a few payments.

ESOPs were initially created to provide for the retirement benefits of a firm's employees. However, about half of all ESOPs are used to create a market for the shares of current owners wishing to harvest. Where most retirement plans limit the amount of stock in any one company the plan can own, an ESOP is designed to allow employees to invest primarily in the firm's stock. The U.S. government encourages this by providing significant tax advantages for ESOPs. ESOPs can be either leveraged or unleveraged. In an unleveraged ESOP the company makes an annual contribution to the ESOP for the employees' retirement. The ESOP then uses the money to purchase shares of the company. An unleveraged ESOP usually provides a slower harvest for the entrepreneur.

For the franchisor, an ESOP is problematic because the debt load, as in an LBO/MBO; it requires management to increase free cash flow and thus reduces the franchisor's commitment to growth and possibly to franchisees. For the franchisee, an ESOP can be more attractive. However, remember that the franchisor usually has a right of first refusal and can block an ESOP sale. Also, an ESOP covers all employees, and the company has to disclose a great deal of confidential information. The government changes the rules for ESOPs all the time. You need to check the current rules and take financial advice from the appropriate legal and financial professionals.

Your Harvest Strategy and Valuation of the Franchise

For most people, the proper harvest strategy is closely aligned with the best valuation a firm can achieve. For example, venture capitalists in the United States prefer an IPO strategy because it addresses the largest market and typically secures the best valuation. Therefore, a very aggressive growth rate and a national or international rollout is a prerequisite for venture capital backing of a franchisor. In Europe, where the IPO capital markets are typically less robust, venture capitalists prefer trade sales in which the venture capitalist cashes out completely with lower transaction costs. The franchisor in Europe must have a clear vision of who will acquire it before it seeks venture capital backing.

Venture capitalists tend to rely on some multiple of earnings as a means to value both the franchisor and franchisee firms. But earnings have many definitions: net income, operating income, earnings before interest and taxes (EBIT), and earnings before interest, taxes, depreciation, and amortization (EBITDA). Current earnings provide an anchor to look into the future. Knowing what earnings measure to use and what the amount will be in the future is as much an art as a science for most firms. The firm's valuation is larger when confidence in future earnings is high. Firms do sophisticated market research and financial projections to convince investors or buyers that they know what the future will look like. However, in franchising, development of the system provides a very rational roadmap to the future. This clarity is rooted in the performance of the individual unit and the scale potential of the system. When you have shown you can accurately project outlet performance, then the income stream is more assured. Greater confidence in the future income stream lessens the debate over valuation.

For the franchisee, valuation becomes simpler as the system matures. That's because unit performance becomes relatively predictable and the earnings from the units are normalized. As franchises are bought and sold, a set of comparables emerge from these transactions. Actual earnings in a franchise are less valuable than revenue as a measure. The assumption is that if you are operating a store per the business model, a certain level of revenue will yield predictable earnings. If the earnings are not present, it is assumed that the operator is executing poorly or exercising creative accounting. A valuation rule of thumb for a single franchise store is that you'll get paid one year of annual revenue in a sale of the store. However, store values vary by each individual franchise system.

Conclusion

Before taking the leap into franchising, every entrepreneur must ask the question, If I put my assets at risk, will I make enough money to make me happy, in a period of time I think is reasonable? If the business is providing even a good living but does not create wealth, then there will be no harvest. Even though there will be no harvest, you will eventually exit the business. With no harvest, exit means liquidation of the assets or bankruptcy.

You must also understand the emotional impact of harvest, especially if that means you will be exiting the firm. Franchise organizations necessarily create bonds among the franchisees and the franchisor, because their success and growth are intertwined. For most entrepreneurs, the company becomes a dominant part of their lives. It is impossible to separate the harvest strategy from personal goals, because peoples' ambitions are so varied. Each of us has an internal scale that measures value and seeks a natural balance between our careers and personal lives. This balance is so personal that no calculation will be accurate or do it justice. We believe that franchising is a way of life that is exciting and rewarding. Although this book prescribes ways to use franchising as a pathway to personal wealth, we understand that wealth can be different for each person.

Although we've covered an enormous amount of detail throughout this book, we firmly believe in these simple guidelines that we refer to as the 4-A's: Find an "A" concept—one that is measurable against an expectation of ROI. Find an "A" market—one that addresses a customer's need. Find an "A" location—one that links your concept to the customer. Find an "A" operator—one that understands the franchise relationship as a partnership and is passionate about the concept. Do all of these right, and ongoing operation and relationship issues will be manageable, positive, and profitable.

Index

8 reasons why you should read the Financial Times for 4 weeks RISK-FREE!

To help you stay current with significant
developments in the world economy ...
and to assist you to make informed business
decisions — the Financial Times brings you:

 Fast, meaningful overviews of international affairs ... plus daily briefings on major world news.

 Perceptive coverage of economic, business, financial and political developments with special focus on emerging markets.

More international business news than any other publication.

 Sophisticated financial analysis and commentary on world market activity plus stock quotes from over 30 countries.

 Reports on international companies and a section on global investing.

Specialized pages on management, marketing, advertising and technological innovations from all parts of the world.

Highly valued single-topic special reports (over 200 annually) on countries, industries, investment opportunities, technology and more.

The Saturday Weekend FT section — a globetrotter's guide to leisure-time activities around the world: the arts, fine dining, travel, sports and more.

FT FINANCIAL TIMES
World business newspaper

The *Financial Times* delivers a world of business news.

Use the Risk-Free Trial Voucher below!

To stay ahead in today's business world you need to be well-informed on a daily basis. And not just on the national level. You need a news source that closely monitors the entire world of business, and then delivers it in a concise, quick-read format.

With the *Financial Times* you get the major stories from every region of the world. Reports found nowhere else. You get business, management, politics, economics, technology and more.

Now you can try the *Financial Times* for 4 weeks, absolutely risk free. And better yet, if you wish to continue receiving the *Financial Times* you'll get great savings off the regular subscription rate. Just use the voucher below.